Procreate for Digital Artists

Sharpen your digital art skills with over 50 expert-led walkthroughs

Mellisa Aning

‹packt›

Procreate for Digital Artists

Portfolio Director: Pavan Ramchandani
Relationship Lead: Tejashwini R
Project Manager: Divij Kotian
Content Engineer: Esha Banerjee
Technical Editor: Vidhisha Patidar
Copy Editor: Safis Editing
Proofreader: Esha Banerjee
Indexer: Manju Arasan
Production Designer: Aparna Bhagat
Growth Lead: Nivedita Singh

First published: September, 2025

Production reference: 1080825

Published by Packt Publishing Ltd.
Grosvenor House
11 St Paul's Square
Birmingham
B3 1RB, UK.

ISBN 978-1-83508-298-0

www.packtpub.com

To aspiring artists and dreamers who are passionate about their craft, keep believing in yourself and let your passion inspire others along your art journey.

- Mellisa Aning

Created by Mellisa Aning

Title: Letter from Spring

Contributor

About the author

Mellisa Aning, also known as *Gummy* and *Happyyu*, is a self-taught illustrator from Malaysia. She began her artistic journey as a freelancer in 2019 and has since collaborated with numerous clients and companies around the world, including TOi Puzzles, CASETiFY, QUALIA, and Youtooz. She is also the creator of a popular online tutorial on character creation, *From Coloring Technique to Creating Your Own Unique Character*. With over five years of professional experience using Procreate, Mellisa loves creating art that feels cozy, joyful, and safe—bringing warmth and smiles to everyone who sees it.

> **Where to find Mellisa's work**
>
> Instagram: `https://www.instagram.com/gummyy.y/?hl=en`
>
> Website: `https://happyyu.carrd.co/`

Thank you to my amazing family and friends for being by my side throughout this artistic journey. Your support filled my journey with warmth, courage, and joy!

– Mellisa Aning

Created by Surabhi Banerjee

Title: Kalamkari Katha

Created by Vivian Wong

Title: Nostalgic Snack Shack

About the reviewers

Surabhi Banerjee is a Bangalore-based architect/illustrator with a passion for storytelling through her clear-line drawings. Her work, marked by the ligne claire style, showcases personal narratives with strong lines and minimal shading. She has collaborated with leading brands such as KFC, Hershey's, Facebook, Yash Raj Films, Vidhu Vinod Chopra Films, Coca-Cola, Budweiser, Naturals Ice Cream, Lamborghini, Titan, MUBI, Jaquar, Chicago Botanical Garden, St+art India, Sony Music India, and Antiquity, gaining rich and diverse professional experience.

Vivian Wong is an illustrator based in London and Hong Kong, with a passion for drawing since the age of five. She has created a charming world of original characters, including *Gu* and *Bu* and the *Bread Family*. Each member of the *Bread Family* is inspired by different types of bread, with *Gu* and *Bu* representing fried and steamed *mantou*, a popular Chinese bun. Vivian's artwork often takes her characters on whimsical and colorful adventures, filled with delicious food and magical, Ghibli-inspired landscapes. Through her art, she hopes to bring joy and smiles to her audience, leaving a lasting and memorable impression with her adorable characters!

Table of Contents

Preface   xvii

Your book comes with exclusive
perks – here's how to unlock them   xx

1

Crafting Stunning Backgrounds with Advanced Techniques   1

Technical requirements	2	What you need	14
Getting to know your brushes and		Following the steps	14
materials	2	Understanding the technique	16
Textured brushes	5	**Adding texture for more depth and**	
Brush information	6	**personality**	**17**
Know more…	7	What you need	17
Using reference images for inspiration	**8**	Following the steps	17
What you need	9	Know more…	19
Following the steps	9	**Using background color to set the**	
Preparing a color palette based on		**mood**	**21**
a reference image	11	Color tones: warm and cool	22
Understanding the technique	13	Understanding the technique	23
		Know more…	24
Starting with a simple composition		**Summary**	**26**
for background drawing	**13**		

2

Drawing Intricate Details with Precision   27

Learning how to draw fluffy clouds	28	Understanding the technique	29
Following the steps	28		

Learning how to draw delicate trees   29

Following the steps   30

Understanding the technique   31

Learning how to draw soothing grass   32

Following the steps   32

Understanding the technique   33

Learning how to draw a flower field scene   33

Following the steps   34

Understanding the technique   35

Learning how to draw gravel   35

Following the steps   36

Understanding the technique   36

Learning how to draw a fence   37

Following the steps   37

Understanding the technique   38

Learning how to draw little houses   38

Following the steps   38

Understanding the technique   39

Learning how to draw a green field   40

Following the steps   40

Understanding the technique   41

Learning how to draw a lake   41

Following the steps   42

Understanding the technique   42

Learning how to draw snow   43

Following the steps   43

Understanding the technique   44

Know more...   44

Summary   44

3

Mastering Perspective for Dynamic Scenes   47

How to apply natural perspective in background drawing   48

Size perspective   52

Detail perspective   55

How to use the linear perspective built-in system   60

One-point perspective   60

Two-point perspective   61

Three-point perspective   63

How to identify linear perspective in real-life images   65

Identifying a one-point perspective in a real-life image   65

Identifying a two-point perspective in a real-life image   68

Identifying a three-point perspective in a real-life image   71

How to implement linear perspective techniques in background illustration   75

Drawing background scenery using a one-point perspective   75

Drawing background scenery using a two point-perspective   76

Drawing background scenery using a three-point perspective   78

Summary   81

4

Enhancing Lighting to Elevate Your Artwork   83

Observing lighting and shadows using real-life images and reference images   84
Light and shadow on shiny surfaces   84
Light and shadow on rough surfaces   86
Understanding the technique   88

Understanding lighting and shadow techniques   89
What you need   89
Identifying a soft light source   89
Identifying a bright light source   91

Using light and shadow to illustrate a peaceful morning scene   94
Following the steps   94
Understanding the technique   97
Know more...   97

Using light and shadow to illustrate a bright afternoon scene   98
Following the steps   98
Understanding the technique   100

Using light and shadow to illustrate a warm evening scene   101
Following the steps   101
Understanding the technique   103

Using light and shadow to illustrate a calm night scene   104
Following the steps   104
Understanding the technique   106

Mastering lighting and shading in the easiest way   107
Following the steps   107
Understanding the technique   111
Know more...   114

Summary   114

5

Exploring Color Theory for Vibrant Illustrations   117

Creating color harmony with Procreate   118
Creating monochromatic schemes   118
Creating analogous schemes   120
Creating complementary schemes   122
Creating triadic schemes   124
Understanding the technique   126

The importance of color value and how to use it in art   127
Following the steps   127
Understanding the technique   130

How and when to use warm and cool colors   130
Applying warm tones   130
Applying cool tones   132
Understanding the technique   134

Improving contrast in art — 136

Following the steps — 136

Understanding the technique — 138

Choosing random colors to create a color palette — 139

Following the steps — 139

Understanding the technique — 141

Know more... — 141

Creating a color palette using Gradient Map — 142

Following the steps — 142

Understanding the technique — 144

Using color harmony, color value, and contrast in art — 145

Following the steps — 145

Understanding the technique — 148

Summary — 150

6

Crafting a Mood and Atmosphere with Useful Techniques — 151

Color emotions and how to apply them to our art — 152

Breaking down color emotions — 152

Learning which colors create a happy atmosphere — 153

Following the steps — 154

Understanding the technique — 155

Know more... — 155

Learning which colors create a sad atmosphere — 156

Following the steps — 156

Understanding the technique — 158

Learning which colors create a mysterious atmosphere — 158

Following the steps — 158

Understanding the technique — 160

Learning which colors create an intense atmosphere — 160

Following the steps — 160

Understanding the technique — 162

Learning which colors create a heartwarming atmosphere — 162

Following the steps — 162

Understanding the technique — 164

Know more... — 164

Discovering the connection between colors and composition — 165

Following the steps — 165

Understanding the technique — 167

Summary — 169

7

Storytelling Through Art: Creating Visual Narratives — 171

Brainstorming and writing down ideas — 172

Following the steps — 172

Understanding the technique — 173

Creating a mood board for references 173

Following the steps   174
Understanding the technique   176
Know more...   176

Sketching out the storyline   177

Following the steps   177
Understanding the technique   179

Improvising the story and sketch   179

Following the steps   180

Understanding the technique   181

Integrating color emotion into
the sketch   182

Following the steps   182
Understanding the technique   183

Finalizing the story and illustration 184

Following the steps   184
Understanding the technique   187

Summary   188

8

Designing Characters That Blend Seamlessly into Backgrounds   191

Brainstorming and sketching out
character designs   192

Following the steps   192
Understanding the technique   194

Finalizing character designs   195

Following the steps   196
Understanding the technique   197

Drawing character designs from
different perspectives   198

Following the steps   198
Understanding the technique   199

Drawing facial expressions   200

Following the steps   200
Understanding the technique   202

Preparing a character sheet for a
portfolio   202

Following the steps   203
Understanding the technique   206

Adding a character to a background
drawing   206

Following the steps   207
Understanding the technique   208

Perfectly blending a character into
the background drawing   209

Following the steps   209
Understanding the technique   211

Summary   212

9

Perfecting Composition for Visually Striking Art   213

Getting started with background
composition   214

Following the steps   215

Understanding the technique   217
Common mistakes and how to fix them   217

Learning how to use C-shape
composition in art   218
Following the steps   218
Understanding the technique   220
Common mistakes and how to fix them   220

Learning how to use V-shape
composition in art   220
Following the steps   221
Understanding the technique   222
Common mistakes and how to fix them   223

Learning how to use unbalanced
composition in art   223
Following the steps   223
Understanding the technique   225
Common mistakes and how to fix them   226

Learning how to use balanced
composition in art   226
Following the steps   226
Understanding the technique   228
Common mistakes and how to fix them   228

Learning how to use diagonal
composition   228
Following the steps   229
Understanding the technique   230
Common mistakes and how to fix them   231

Learning how to use cross
composition in art   231
Following the steps   231
Understanding the technique   233
Common mistakes and how to fix them   234

Learning how to use circular
composition in art   234
Following the steps   234
Understanding the technique   236
Common mistakes and how to fix them   236
Know more…   236

Learning how to use Golden Section
composition in art   236
Following the steps   238
Understanding the technique   240
Common mistakes and how to fix them   240
Know more…   241

Summary   241

10

Step-by-Step Guide to Drawing Compelling Backgrounds   243

Important note   244

Learning how to draw a serene
morning landscape   245
Following the steps   246
Understanding the technique   251
Know more…   251

Learning how to draw a joyful
afternoon landscape   253
Following the steps   253
Understanding the technique   258
Know more…   259

Learning how to draw a nostalgic
evening landscape   260
Understanding the technique   266
Know more…   266

Learning how to draw a peaceful
night landscape   267

Following the steps   267

Understanding the technique   273

Know more...   274

Drawing challenge: Create a
background scenery   275

Following the steps   275

Understanding the technique   278

Drawing mission: Let's create together!   279

Summary   279

Index   281

Other Books You May Enjoy   288

Preface

Procreate is a powerful and easy-to-use drawing app for iPad. It's loved by artists for its natural brushes, smooth layer system, and helpful tools such as perspective guides and color features. You can sketch, paint, animate, and explore your ideas freely—all with just one app. No subscription needed—just a one-time purchase. And it works beautifully with the Apple Pencil, so your lines feel just like traditional drawing.

Using Procreate as our main creative tool, we'll walk through techniques that are helpful in background drawing. The walkthroughs in this book are designed to be both practical and to offer guidance to help you grow your confidence while staying true to your unique creative style. This book will guide illustrators in creating backgrounds that feel meaningful and immersive. You'll find easy steps, kind advice, and helpful tools to support your journey, every step of the way.

Who this book is for

This book was created for illustrators who want to take their skills in background drawing to the next level. Since scenery plays a big role in animation, art books, and the game industry, learning how to create backgrounds can be an important first step in your creative journey. Whether you're preparing for professional work or simply exploring new artistic paths, this book offers guidance to help you begin with confidence and joy.

Procreate for Digital Artists is designed for intermediate users familiar with the basics of Procreate. But if you're new to it, don't worry. Each chapter includes friendly tips to help you access and use the tools with ease.

What this book covers

Chapter 1, Crafting Stunning Backgrounds with Advanced Techniques, will help you learn how to create background scenery using Procreate. You will explore the basics, such as brushes, textures, and color, alongside helpful tips for using references, building simple compositions, and setting the mood with thoughtful color choices.

Chapter 2, Drawing Intricate Details with Precision, will show you how to draw nature-inspired background elements such as fluffy clouds, delicate trees, soft grass, flower fields, and cozy little houses. These details will help set the scene and make your illustrations feel full of life. We'll also explore how to use contrast, color value, and Procreate tools such as Curves and Hue, Saturation, and Brightness to bring balance to the background scenery.

Chapter 3, Mastering Perspective for Dynamic Scenes, will help you explore how to use both natural and linear perspectives to add depth and realism to your backgrounds. You'll learn simple ways to apply atmospheric, size, and detail perspective, along with helpful step-by-step guides using Procreate's built-in tools for one-point, two-point, and three-point perspective.

Chapter 4, Enhancing Lighting to Elevate Your Artwork, will guide you in using lighting and shadows to bring your artwork to life. You'll discover how light affects different surfaces, and how to create morning, afternoon, evening, and night scenes with the right colors and moods. With easy walkthroughs and helpful tools in Procreate, you'll learn to add highlights, shadows, and reflected light in a way that feels natural.

Chapter 5, Exploring Color Theory for Vibrant Illustrations, will help you learn how to make your art shine through color. You'll discover how to choose colors that complement each other, create mood with warm and cool tones, and understand how to use contrast and color value to add depth. With friendly Procreate walkthroughs that include tips on color harmony, making palettes, and using the Gradient Map, you'll feel more confident and creative with every brushstroke.

Chapter 6, Crafting a Mood and Atmosphere with Useful Techniques, will help you explore how colors can shape the feeling of your illustrations. You'll learn how different hues, such as warm yellows or cool blues, can help you express emotions such as happiness, sadness, mystery, intensity, or comfort. Through simple Procreate walkthroughs and easy tips, you'll build color palettes that match the story you want to tell. By understanding how color and composition work together, you'll discover how to guide the viewer's eye and bring emotional depth to your art.

Chapter 7, Storytelling Through Art: Creating Visual Narratives, will guide you through creating visual stories that make your artwork more meaningful and memorable. You'll learn how to brainstorm ideas, sketch scenes and characters, and build your narrative step by step—starting from a mood board to a finished illustration. With easy techniques and supportive tips, you'll explore how colors, settings, and emotions all come together to tell a story your viewers can truly feel.

Chapter 8, Designing Characters That Blend Seamlessly into Backgrounds, will help you explore how to create characters that feel naturally connected to the backgrounds they live in. Step by step, we'll explore how to brainstorm personality traits, sketch ideas, and finalize characters. You will also learn to draw the characters from different angles and show varied expressions. And finally, you will discover how to place them into a setting and blend everything together to tell a heartfelt story.

Chapter 9, Perfecting Composition for Visually Striking Art, will help you learn how to arrange elements in your illustrations to create beautiful, balanced, and eye-catching backgrounds. Through walkthroughs, you'll explore techniques such as C-shape, V-shape, circular, and Golden Spiral compositions. You'll learn to direct the viewer's attention, add depth, and craft meaningful, story-rich scenes full of charm.

Chapter 10, Step-by-Step Guide to Drawing Compelling Backgrounds, will guide you in creating beautiful backgrounds that support your characters and tell a story. We'll explore how to set the mood, show distance with depth and perspective, and use layering techniques to make your art feel natural and engaging. Step by step, you'll draw landscapes set in morning, afternoon, evening, and night—guided gently, with plenty of room to explore and play. By the end, you'll feel more confident in designing backgrounds that add feeling, atmosphere, and meaning to your work.

To get the most out of this book

To follow along with the walkthrough in this book, you'll need an iPad running iPadOS 16.3 or later and the Procreate app (version 5.3.15) or newer. For best results, ensure your device is up to date and capable of supporting the latest version of Procreate.

In this book, the walkthroughs are here to gently guide you as you create your first background scenery or explore new ideas for your art. Feel free to draw in your own way, using your unique style. And if you're working in a different drawing program, that's absolutely okay—these tips are meant to support you, no matter what tools you use.

Download the images

We also provide a PDF file that has color images of the screenshots and images used in this book. You can download it here: `https://packt.link/gbp/9781835082980`.

Conventions used

Bold: Indicates a new term, an important word, or words that you see onscreen. Here is an example: "**Atmospheric perspective** is a technique used in art to create the illusion of depth and distance by depicting the changes in color and contrast of objects as they recede into the background."

> **Tips or important notes**
> Appear like this.

Your book comes with exclusive perks – here's how to unlock them

Unlock this book's exclusive benefits now

UNLOCK NOW

Scan this QR code or go to packtpub.com/unlock, then search this book by name. Ensure it's the correct edition.

Note: Have your purchase invoice ready before you start.

Enhanced reading experience with our next-gen reader:

- **Multi-device progress sync**: Learn from any device with seamless progress sync.

- **Highlighting and notetaking**: Turn your reading into lasting knowledge.

- **Bookmarking**: Revisit your most important learnings anytime.

- **Dark mode**: Focus with minimal eye strain by switching to dark or sepia mode.

Learn smarter using our AI assistant (Beta):

- **Summarize it**: Summarize key sections or an entire chapter.

- **AI code explainers**: In the next-gen Packt Reader, click the **Explain** button above each code block for AI-powered code explanations.

> **Note:**
> *The AI assistant is part of the next-gen Packt Reader and is still in beta.*

Learn anytime, anywhere:

- Access your content offline with DRM-free PDF and ePub versions—compatible with your favorite e-readers.

Unlock your book's exclusive benefits

Your copy of this book comes with the following exclusive benefits:

- Next-gen Packt Reader
- AI assistant (beta)
- DRM-free PDF/ePub downloads

Use the following guide to unlock them if you haven't already. The process takes just a few minutes and needs to be done only once.

How to unlock these benefits in three easy steps

Step 1

Keep your purchase invoice for this book ready, as you'll need it in Step 3. If you received a physical invoice, scan it on your phone and have it ready as either a PDF, JPG, or PNG.

For more help on finding your invoice, visit `https://www.packtpub.com/unlock-benefits/help`.

Note: Did you buy this book directly from Packt? You don't need an invoice. After completing Step 2, you can jump straight to your exclusive content.

Step 2	
Scan this QR code or go to `packtpub.com/unlock`.	

On the page that opens (which will look similar to Figure X.1 if you're on desktop), search for this book by name. Make sure you select the correct edition.

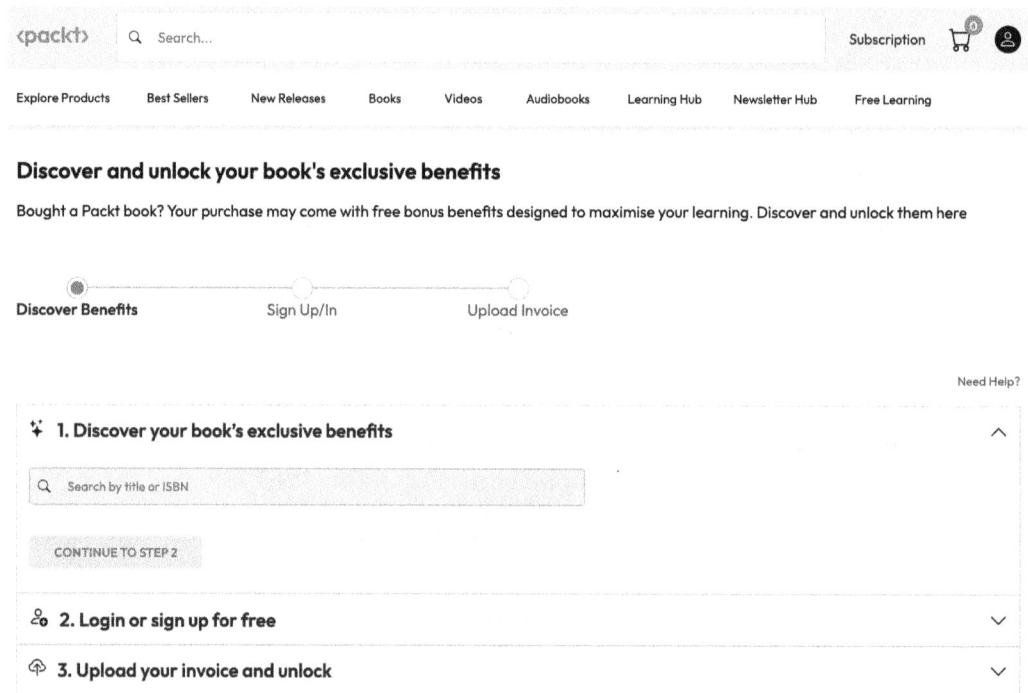

Figure X.1: Packt unlock landing page on desktop

Step 3

Sign in to your Packt account or create a new one for free. Once you're logged in, upload your invoice. It can be in PDF, PNG, or JPG format and must be no larger than 10 MB. Follow the rest of the instructions on the screen to complete the process.

> **Need help?**
>
> If you get stuck and need help, visit `https://www.packtpub.com/unlock-benefits/help` for a detailed FAQ on how to find your invoices and more. The following QR code will take you to the help page directly:

> **Note:**
> If you are still facing issues, reach out to `customercare@packt.com`.

The next-gen Packt Reader is included for free with the purchase of this book. Scan the QR code OR go to packtpub.com/unlock, then use the search bar to find this book by name. Double-check the edition shown to make sure you get the right one.

Get in touch

Feedback from our readers is always welcome.

General feedback: If you have questions about any aspect of this book, email us at customercare@ packtpub.com and mention the book title in the subject of your message.

Errata: Although we have taken every care to ensure the accuracy of our content, mistakes do happen. If you have found a mistake in this book, we would be grateful if you would report this to us. Please visit www.packtpub.com/support/errata and fill in the form.

Piracy: If you come across any illegal copies of our works in any form on the internet, we would be grateful if you would provide us with the location address or website name. Please contact us at copyright@packt.com with a link to the material.

If you are interested in becoming an author: If there is a topic that you have expertise in and you are interested in either writing or contributing to a book, please visit authors.packtpub.com.

Unlock Bonus Resources

Scan the QR code or visit the link to get access to exclusive resources curated for you.

https://packt.link/xHrUM

Share Your Thoughts

Once you've read *Procreate for Digital Artists*, we'd love to hear your thoughts! Scan the QR code below to go straight to the Amazon review page for this book and share your feedback.

https://packt.link/r/183508298X

Your review is important to us and the tech community and will help us make sure we're delivering excellent quality content.

Crafting Stunning Backgrounds with Advanced Techniques

Welcome to the first chapter! **Procreate** is a powerful and versatile digital painting app, widely used by professional and hobbyist artists alike. Developed by Savage Interactive specifically for iPad and Apple Pencil, it offers a wide array of tools and brushes that make it one of the most popular choices for digital illustration.

Like many digital artists, I use Procreate for both personal and professional projects. It's opened up so many creative possibilities, and throughout this book, I'll be sharing the techniques and discoveries I've made along the way.

This guide is designed for digital artists looking to take their background illustration skills to the next level. We'll explore practical techniques and creative strategies that not only refine your art but also help you build stunning, storytelling-rich scenes from scratch. Whether you're aiming to master lighting and shading, deepen your understanding of color theory, or learn how to create captivating atmospheres and character designs, this book has you covered.

Whether you're an intermediate artist ready to level up or an advanced illustrator refining your skills, this guide is packed with techniques, tips, and fun exercises to help elevate your background art. We'll walk through easy methods that make drawing scenery feel simpler and more enjoyable. This book covers everything from choosing the right brushes and using real-life references to mastering composition, color, and texture that will help you create your own masterpiece. Best of all, this book doesn't ask you to follow rigid rules. Instead, you'll discover flexible tools and creative ideas you can adapt to your own workflow and style.

This chapter will guide you through a few essential techniques to help you get started in illustrating your own background scenery illustrations.

Here's what we'll explore in this chapter:

- Getting to know your brushes and materials
- Using reference images for inspiration
- Starting with a simple composition for background drawing
- Adding texture for more depth and personality
- Using background color to set the mood

Now let's start the first chapter that will help bring your background to life. In the next walkthrough, we'll explore the brushes and materials you'll be using throughout this book and a few tips on how to tweak them, so they feel just right for your style.

Technical requirements

To follow along with the walkthrough in this book, you'll need an iPad running **iPadOS 16.3** or later and the **Procreate app (version 5.3.15)** or newer. For best results, ensure your device is up to date and capable of supporting the latest version of Procreate.

Getting to know your brushes and materials

Choosing the right brushes is a big part of getting the look and feel you want in your illustrations. There are so many options out there, but the most important thing is to use brushes that feel good to you. If you're unsure which brush to pick, try doing a few test doodles or strokes on a blank canvas. See how each one flows and whether its texture suits the type of scene you're creating.

For example, in *Figure 1.1*, I used a watercolor brush to create a quick painting, just to explore the brush's flow and texture before diving deeper into the illustration process. This simple test helps me understand how the brush handles layering, texturing, and blending colors – three things that really determine how natural it feels while using the brush.

Figure 1.1 – An example of using the watercolor brush

If you're not satisfied with the brush flow and texture, you can adjust the settings. This will help you create a brush of your own liking. When creating brushes, we can consider the texture, rendering, and flow of the brush. Examples will follow on how to create a good rendering and texture effect for Procreate's brushes.

To create a good rendering effect, you can make changes to the **Rendering mode** and **Wet mix** sections.

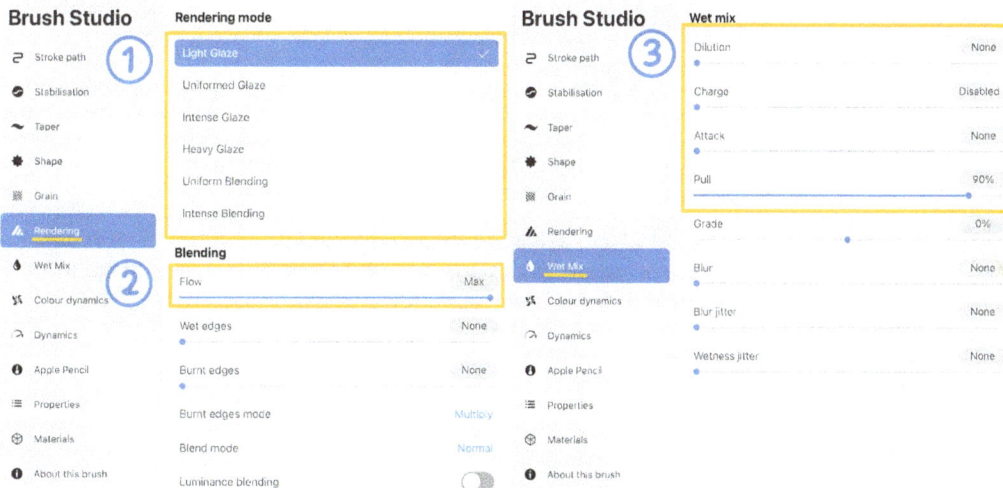

Figure 1.2 – An example of how to make changes to the brush rendering effect

To create a good texture, you can make changes to the **Grain** and **Apple Pencil | Bleed** sections.

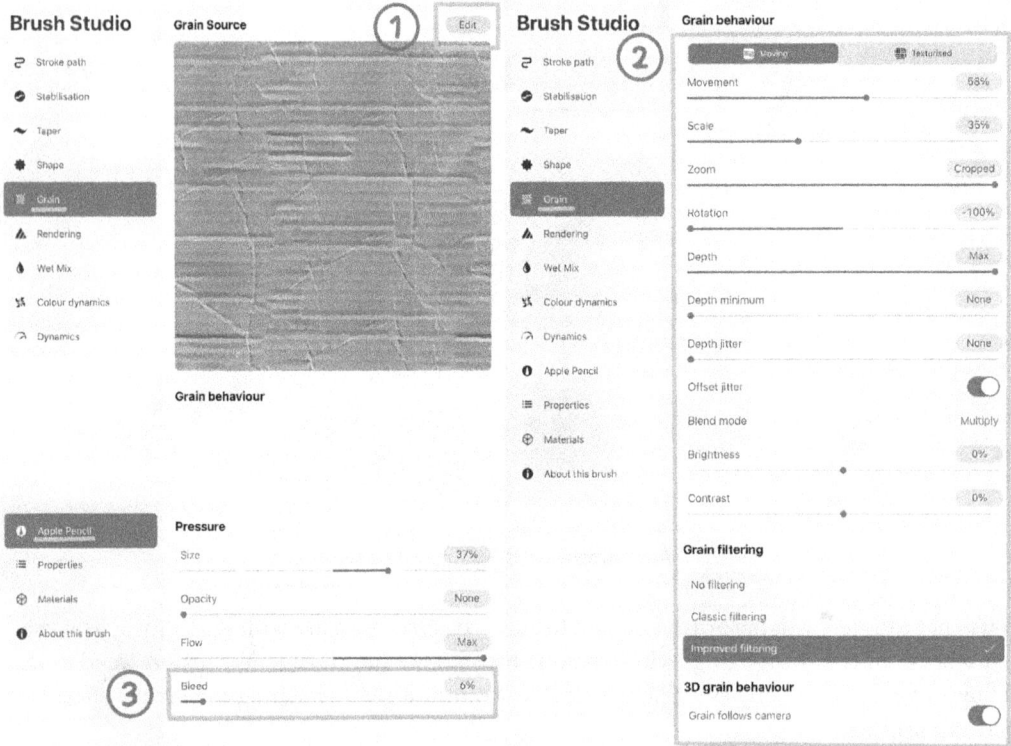

Figure 1.3 – An example of how to make changes to the brush texture

---

Tip

🔍 **Quick tip**: Need to see a high-resolution version of this image? Open this book in the next-gen Packt Reader or view it in the PDF/ePub copy.

🔒 **The next-gen Packt Reader** and a **free PDF/ePub copy** of this book are included with your purchase. Scan the QR code OR go to `packtpub.com/unlock`, then use the search bar to find this book by name. Double-check the edition shown to make sure you get the right one.

To create a good brush flow and brush strokes, you can make changes in the **Stabilisation | Motion filtering** sections.

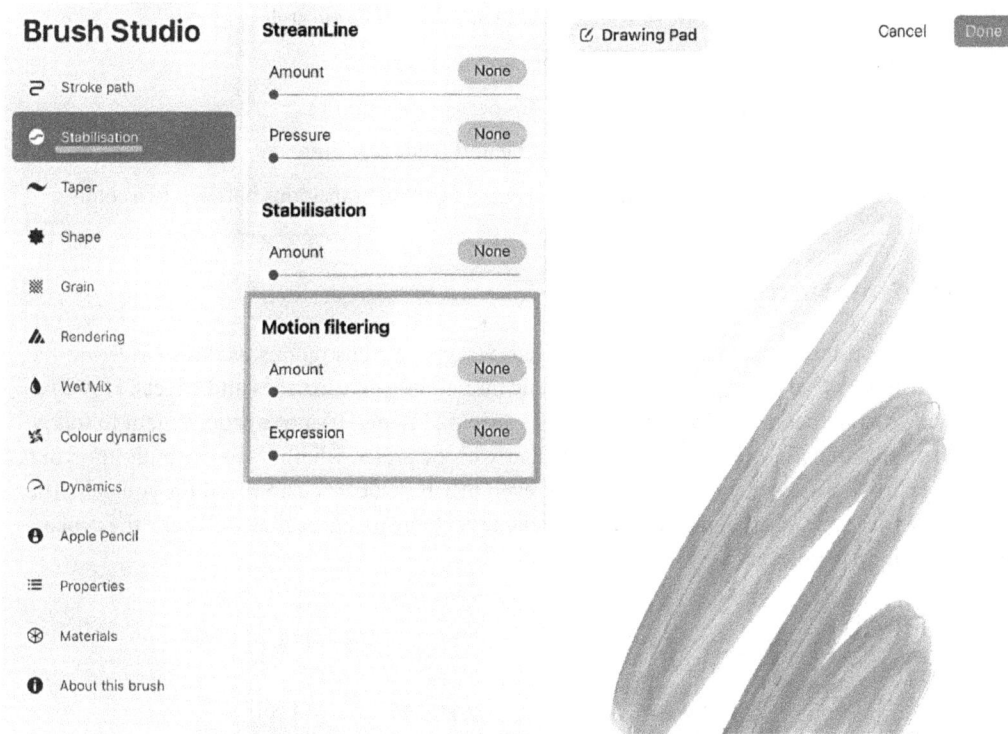

Figure 1.4 – An example of how to make changes to the brushstroke

Textured brushes

Using certain brushes, such as a textured brush, can greatly enhance your background illustrations by introducing more detail and dimension. Textured brushes help break away from plain, flat areas and create surfaces that feel more dynamic and visually engaging. For example, a brush that mimics the texture of paper, fabric, or rough stone can add subtle patterns that make the background appear more natural and lifelike. The added texture also plays a big role in creating depth. By varying the density, size, or intensity of the texture, you can suggest layers within your illustration. Textures can also set a mood or convey a particular story. For instance, a soft, grainy texture might evoke a nostalgic or dreamy atmosphere, while bold and sharp textures can add energy or drama. By experimenting with textured brushes, you can discover new ways to add personality and uniqueness to your artwork.

> **Tips**
>
> If you're still exploring which brushes suit you best, these brushes are a great starting point because they're easy to use and work well across a variety of drawing styles:
>
> **6B Pencil (Sketching)**: Great for rough sketches and linework.
>
> **Studio Pen (Inking)**: Clean and smooth lines. It's perfect for outlines.
>
> **Round Brush (Painting)**: A go-to for soft shading and color blending.
>
> **Soft Brush (Airbrushing)**: Ideal for smooth gradients and subtle transitions between two colors.

Brush information

In this book, I'll be using Happyyu Brush Pack to create background illustrations, as shown in *Figure 1.5*. It's a paid brush pack that offers a variety of versatile oil painting-like brushes and effects. However, it's important to note that using this brush pack is entirely optional. It's not a requirement to follow along. You are free to use any brushes you're familiar with or prefer, whether they're built into your software, free brush packs you've downloaded, or even brushes you've customized for yourself. The key is to work with tools that you feel confident and comfortable using, as that will make the process smoother and more enjoyable.

Figure 1.5 – Brush Pack information

The brushes from *Figure 1.5* are mainly used for the tutorials and step-by-step drawing process in this book. If you decide to use this brush pack, you can refer to *Figure 1.6* to ensure that you can follow the step-by-step walkthroughs in this book without any problems.

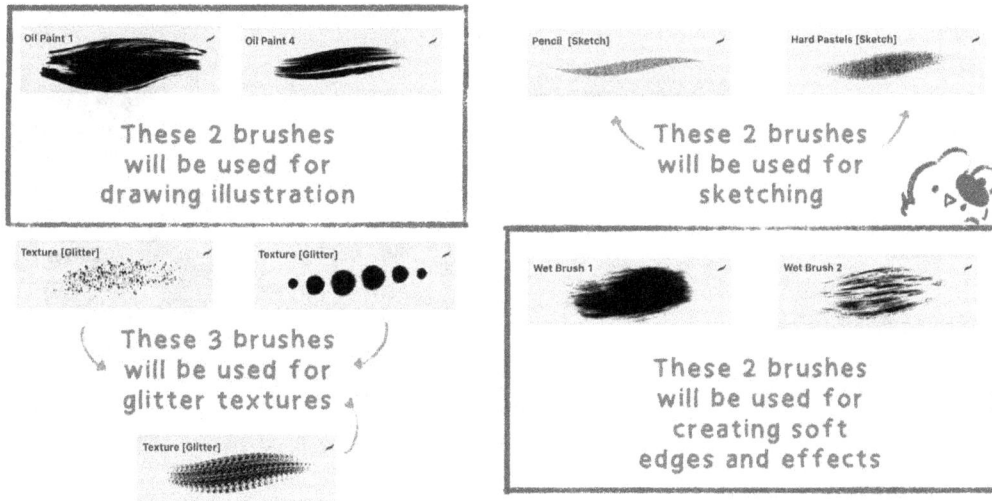

Figure 1.6 – The main brushes from Happyyu Brush Pack that will be used for this book

Know more...

If you're looking to explore new styles and add variety to your illustrations, trying out other brush packs can be a great idea. These free brush packs come with a range of brush types that allow you to experiment with different textures, strokes, and effects. They can help you achieve unique finishes, such as soft watercolor washes, crayon-like brushes, and rough textures. The QR codes and links to the free and paid brush packs follow:

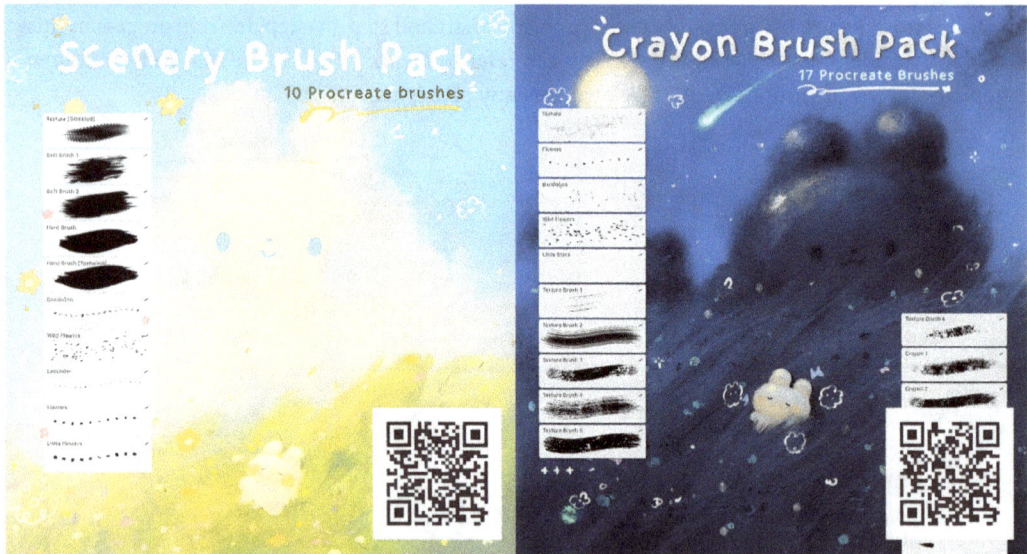

Figure 1.7 – Images of free brush packs provided

Links

Scenery Brush Pack: `https://ko-fi.com/s/cfb60fa5c9`

Crayon Brush Pack: `https://ko-fi.com/s/45c6b97dd0`

Happyyu Brush Pack: `https://ko-fi.com/s/95fcf32bb9`

Now that you're familiar with the brushes and materials we'll be using, let's explore how to draw inspiration from real-life references to build the foundation of your background illustration.

Using reference images for inspiration

To create realistic scenery, using reference images can greatly help in bringing your ideas to life on canvas. Don't feel discouraged about relying on references – they're an excellent learning tool for illustrators to improve their drawing skills. Observing real-life objects and surroundings helps us better understand details and techniques. References are also particularly useful for mastering lighting, as well as improving composition and atmosphere in your background illustrations. In this walkthrough, we'll focus on using reference images to guide the creation of sketches and base colors for background artwork.

What you need

Choose one reference image to help you with sketching out your first ideas. You can use *Figure 1.8*, which I prepared, to do the following step-by-step walkthrough.

Following the steps

For example, let us have a look at the reference image:

Figure 1.8 – Reference image; source: https://unsplash.com/photos/grass-field-DNnxRx9Vkb4

From *Figure 1.8*, search out the first few objects that stand out and list them in order. From my perspective, I noticed a blue sky, a green field, and a flock of sheep.

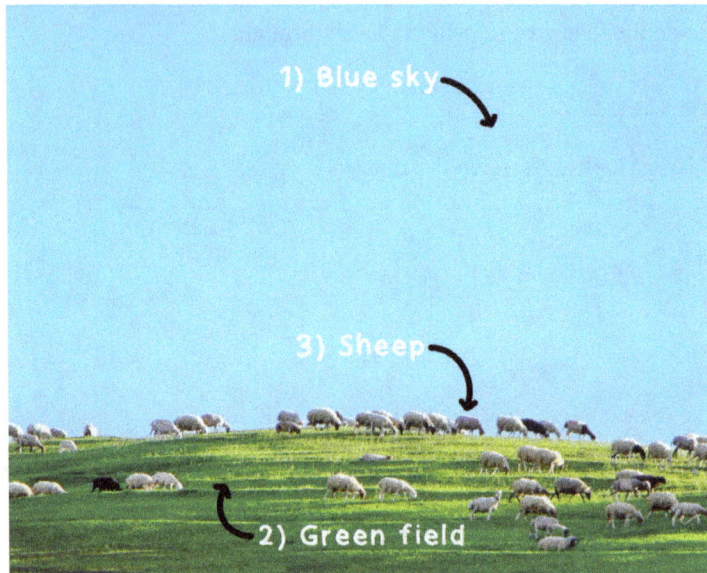

Figure 1.9 – An example of how to identify objects from Figure 1.8; source: https://unsplash.com/photos/grass-field-DNnxRx9Vkb4

Once we identified the first few objects from *Figure 1.8* we marked them down, then sketched out the objects by referencing them in *Figure 1.9*.

Creating a sketch can be done by following the next steps:

1. First, draw the green field and blue sky. In Procreate, you can easily add a reference image next to your drawing, so you can look at both at the same time. Just tap the **wrench icon** at the top, go to **Canvas**, and turn on **Reference**. A small window will pop up. Tap **Image**, then pick the photo you want to use. You can move this window around and zoom in if you need to see the details better. You can also use the color picker on it to grab colors for your art.

2. Next, sketch some of the sheep. There's no need to draw every single one; just include a few to capture the essence of the scene. Copying and pasting can save a lot of time, especially when you're drawing the same thing, such as sheep, many times. You can make each one look a bit different by turning it, changing its size, or flipping it. In Procreate, the **Duplicate** and **Transform** tools can help you do this easily.

3. *Optional*: Draw a character to add more story to the illustration. For example, I will draw a goatherd.

Figure 1.10 – Sketch based on reference image

A sketch has been created by referencing a real-life image of a green field. Now, let us move forward to prepare the base color.

Preparing a color palette based on a reference image

We will move forward to the base color, where we will create a color palette based on *Figure 1.8*.

Adding a base color can be done by following these steps:

1. Begin by identifying the dominant colors in the reference image and saving them using the **color picker tool**. If you want to pick up a color from your canvas, just press and hold your finger on the color area. After a moment, the color will appear in your active color circle. When selecting colors from the reference palette, it's crucial to consistently choose hues that complement each other to maintain overall color harmony. You can learn more about this technique in *Chapter 5, Exploring Color Theory for Vibrant Illustrations*.

Figure 1.11 – An example of preparing the color palette based on a reference
image; source: https://unsplash.com/photos/grass-field-DNnxRx9Vkb4

2.   Based on *Figure 1.4*, apply these colors to the environment sketch created in *Figure 1.10*. Next,
     we'll render the colors using **Wet Brush 1** from Happyyu Brush Pack to achieve a painterly
     effect. However, this brush isn't required – feel free to use any brush that best suits your style
     and workflow.

Figure 1.12 displays the outcome of applying the base color and rendered version from *Figure 1.8* :

Figure 1.12 – The outcome of the illustration after the base color has
been applied and the illustration has been rendered

With that, we've successfully created background scenery inspired by a real-life image. Now, let's take a closer look at how it all comes together.

Understanding the technique

With that, we've successfully completed a background scene inspired by the reference image. Keep in mind that you don't have to follow the reference image exactly; it's meant to guide and inspire you, not limit your creativity. While using a reference helps with understanding key elements such as lighting, composition, and atmosphere, you're free to reinterpret it in your own way. Feel free to add your personal touch to the scene, whether it's adjusting colors, changing the layout, or including extra details that reflect your unique style. Artistic expression is about taking what inspires you and making it your own, so embrace your creativity to explore and enhance the scene in a way that feels right to you. This combination of guidance from a reference and your personal input will make your background both visually appealing and unique.

> **Tips**
>
> You don't have to draw every detail. Keeping things simple makes it easier to make changes and adjustments later as you refine your drawing. Using reference images is a great way to get color palette ideas, but you don't need to follow them exactly. Instead, use them as a guide to help shape the colors in your next illustration.

Once you've gathered ideas from your references, the next step is to learn how to simplify them into an easy-to-manage composition. This makes the drawing process smoother and helps keep the focus on what matters most.

Starting with a simple composition for background drawing

To make drawing backgrounds easier and faster, it's best to focus on keeping things simple. Instead of adding too many details, try to highlight only the key parts of the background that make it interesting. For example, focus on important elements such as shapes, structures, or features that stand out. Using fewer colors also helps simplify the process. You can start with just a few colors that match the mood or scene you're creating. When you're using a reference image, pay close attention to three to six main details or colors that define the scene, such as lighting, objects, or textures. This way, you're not overwhelmed by trying to include everything. In this walkthrough, we will learn how to draw a background using a simple composition.

What you need

In this walkthrough, we'll work with a new reference image to help you better understand how to create a background using a simple composition. This will also show you how to make the most of a reference image for your artwork.

Following the steps

Let's have a look at the reference image. Identify the first three main details and several colors we get from it.

Figure 1.13 – An image of a vast green field; source: https://unsplash.
com/photos/tree-on-body-of-mountain-cX4TlF3l_U8

From *Figure 1.13*, we can notice three main details – the tree, the vast green field, and the sky. The three main colors here are light green, a darker green, and light blue.

Now, let us create a simple background composition by following this walkthrough:

1. List down the three main details and colors we identified from *Figure 1.13*.
2. Create a sketch based on *Figure 1.13* to create a background drawing.

3. Start by applying the three main colors to the background of your drawing. I added a few extra colors to help create a more balanced and harmonious atmosphere in the overall illustration.

Figure 1.14 – An example of a sketch and color palette based on Figure 1.13

4. Based on the information we have gathered, create scenery in your own style.

Figure 1.8 showcases the result achieved by following the step-by-step drawing process for creating a simple composition.

Figure 1.15 – An example of an illustration using Figure 1.13 as a reference

With that, we've successfully designed simple background scenery based on a real-life image. Let's move forward to the section on understanding the technique to learn more about how it all comes together.

Understanding the technique

When you start simple, it's much easier to see the overall composition of your background and identify areas that might need adjustments or improvements. This clarity makes it simpler to refine your work as you go, whether you're adding details or reworking certain elements. Additionally, because the composition is already straightforward, you'll find it easier to incorporate any creative touches or changes you might think of along the way.

Once the base of your background is in place, you can gradually layer in more details and focus on enhancing it through techniques such as detailing and rendering. This step-by-step approach not only keeps your work organized but also allows you to make thoughtful adjustments without feeling overwhelmed. Overall, starting simple gives you the flexibility and control to create visually appealing art while staying open to creativity throughout the process.

With your illustration ready, it's time to bring your background drawing to life by layering in texture. This will help your scenery feel more natural, engaging, and full of depth. Next, we will learn how to apply texture to our illustrations.

Adding texture for more depth and personality

Adding texture to the background of an illustration makes the image feel more natural and less flat. Texture can include things such as rough patterns, soft gradients, or even details that imitate real-life surfaces such as wood, fabric, or stone. These elements help the artwork feel more alive and relatable, like it has a personal touch. Playing around with different textures also allows you to improve how the illustration looks overall. It can draw attention to specific parts of the image, make it visually interesting, and give it a sense of depth. Plus, texture adds a sense of uniqueness to your work, making it stand out. In this walkthrough, we will learn how to use textured materials to add texture to our illustration.

What you need

Gather and prepare a textured material image. The texture materials will be used for this walkthrough to add texture to the illustration.

Following the steps

For example, let us have a look at the following texture material:

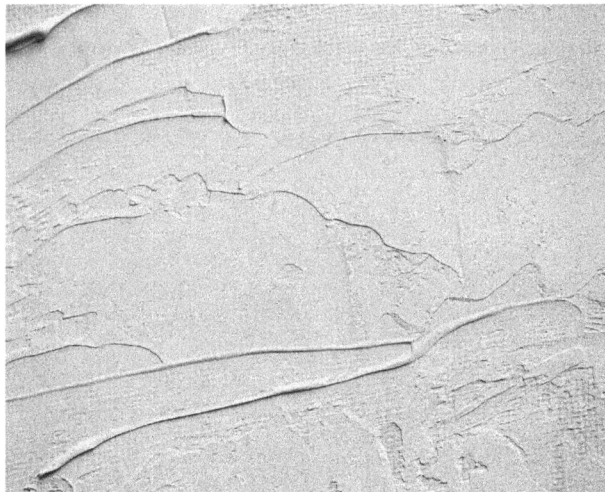

Figure 1.16 – An example of a textured material; source: https://unsplash.com/
photos/a-close-up-of-a-white-wall-with-peeling-paint-mjC9apK53a8

Let us learn how to apply texture effectively to our art:

1. We can start by preparing an illustration as a base layer, **Base Layer (illustration)**.

2. Then, add an additional layer on top of it as a textured material. Textured materials such as paper, canvas, fabric, or a material of your own preference can be added to this layer.

Figure 1.17 – An example of layers for texture

3. Once added, change the blending mode based on your preference. For texture layer placement, you can refer to *Figure 1.17*.

4. Blending modes that are often used for texture are **Overlay**, **Multiply**, **Soft Light**, and **Color Burn**. A mixture of these blending modes can create a stunning effect in your illustration as well.

Figure 1.18 – An example of texture applied to an illustration

Tips

For textured materials, it is recommended to use a black and white texture for better results. To enhance texture details, you can increase and adjust the sharpness using Procreate's built-in **Sharpen** settings. Tap the **magic wand icon** at the top of the screen. That opens the **Adjustments** menu. Then choose **Sharpen** to make your artwork look a bit clearer. You can slide left or right to change how strong the sharpening effect is.

Know more...

Other than adding a texture material into the illustration, using a textured brush can create a wonderful effect, as seen in *Figure 1.19*:

Figure 1.19 – An example of using textured brushes

There are many textured brushes available in Procreate, such as *Oberon*, *Styx*, *Fresco*, *Gouache*, as seen in *Figure 1.19*. By using textured brushes, you can add your own artistic touch to your illustration. Please do not be afraid to add some imperfections or uniqueness to make your background more aesthetically appealing. The imperfections can be specific brush strokes or rendering styles. You can refer to *Figure 1.19* as an example. As you can see, I did not draw everything perfectly to avoid it looking too stiff. If you have a specific texture you'd like to apply to your illustration, you can create your own texture materials and brushes as well. This will make your illustration more unique. I will share an example of how to change the texture in a brush setting.

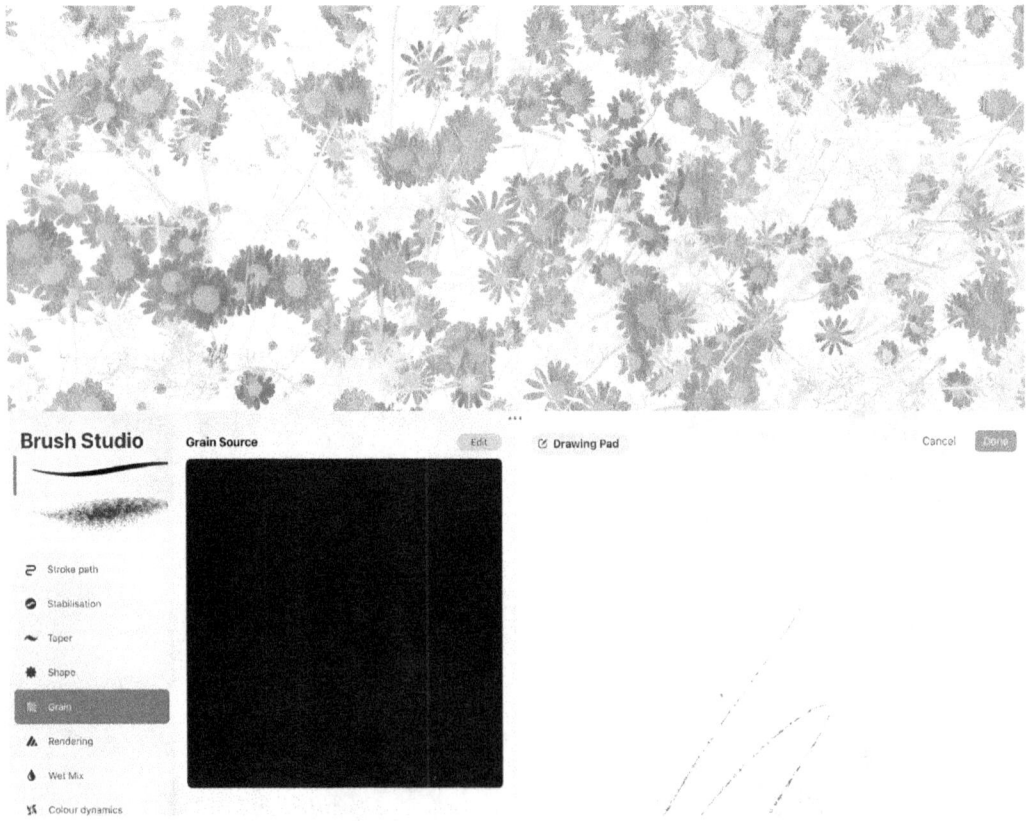

Figure 1.20 – Example of using texture material and brush settings

Tips

You can refer to *Figure 1.20* with regard to changing the texture in a brush setting. You can find the texture setting in the **Grain** section. Just tap **Edit** next to **Grain Source**, and then you can upload your own texture image there. Another way is by combining brushes in Procreate. It is a fun way to create custom tools with unique textures and effects. Here's how to combine two brushes in Procreate:

1. First, make a copy of each brush you want to combine so you don't change the originals. Put both brushes in the same folder. You can drag and drop the brush from other brush set folders. Just touch and hold the brush, then drag it over to the target brush set folder. It'll move there once you drop it.

2. Tap one brush to pick it, then swipe right on the second one to select both.

3. Tap **Combine** at the top. This creates one new brush with both textures.

4. Tap the new brush to open its settings, where you can change how the two brushes mix together.

If you want to separate them later, tap the brush, then choose **Uncombine**.

After adding texture, the final touch to enhance your background is color. Let's take a look at how thoughtful color choices can influence the mood and harmony of your scene.

Using background color to set the mood

Color is a key part of creating beautiful and eye-catching illustrations in art. To make your artwork look balanced and pleasing, it's important to choose colors that work well together. Different colors can bring out different feelings and ideas. Hence, the color palette can be divided into two different tones, namely, warm color tones and cool color tones.

Color tones: warm and cool

Using warm color tones such as orange, yellow, red, and brown can create a pleasant and cozy environment.

For example, let us have a look at a reference image:

Figure 1.21 – An example of an illustration with warm color tones

Next, we will see what cool color tones look like. Using cool color tones such as blue, green, and purple can evoke relaxation and calm feelings. If you notice, in *Figure 1.22*, I'm using a yellow warm color as well, but due to the dominance of cool color tones, it makes the illustration look more cool than warm.

Figure 1.22 – An example of a cool color tone illustration

Understanding the technique

When selecting a color tone for your background illustration, it's essential to think about the mood and atmosphere you want to convey. This choice plays a key role in shaping the overall feel of your artwork and communicating a clear message to your audience. Let's explore an example of how warm and cool color tones can be used effectively:

Figure 1.23 – An example of warm and cool color tones

Warm tones, such as reds, oranges, and yellows, often create feelings of comfort, energy, or warmth. They are perfect for backgrounds that aim to feel inviting, lively, or even nostalgic. For example, a sunset scene might use rich warm hues to convey serenity and beauty. On the other hand, cool tones, such as blues, greens, and purples, tend to evoke calmness, tranquility, or even mystery. These tones work well for backgrounds that are serene, refreshing, or dramatic. Considering the emotional connection between color and mood allows you to tailor your illustration to the message you want to communicate. Understanding these aspects will guide your choices in color tones and help your artwork resonate with viewers.

> **Tips**
>
> Lighter shades can create a soothing and gentle atmosphere, while darker shades can be used to create mysterious and intense atmospheres. This can be grouped as color emotion. Details and explanations of color emotion can be found in *Chapter 6, Crafting Mood and Atmosphere with Expert Techniques*.

Know more...

Changing the hue of your illustration can be a quick and easy way to generate a new color palette. For example, you can use Procreate's built-in **Hue**, **Saturation**, and **Brightness** settings to adjust the color hue. In *Figure 1.24*, we can see that, by changing the **Hue** setting percentage, we can create a new color palette easily:

Figure 1.24 – An example of using Procreate's Hue tool

Another thing we need to consider is the color saturation level. I will show an example of a high-saturation illustration and a low-saturation color illustration.

Figure 1.25 – An example of a high-saturation illustration

Figure 1.25 shows an example of a high-saturation illustration. A high saturation color illustration will create vibrant and eye-catching scenery, thus making it suitable for advertising purposes. Let's have a look at the following example of a low-saturation illustration.

Figure 1.26 – An example of a low-saturation color illustration

Moving forward, *Figure 1.26* shows an example of a low-saturation color illustration. Low-saturation colors can create a soft and calming effect, making them suitable for healing illustrations. To achieve this effect, use muted colors such as soft blue, hazy yellow, and gray. It's best to avoid bright or vibrant hues, as they can distract from the mood of the illustration. You can include warm tones too, but keep them subtle, using low-saturation yellows such as the one shown in *Figure 1.26*, for example. This is to maintain a balanced atmosphere without overpowering the other details.

Adjusting the color saturation in your illustration plays a key role in shaping how your audience experiences your work. By fine-tuning saturation levels, you can guide the viewer's attention, create mood, and emphasize certain elements without overwhelming the composition. Higher saturation can evoke energy, excitement, or warmth, perfect for lively scenes, while lower saturation tends to feel softer, calmer, or more introspective. Making careful choices about saturation helps your artwork stay balanced while also expressing the mood or story you want to tell.

Summary

In this chapter, we explored how to bring background illustrations to life in a way that feels enjoyable and approachable. We learned how to choose brushes that fit our style and how to adjust the brushes so drawing feels smooth and natural. And, in the course of this chapter we learned how to use reference images as tools to spark new ideas and make our art feel more real.

We also discovered the power of keeping things simple when building a scene, which gives us the scope to make changes and also add personal touches. Adding texture gave our backgrounds depth and an interesting look, while thoughtful color choices helped set the mood, whether bright and bold or soft and calming.

In the next chapter, we'll move on to learning how to draw important background details such as trees, grass, and gravel to give your illustrations more depth and detail.

Unlock this book's exclusive benefits now

Scan this QR code or go to `packtpub.com/unlock`, then search this book by name.

2
Drawing Intricate Details with Precision

Background scenery in art helps to enhance the overall composition, contributes to building a story and adds depth to the main subject. Artists use background scenery to convey mood and to establish a theme to create a sense of place and time. Adding perspective, color value, and detail to a background can complement the main subject, thus helping to create contrast in your illustration. For example, drawing a desaturated background with a vibrant character as the focal point will create a contrast and attract viewers' eyes to look at it. In Procreate, we can use the **Curves** and **Hue, Saturation, Brightness** tools to enhance the color contrast in our art. In *Chapter 5*, we will delve deeper into the concept of color contrast and explore it more thoroughly.

Drawing backgrounds consists of drawing things we see in our surroundings, such as clouds, trees, rivers, grass, flowers, houses, and so on. In this chapter, we will learn how to draw important details such as clouds, trees, grass, and nature-related elements that are usually drawn in the background. By the end of this chapter, you will have improved your skills in drawing details for background illustrations by following the step-by-step walkthroughs provided.

With the help of walkthrough examples, we'll cover the following topics:

- Learning how to draw fluffy clouds
- Learning how to draw delicate trees
- Learning how to draw soothing grass
- Learning how to draw a flower field scene
- Learning how to draw gravel
- Learning how to draw a fence
- Learning how to draw little houses
- Learning how to draw a green field

- Learning how to draw a lake
- Learning how to draw snow

Learning how to draw fluffy clouds

Clouds are often drawn in a background scenery illustration to create a realistic view based on what we see around us. Clouds come in various shapes and sizes, and it can be challenging to replicate this variety in a drawing. To realistically capture the fluffy and soft appearance of clouds, we need to have a good understanding of shading and blending techniques. We can get better at drawing clouds by observing the clouds around us. This can be done by taking pictures of clouds and redrawing them on the canvas. The main problem we encounter in drawing clouds is the difficulty in finding the right colors and knowing how to blend them to recreate the fluffy shapes of the clouds. Other than that, determining where to add shadows and lighting on clouds can be challenging. It's important to avoid making clouds that look too uniform or repetitive as it will affect the whole background scenery. In this walkthrough, we will learn a simple, step-by-step method for easily drawing fluffy clouds, ensuring you can capture their essence beautifully.

Following the steps

Before moving on to the step-by-step process, please refer to *Figure 2.1*, which will guide you and help you follow the walkthrough effectively.

Figure 2.1 – Drawing fluffy clouds

You can use the following steps to draw fluffy clouds:

1. First, draw a base for the clouds using white color on a blue-colored base (*STEP 1* in *Figure 2.1*).

2. Decide where the light source placement will be and paint a shadow on the area that is hidden from the light source, as shown in *STEP 2*.

3. Add highlights using white color and add reflected lights with light yellow and blue tones (*STEP 3*).

4. Lastly, add some additional details such as specks of lights and soft clouds on the sky's base color to complete it (*STEP 4*).

Understanding the technique

Drawing clouds is all about capturing their whimsical and fluffy essence. To achieve this, it's important to understand the cloud's shape and where to place lighting and shadows. Start by determining the light source. For instance, as shown in *Figure 2.1*, if the light source comes from the left, the shadows will fall on the right side of the clouds. Keep in mind that shadows always form on the side opposite to the light source.

When adding shadows, visualize the clouds in three dimensions and paint the shadows accordingly to reflect their form. To make the process easier, you can use reference images as a guide. In *Figure 2.1*, I utilized light yellow and blue tones for reflected light, enhancing the clouds' appearance and giving them a softer, more dynamic look.

To ensure the clouds appear natural, maintain a balanced color value in the overall illustration. For example, if the cloud shadows are painted too dark, the clouds may look rigid and fail to blend seamlessly with the background. Aim for a harmonious composition to bring your artwork to life.

> Tip
>
> Keep observing clouds around you (how the lighting affects them, how they blend seamlessly with the sky, and the shapes of the clouds forming in the sky), as it will help you improve in painting clouds easily. You can also use cloud photos as a reference to draw clouds.

Learning how to draw delicate trees

Drawing trees involves a deep understanding of the form and shape of the tree. Practicing drawing diverse types of trees can help us become better at drawing trees. Trees can be challenging to draw due to the complex details in their foliage and the difficulty of getting the proportions right. Trees come in all shapes and sizes so to become better at drawing them, we can observe the trees around us and try to recreate them. Moreover, we can use ready-made tree foliage brushes that are available on the internet to easily recreate a tree, adding details as necessary. This can save time and make the process easier. The downside is if we do not know how to draw trees, even with the help of a brush, we are unable to recreate a tree that looks natural.

Figure 2.2 shows a few examples of combining two different concepts to create unique trees.

Figure 2.2 – Trees in different concepts

Creating unique trees

To create a unique tree, you can mix up two different concepts, such as a cat tree, a mushroom tree, an ice cream tree, and a whimsical tree, as shown in *Figure 2.2*. By doing this, we can create a fun concept and draw the viewers' attention to it.

Now we have seen some examples of how unique trees look, let us move forward to drawing a tree. In this walkthrough, we will learn how to draw trees easily without having to draw complex details.

Following the steps

Before moving on to the step-by-step process, refer to *Figure 2.3* as guidance to follow the walkthrough effectively.

Figure 2.3 – Drawing a tree

You can use the following steps to draw a gentle tree:

1. Firstly, draw a tree's trunk and some branches as the base for the tree foliage.

2. Decide where the light source placement is coming from and paint the shadow formed on the area that is hidden from the light source.

3. Add highlights using a bright yellow color and shadow using a darker green color.

4. Lastly, add the final details to the tree and the reflected light to complete it.

Understanding the technique

To draw a tree, we start by drawing its trunk. From the top of the trunk, draw several branches extending outward. The branches should vary in length and thickness, becoming thinner as they move away from the trunk. Make sure to add some smaller branches coming off the main ones to create a more natural look (*STEP 1* in *Figure 2.3*). To create the tree foliage, draw a series of overlapping, irregular shapes around the branches. These shapes can be cloud-like or more detailed, depending on the type of tree you are drawing. Make sure to vary the size and shape of the foliage to give the tree a more realistic appearance (*STEP 2*). This variation can be achieved by adjusting Procreate's pressure sensitivity settings or applying a lighter touch with your Apple Pencil on the canvas. This allows you to control the size of the branches and the tree's foliage more effectively. Then, add some shading to the foliage to give it depth and dimension. For the trunk and branches, add more texture and shading to enhance the overall look (*STEP 3*). Lastly, refine the edges using the **Smudge** or **Sharpen** tool and add any final details. You can add some grass or other elements around the base of the tree to complete the scene (*STEP 4*).

Learning how to draw soothing grass

Grass has a unique texture that can be difficult to replicate. We have to use varied brush strokes and shades of green to mimic the natural look of grass. We can use short, quick strokes to recreate the sharp appearance of grass. By varying the pressure we put on our brush strokes, we can create different thicknesses and shapes. We can use a customized grass brush to draw grass easily. This is a great method to help us save time, but it can be limiting as we are unable to recreate a grass look based on our own preference. Understanding how to draw grass can help us break the limitations and enable us to draw unlimited grass scenery. In this walkthrough, we will learn how to draw grass manually without using a ready-made brush by following a simple step-by-step drawing process.

Following the steps

Before moving on to the step-by-step process, refer to *Figure 2.4* as guidance to follow the walkthrough effectively.

Figure 2.4 – Drawing grass

You can use the following steps to draw soothing grass:

1. Firstly, draw a base for the grass using a green color on a light brown color base.

2. Decide on the light source placement and paint a shadow on the area that is hidden from the light source.

3. Add highlights using a light green color and shadows with darker color tones.

4. Lastly, add some additional details such as small flowers and reflected light.

Understanding the technique

Start with a base; draw a base for the grass using a green color on a light brown color base. This will give you a foundation to draw upon and provide you with directions to draw the grass (*STEP 1* in *Figure 2.4*). Then, decide where the light source is placed as it will help you determine where to add shadows. Shadows can be added to areas that are hidden from the light source (*STEP 2*). Proper shading can give your grass a more three-dimensional look and add charm to the color. Use a light green color for highlights and darker color tones to enhance the shadows (*STEP 3*). If you find blending the colors difficult, you can use **blending modes** such as **Soft Light** for highlights and **Multiply** for shadows for a smoother workflow. This contrast will help in making the grass look more realistic and vibrant. Finally, add some details such as little flowers, bright yellow for highlights, dark green for shadows, and a teal color for reflected light on the grass (*STEP 4*). Grass can sometimes appear to have blue or teal tones because it reflects the color of the sky. Adding these colors to your drawing can make the grass look more realistic and natural. These small details can make a significant difference in the overall look of your grass drawing. To make it easier to add small details during the detailing process, you can adjust the brush sizes accordingly.

Learning how to draw a flower field scene

Flowers have delicate textures that can be challenging to draw. Drawing flower field scenery requires a deep understanding of petal textures and how they appear from different perspectives. This is to ensure we can create a realistic flower drawing. It is important to remember that *realistic* does not mean *perfect*; it means that we get to draw an object that looks almost identical to a real-life object. To get better at drawing flowers, we can take pictures of flowers and observe them. Play around with the lighting and discover how external circumstances such as weather can create a different texture and appearance of the flowers. This method will surely help us in drawing flowers, but it may take time for us to master it. In this walkthrough, I will share the quickest way to draw flowers using specific tools in Procreate.

Following the steps

Before moving on to the step-by-step process, please refer to *Figure 2.5* as guidance to follow the walkthrough effectively.

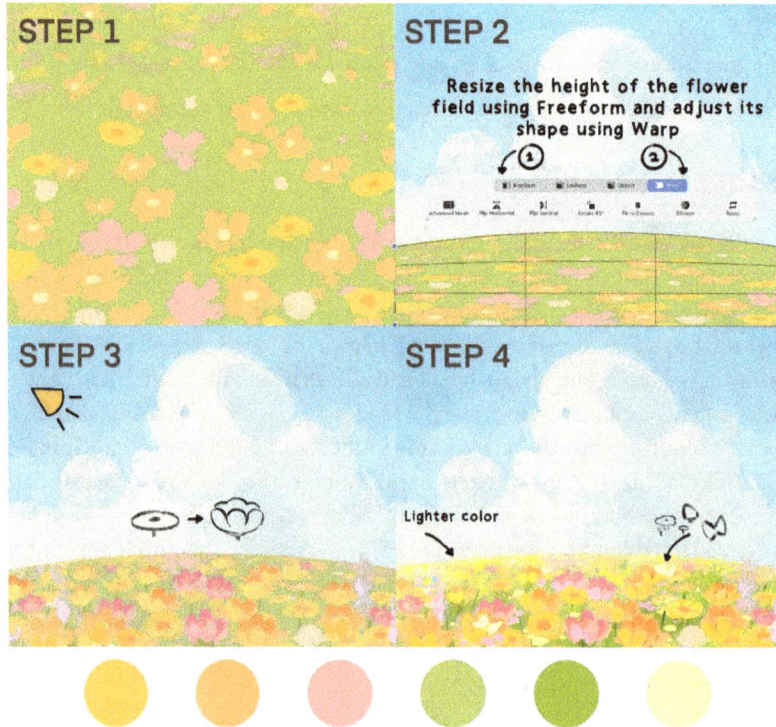

Figure 2.5 – Drawing a flower field

You can use the following steps to draw a field of flowers:

1. Firstly, draw a base for the green field using a green color and draw some flowers on it.

2. Create a bright blue sky with soft white clouds beneath the flower field layer, following the layout in *STEP 2*. If needed, refer to the earlier cloud tutorial for guidance.

3. Using the **Warp tool** in Procreate, reshape the green background color, as shown in *STEP 2* in *Figure 2.5*.

4. Add details to the flowers and redraw them in 3D form to make them more realistic.

5. Lastly, add highlights and additional details such as butterflies and smaller flowers on the flower field to complete it.

Understanding the technique

To draw a flower field scene, start by painting the whole canvas with a green color. Then, draw different shapes of flowers with different colors on top of the green layer, as shown in *STEP 1*. We draw different flowers to add variation to the flower field. Then, use the **Warp** tool to reshape the flower field. To do this, tap the **Transform** button in the toolbar and select **Warp** from the options. This will activate the **Warp** mesh, which overlays your artwork with a grid. You can drag the corners, edges, or inner parts of the mesh to warp your artwork in any direction. This is great for creating folds, curves, or unique distortions, as shown in *STEP 2*. You can reshape the flower field based on your own preference. Once it has been reshaped, enhance the flowers' appearance by adding details to make them appear more realistic. You can add details to the petals and add shadows to make them more three-dimensional. In the last step, add highlights to create a softer look using **Soft Brush** (or any brush you prefer) to add depth to the flower field. As you can see in *STEP 4*, I added highlights to the furthest flowers to make them look more distant. The farther away it gets, the less detailed and the smaller the flowers appear.

You may also add butterflies to enhance the overall look of the flower field. By mastering this simple walkthrough, we can create natural flower scenery and successfully capture the beauty of nature.

Learning how to draw gravel

Capturing the intricate textures and details of rocks and dirt can be difficult. Each rock has unique cracks, lines, and surfaces that need to be represented accurately while dirt has smaller details that you need to draw to make it look realistic. To ensure that both are represented correctly, we need to add depth and perspective. When drawing background scenery, we tend to avoid paying attention to rocks and dirt. However, if we understand how to draw them, we can create better ground scenery. Remember not to add too many rocks as it will lead to creating a whole new scene and changing the aesthetics of the gravel background. Sometimes it can overshadow the main subject in a drawing, thus making people move past your art very quickly as they are unable to focus on one thing.

Following the steps

Before moving on to the step-by-step process, please refer to *Figure 2.6* as guidance to follow the walkthrough effectively.

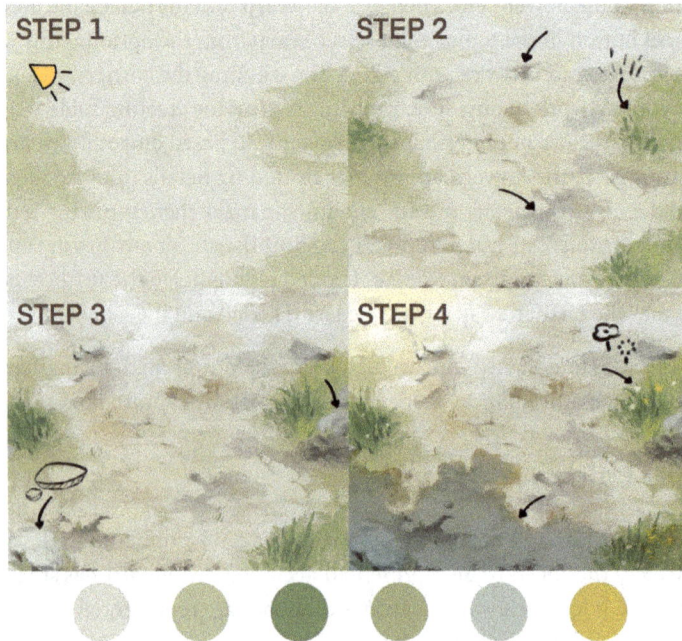

Figure 2.6 – Drawing gravel

You can use the following steps to draw gravel:

1. Firstly, draw a base for the gravel using a desaturated yellow color as the base.

2. Add some dirt texture and grass to make it look more realistic.

3. Add some rocks and additional shadows to the texture and highlight the area that the light source hits.

4. Lastly, add some additional details, such as a tree's shadow and some small flowers, and increase the color saturation.

Understanding the technique

Start by drawing a base for the gravel using a desaturated yellow or light grayish-yellow color. This will be the base for your rocks and dirt (*STEP 1*). Incorporate some dirt texture and grasses to make the scene look more realistic. This can be done by varying the brush strokes and colors to mimic the natural look of dirt and grass. You can apply a grainy or rough texture to it for easiness and to save more time (*STEP 2*). Then, draw some rocks of different sizes and shapes. Adding shadows to the rocks will give them depth and make them appear more three-dimensional (*STEP 3*). To achieve this, you can either use Procreate's blending modes, such as **Multiply**, or apply a darker shade of the object's base color to create the shadows. Adding highlights to the areas where the light source hits the rocks and dirt will create a sense of depth and realism. Shadows should be added to the areas hidden from the light source. Finally, add some details, such as the shadow of a tree and small flowers, and increase the color saturation to enhance the overall look of the scene (*STEP 4*).

Learning how to draw a fence

A fence is a fun way to add charm to our background scenery. It also can add depth to our background scenery by drawing the fence bigger at the nearest point and smaller at the farthest. Maintaining consistency in spacing between the fence posts is one of the crucial things when drawing a fence, which can be done using Procreate's 2D Grid found at **Drawing Guides | 2D Grid**. Drawing them in uneven shapes or forms can create an eerie or abandoned atmosphere. One challenge that we face in drawing fences is capturing the wooden texture. The number of details we need to draw for wooden texture can be difficult if we are unfamiliar with it. In this walkthrough, I will share a step-by-step process to help you draw fences easily.

Following the steps

Before moving on to the step-by-step process, please refer to *Figure 2.7* as guidance to follow the walkthrough effectively.

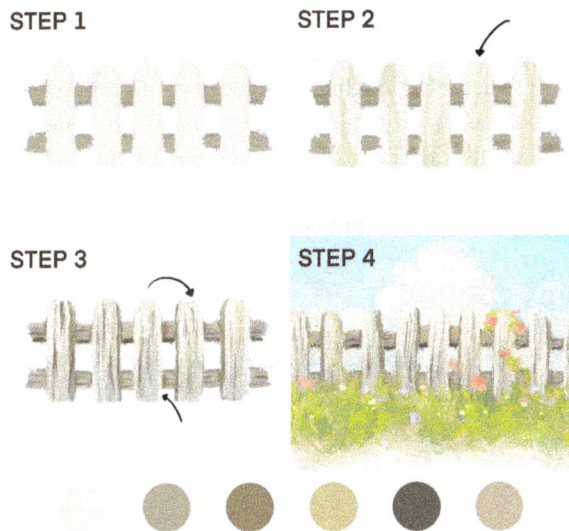

Figure 2.7 – Drawing a fence

You can use the following steps to draw a fence:

1. Firstly, draw a base for the fence using a cream color and a desaturated light brown.

2. Then, using a darker color from the base color, draw uneven lines for texturing purposes.

3. Draw a wooden texture on the fence and add some shadows to make it look realistic.

4. Lastly, duplicate the fence and add a background with clouds and grass to complete it.

Understanding the technique

Start with drawing fence posts with two different colors (*STEP 1*). In this walkthrough, I used a cream color and desaturated brown color. You are free to use any colors you prefer for your fence. Then, paint some uneven horizontal lines using a darker color, which serves as the base for texturing purposes. Once added, add a wooden texture by using a darker color (*STEP 2*). Please avoid drawing it too perfectly as it may look too stiff and unnatural. Add shadows to the area that is hidden from the light source (*STEP 3*). Finally, duplicate the fence to fill in the background or place it where needed (*STEP 4*). Now, the fence is ready to use, and you can paste it on your background scenery. You can reshape it using the **Warp** and **Distort** tools in Procreate to make it look more natural and random. You can add background scenery to the fence drawing to complete it.

Learning how to draw little houses

Drawing houses is the easiest method to create a cozy and welcoming background scenery. By drawing houses, we can create a storyline, and when the viewer sees it, they can imagine that someone may have once lived in that house or a family is living there. This will create an emotional response from viewers, and they can connect with the art. A house often represents security and comfort; thus, this will help viewers feel a sense of safety after looking at it. Drawing small houses can help to create depth in the background illustration, too, by varying the house sizes. We are sometimes afraid of drawing houses due to the number of details they have. There is no right way to draw a house in art; you can draw the house however you prefer. In this walkthrough, I will help you draw a house in the easiest way, and you will no longer have to worry about drawing complex details on houses.

Following the steps

Before moving on to the step-by-step process, please refer to *Figure 2.8* as guidance to follow the walkthrough effectively.

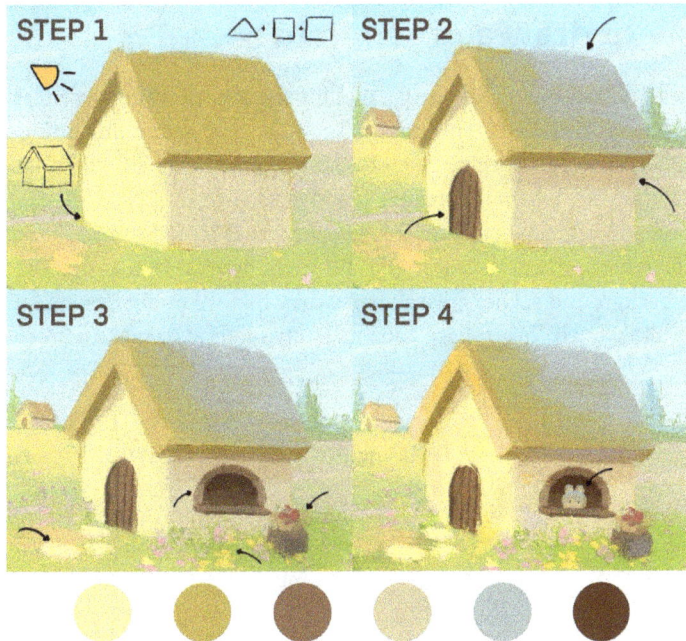

Figure 2.8 – Drawing a little house

You can use the following steps to draw a little house:

1. Firstly, draw a house shape, as shown in *STEP 1* in *Figure 2.8*.

2. Then, add details such as a door and shadows, and use a blue color for the reflected light.

3. Add details such as a path, small flowers, windows, and any decoration around the house.

4. Lastly, add any character you prefer to the house.

Understanding the technique

For little houses, you can draw simple shapes such as squares, rectangles, and triangles as the main base. Then, adjust the shape by adding a shadow on it to turn it into a three-dimensional shape. You can refer to *STEP 1* in the previous figure for guidance. Once the house base is created, draw a door and add additional shadows to create contrast. On the rooftop, you can add light blue as reflected light. You can use Procreate's **Soft Light** blending mode to paint this (*STEP 2*). The reflected light on the rooftop was created because the light bounces from the blue sky and hits the rooftop. Add extra details such as a garden path, small flowers, a window, and other decorations in the surroundings to make it livelier (*STEP 3*). Finally, add a character to add some story to the house (*STEP 4*). This will create a more joyful and serene view. Adding a character to the house is purely optional and not a necessity.

Learning how to draw a green field

A green field provides a natural and calm setting, making the overall scene more pleasing to look at. The color green is often associated with calmness, tranquility, and nature. Including a green field in the background can help convey a specific mood or atmosphere in the artwork and can add depth and perspective to the drawing. It helps to create a sense of distance and space, making the scene look more natural. Other than that, green fields can enhance the visual aesthetic of the background scenery by adding various elements such as grass, flowers, and small houses. Due to the limited shapes that can be drawn in the background scenery, we always worry that we might draw it looking too plain and boring. In this walkthrough, I will share and create my method to make a green field look nice and interesting.

Following the steps

Before moving on to the step-by-step process, please refer to *Figure 2.9* as guidance to follow the walkthrough effectively.

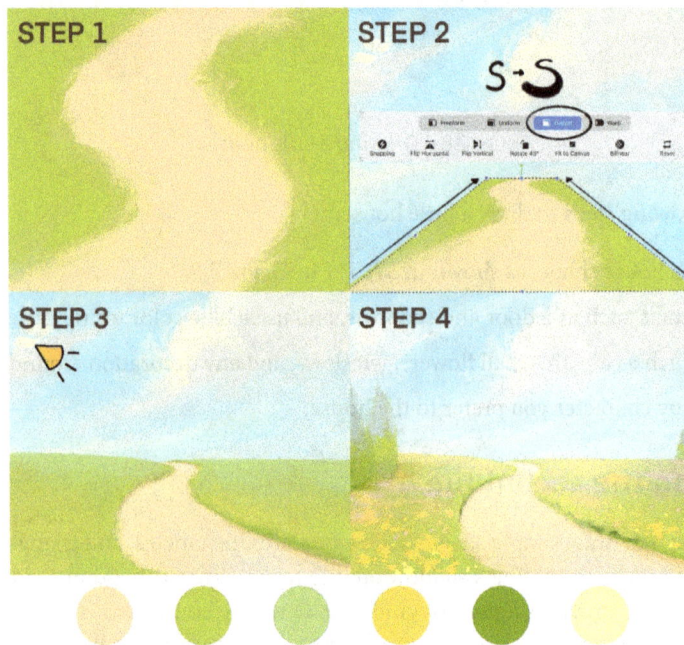

Figure 2.9 – Drawing a green field

You can use the following steps to draw a green field:

1. Firstly, draw a base for the green field using green and light brown colors, as shown in *STEP 1* in *Figure 2.9*.

2. Create a bright blue sky with soft white clouds beneath the green field layer, following the layout in *STEP 2*. If needed, refer to the earlier cloud tutorial for guidance.

3. Then, reshape the green field using the **Distort tool** to your own preference.

4. Add a blueish-green color and yellowish-green to the green field.

5. Lastly, add details such as flowers and trees to complete it.

Understanding the technique

To draw a green field easily, you can start by filling out the canvas with a green color and adding an S-like shape on top of it using a light brown color to form a road (*STEP 1*). Then, go to Procreate's settings and use the **Distort** tool to reshape it (*STEP 2*). This can help to add distance and perspective to your background scenery. The **Distort** tool in Procreate is part of the **Transform** options, which allow you to manipulate the shape of your artwork to create perspective effects. To use it, first, select the layer you want to adjust and tap the **Transform** button. Then, choose the **Distort** mode from the toolbar. This will display a bounding box around your selected layer. You can drag the corner nodes of this box to reshape your artwork, giving it a tilted or angled effect that mimics three-dimensional depth. As you can see, the road's perspective and composition can be changed easily using the **Distort** tool. Then, fill in the empty spaces with colors. Use light blue colors on the farthest and a vibrant olive color on the nearest green field (*STEP 3*). This is to create a sense of distance in the background scenery. Finally, add some trees and small flowers to enhance the overall atmosphere (*STEP 4*). The last step is optional, and it is not necessary to add flowers to finalize it. The additional details will depend on what emotion or atmosphere you would like to express through your illustration.

Learning how to draw a lake

A lake often evokes a sense of calm and tranquility. Including elements such as a still lake or a gently flowing stream can create a peaceful and serene atmosphere in the background scenery. On the other hand, drawing water in motion such as a waterfall, waves crashing against the shore or a gushing river can add a sense of movement and energy to the background scenery. The reflected objects or things that appear on the water reflection can add charm and draw viewers to look at them. Drawing water can be challenging, especially capturing the movement of the water and knowing which colors to use for water scenery such as lakes, seas, and so on. In this walkthrough, we will learn how to add a lake to the scenery such that it looks natural and serene.

Following the steps

Before moving on to the step-by-step process, please refer to *Figure 2.10* as guidance to follow the walkthrough effectively.

Figure 2.10 – Drawing a lake

You can use the following steps to draw a lake:

1. Firstly, draw the base for water using green and blue colors.

2. Then, add a reflection on the water and some different green shades for the grass. Optionally, add a character as the main focal point. I will draw a duck and bunny as the main focal point.

3. Draw ripples of water around the character and then add shadows and additional reflections on the water.

4. Lastly, add some details such as small flowers, highlights, and shadows to complete it.

Understanding the technique

To recreate a lake scene, fill in the canvas using a green and blue color as the base color. You can draw the shape of the lake based on your own preference (*STEP 1*). Then, add different shades of green to make the grass look more vibrant. Adding a character can create a focal point that attracts viewer attention, which is why I drew a duck and bunny (*STEP 2*). Add the reflections of the objects around the lake on the water. The reflection of an object doesn't need to be perfect; just draw it so it looks similar enough to the original. This will help the viewer to visualize the whole scene. Add ripples of water around the character to create motion (*STEP 3*). Keep in mind that if ripples are added to the water where the object's reflection is drawn, the shape of the reflection will become distorted and appear altered. Finally, enhance the details around the lake to complete it. You can add additional details such as flowers, highlights, and shadows to create a contrast (*STEP 4*).

Learning how to draw snow

Snowy scenery conveys a sense of quiet and solitude, but it is often associated with winter and the holiday season as well. Adding snow to an artwork can evoke seasonal and festive feelings, making the piece feel cozy and significantly influencing the atmosphere of the piece. It depends on what emotions you would like to express through your illustration. Due to the limited color scheme that we get to see in a snowy environment, it can be challenging to find the right color to use. The problems will arise when we add shadow, and we are unsure what color shadow we should use to prevent it from looking plain and empty. In this walkthrough, we will learn how we can draw a serene view of a snowy season.

Following the steps

Before moving on to the step-by-step process, please refer to *Figure 2.11* as guidance to follow the walkthrough effectively.

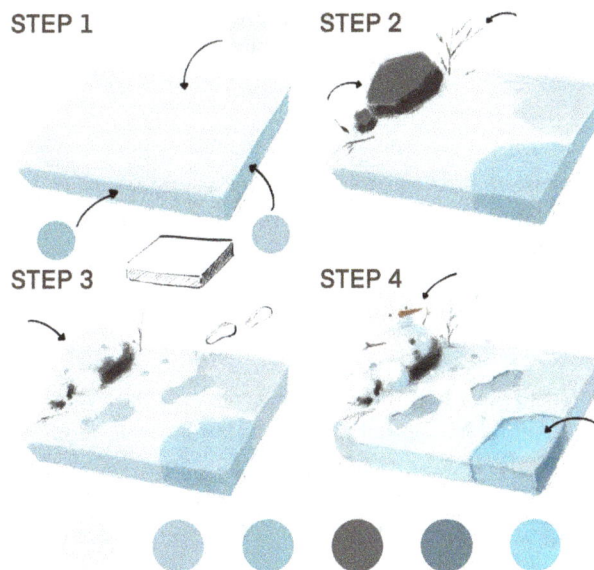

Figure 2.11 – Drawing snow

You can use the following steps to draw snow:

1. First, draw a base for the snow using three different shades of blue.

2. Then, add details such as stones, small branches, and a freezing lake to make it look realistic.

3. Add snow on top of the objects drawn in *STEP 2*.

4. Lastly, add additional details such as a snowman, footprints, enhanced shadows, and reflected light using a vibrant blue color to complete it.

Understanding the technique

Drawing snow can be done by preparing three different shades of blue and using them as the base colors (*STEP 1*). Then, add stones and some branches to make it more realistic. You can add a frozen lake to add more charm to it (*STEP 2*). Since it is a snowy scene, draw snow piling up on the objects you have already drawn, such as the stone (*STEP 3*). You can add footprints to add a story to your illustration. This can help the viewer imagine that someone might have walked past previously, or someone is walking around to find firewood. Finally, add additional details such as a snowman to add fun to the atmosphere. Enhance the snow colors by adding vibrant blue colors to make the colors stand out (*STEP 4*). You are free to add any other details you prefer to finalize it. Remember that in art, it is not necessary to make everything look perfect as this will make the illustration look unnatural. Draw in any way that feels right to you and brings out your unique vision to create a truly one-of-a-kind illustration.

Know more...

You can also use the **Snow brush** in Procreate to make it look more realistic and to save time. If you'd like the snow to have more texture, you can use a texture brush in Procreate such as the **Soft Pastel** or **Tamar brush**.

Summary

This chapter teaches you how to draw beautiful natural scenery and everyday elements step by step, in a way that feels calm and enjoyable. You start with soft clouds, using gentle shapes and blending to make them look light and fluffy. Then you learn how to draw trees, focusing on simple trunks and leaves, followed by adding light and shadow to give them depth. Next comes grass, where short strokes and soft colors help create a peaceful feeling. In the flower field section, you play with shapes, colors, and the Warp tool to give movement to the scene. Drawing gravel teaches you to add realistic ground textures with rocks and shadows, while fences add charm and structure to a background.

The little houses section shows how simple shapes can tell a warm, inviting narrative. Then you learn to draw a green field, adding colors and perspective to build a calm, open space. In the lake tutorial, you use soft reflections and ripples to create a quiet and serene water scene. Finally, you explore snow, layering blues and gentle details to capture the peaceful feeling of a snowy day. Each section reminds you that natural details don't have to be complex. What matters most is expressing feelings through shape, light, and texture while letting your own style and imagination guide the way.

In the next chapter, you'll explore how to use perspective to bring depth and movement into your art. With simple tips on natural and linear perspective, you'll learn to make scenes feel more alive and expressive.

Unlock this book's exclusive benefits now

Scan this QR code or go to packtpub.com/unlock, then search this book by name.

3
Mastering Perspective for Dynamic Scenes

Implementing perspective in art requires a deep understanding of how and when to use it. Perspective can be divided into two main categories: natural perspective and linear perspective. Natural perspective involves painting based on what you see, capturing the essence of the scene as it appears to the eye. On the other hand, linear perspective involves drawing objects by following a set of rules to accurately represent their dimensions. Many artists find perspective challenging because of its complex structure, which can make it difficult to apply effectively in their work. However, mastering perspective is essential for creating realistic artwork.

In this chapter, we will explore how to effectively incorporate perspective into our art. We will learn about the concepts of natural and linear perspective, providing step-by-step guidance on how to apply these techniques to our drawings and paintings. By the end of this chapter, you will have gained the confidence and skills needed to use perspective to enhance your artwork, making it more dynamic and visually appealing.

With the help of walkthroughs, we'll cover the following topics:

- How to apply natural perspective in background drawing
- How to use the linear perspective built-in system
- How to identify linear perspective in real-life images
- How to implement linear perspective techniques in background illustration

How to apply natural perspective in background drawing

Natural perspective and linear perspective are two different techniques in art to add perspective to background drawing. For natural perspective, you will focus on drawing what you see instead of following certain guidelines and rules, whereas, for linear perspective, you need to follow specific guidelines to add perspective in background drawing, which we will learn about together as this chapter goes on. The aim of natural perspective is to draw an object the way you see it. There are a few easy ways we can do that, but first, we need to understand how atmospheric perspective, size perspective, and detail perspective work. Natural perspective can be hard to use initially, but in this chapter, we will learn how to apply these perspective techniques to our background scenery.

Atmospheric perspective is a technique used in art to create the illusion of depth and distance by depicting the changes in color and contrast of objects as they recede into the background. For example, distant objects appear lighter, bluer, and less detailed compared to nearer subjects.

If you walk around and pay attention to your surroundings, you will notice that distant objects such as houses, trees, and hills will appear paler and purple-bluish in color. No matter what the object's real color is, it will appear a little purple-bluish when it is far from you. The farther the object is, the paler it will look.

For example, let us have a look at the following figure for reference:

Figure 3.1 – An example of atmospheric perspective (source: https://unsplash.com/ photos/a-lush-green-hillside-with-trees-and-hills-in-the-background-lbhS3vP_ybY)

We notice that the color of the nearest trees and hill is more vibrant compared to the distant hills and trees. This is due to particles in the air between you and the object that act like a filter that causes a shift in color. The best way to add depth to our background drawing is by using the atmospheric perspective method, and we will learn how to use it effectively in our art by following a simple step-by-step drawing process.

Following the steps

Adding atmospheric perspective can be done as follows:

1. In a blank sheet in Procreate, prepare a simple background scenery with hills. You can follow *Figure 3.2* or create your own background.

Figure 3.2 – Example of hill scenery

2. Add a new layer on top of the Layer 1 background scenery. Let us name the new layer *Distant Hill* to avoid confusion. Please check *Figure 3.3* for guidelines.

3.   Change the new layer's blending mode to **Soft Light**.

Figure 3.3 – Layer names and settings

4.   Using light blue colors, paint the distant hill. Please refer to the *Distant Hill layer* in *Figure 3.3* if you are not sure how to do it.

Figure 3.4 – Example of colors used to paint the distant hill

Tip

You can change the opacity of the Distant Hill layer to your own preference by tapping the layer using two fingers at the same time and the opacity slide bar will appear, ready to use.

Figure 3.5 shows the result of adding atmospheric perspective to the background scenery. The scenery looks more natural and realistic:

Figure 3.5 – Example of hill scenery after lighter blue colors are added to create atmospheric perspective

Now, we have successfully added atmospheric perspective to the background scenery using different color values. Let us move forward to the explanation of how it works.

Understanding the technique

The rule in painting a realistic background scenery is to paint what you see and trust your eyes. If you see the object as bluish or paler, paint it like that. To recreate the bluish effect in your background scenery, use the **Soft Light** blending mode. **Soft Light** in Procreate is like a magic filter for your art. It gently blends colors to make lighting, shading, and atmosphere look softer without overpowering your original design. Think of it as a way to subtly adjust the mood of your artwork, making it feel livelier. By doing this, you can create a background drawing that looks natural and realistic. It is important to remember that not all objects will look purple or bluish, so it is advisable to use your own judgment in coloring the object. Adding atmospheric perspective to the background scenery will create depth in the illustration, making it look more vast.

Size perspective

Size perspective is how we see or think about the size of something compared to other things. It helps us understand how big or small something is in relation to its surroundings. For example, when you look at a picture of a tiny animal next to a huge building, the size perspective helps you realize just how small that animal really is. It also applies to the connection between the distance of an object with another object.

Imagine that you are standing and facing a long road. If you pay attention to the road, you will notice that the farther the road is from you, the smaller it gets. By drawing distant objects smaller than the ones nearest to you, you can add a sense of depth to your background scenery. The advice here is to trust your eyes and paint them how you see them. If the distant trees look smaller, draw them smaller, even though you know that all the trees are roughly the same size. Size perspective helps us better understand the scale of things to make our background drawing look more realistic.

Let's have a look at the following example:

Figure 3.6 – An example of size perspective (source: https://unsplash.com/
photos/a-dirt-path-in-a-grassy-field-with-dead-trees-ejb7MHasSME)

As you can see in *Figure 3.6*, the road gets smaller and narrower as it gets farther from you. The size of the road can convey the distance of the road; thus, it can introduce a sense of depth into the background scenery. Trees and other objects play the same role in this situation as well. When something is close to you, it looks bigger because it's near your eyes, so you can see more of it. But when something is far away from you, it looks smaller because it's further from your eyes, so you can't see it as clearly or in as much detail. This happens because of how our eyes and brain understand distance and size. It's like when you see a tall building up close: it seems huge, but if you see the same building from far away, it looks tiny. This helps us understand how far things are and how they fit into the space around us.

Next, let us try to recreate size perspective by executing the following steps.

Following the steps

Adding size perspective can be done as follows:

1. Prepare straight blocks of color, as seen in *Figure 3.7*. The green color shows the grass area while the light brown color shows the road.

Figure 3.7 – Example of the color and design

2.   Using the **Distort** tool, adjust the shape of the road, as shown in *Figure 3.8*.

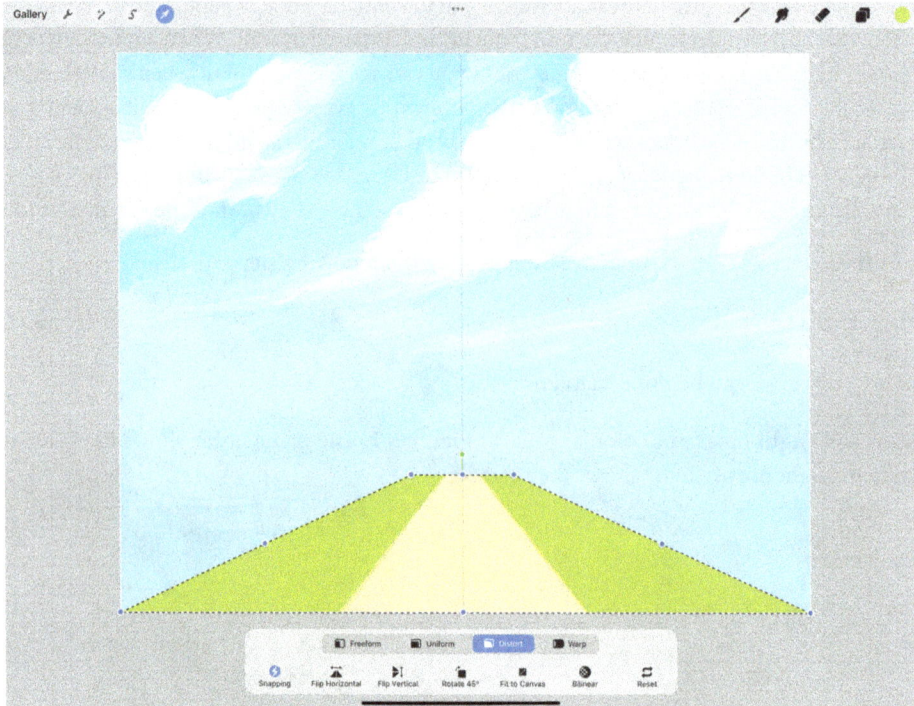

Figure 3.8 – Example of using the Distort tool

3.   Next, fill in the empty spaces and add some trees. Draw them from bigger to smaller sizes, as shown in *Figure 3.9*.

Figure 3.9 – Final result of using size perspective

Figure 3.9 shows the result of adding size perspective to the background scenery. By making the size of the trees smaller as they get further away, we can create depth in our background scenery. Using the size perspective in your drawing helps guide the viewer's eyes to the most important part, like leading them on a journey through the art. It makes them feel like they're walking along a path toward something special or important, creating a sense of depth and adventure in the artwork.

Understanding the technique

Adding size perspective can help you make the background look more realistic, but you do not necessarily have to add a perspective technique to your background scenery if you prefer the illustration to be easier to understand. It is more based on your own aesthetic preference, and you are free to draw as you like.

Know more...

Procreate's perspective tools, such as the **Drawing Guide**, can help you apply the size perspective technique to your background drawings. We'll explore this method further in this chapter.

Detail perspective

Detail perspective (also known as **depth of field**) refers to looking at something closely and focusing on its small parts or characteristics rather than seeing the bigger picture. It involves paying attention to the specifics, such as colors, textures, and shapes, which can reveal valuable information about the overall main focal point.

Like a camera, our eyes can only focus on one object at a time, while the surrounding objects become blurry. If you hold a pencil in your hand and focus on it, you will notice that the surrounding objects look blurry. This can help show the distance of one object, thus helping you create perspective in your background scenery. Detail perspective refers to the portion of an image that appears sharp and focused, while other areas are intentionally blurred to create a sense of depth and to draw attention to specific parts.

For example, let us have a look at the following scenery photograph:

Figure 3.10 – Reference showing how the nearest objects are blurry compared to the distant focal object (source: https://unsplash.com/photos/a-grassy-field-with-a-power-line-in-the-background-21KUVpTNwlQ)

From the preceding figure, we notice that the transmission power line is the focal point; thus the nearest grass becomes blurry and fuzzy. As we can see, the nearest grass loses its detail compared to the transmission power line. This suggests that we are looking at something far away.

Let us look at a second example here:

Figure 3.11 – Reference showing nearest objects clearer than distant objects (source: https://unsplash.com/photos/a-field-of-green-grass-with-purple-flowers-7Ulud_NeEzY)

If we look closely, we notice that the nearest flowers and grass look more detailed compared to the ones in the background. The blurry area shows that the grass in the background is far away from the nearest flowers and grass. It works similarly to the method shown in *Figure 3.10*, where the nearest object is blurry while the distant object is more detailed. Both methods can be used to add depth to our background scenery. Now, I will share a step-by-step *detail perspective* tutorial on how we can use this technique in our background scenery.

Following the steps

Adding the detail perspective can be done as follows:

1. Prepare a background scenery with bunnies as the main focal point. You can draw anything you prefer for your background scenery.

Figure 3.12 – Example of a background scenery illustration

2. Add details such as flowers or grass to the front as the main focal point in separate layers, as shown in *Figure 3.13*.

Figure 3.13 – Example with grass and flowers added to the front

3. Then, use **Gaussian Blur** on the layer of the nearest details, which are the flowers and grass. *Figure 3.14* shows the result we get by blurring out the nearest details:

Figure 3.14 – Example of nearest objects blurred out (grass and flowers)

4.   Let us do it again by blurring out the details in the background with **Gaussian Blur**, then adding details to the nearest grass and flowers.

Figure 3.15 shows the result we get by blurring out the background details:

Figure 3.15 – Example of distant objects blurred out (bunnies and clouds)

By following the steps, we have successfully created two different detail perspective techniques easily with the help of **Gaussian Blur**. Let us look at how this method works.

Understanding the technique

If we compare *Figure 3.14* and *Figure 3.15*, we can see that blurry and fuzzy-looking objects can create depth and add a sense of distance in the background scenery. If we add the same number of details to every part of the object in the illustration, the background scenery will lose some depth and appear flat. To make it easier, think of having a foreground, middle ground, and background. Choose one area to be the main focal point of your artwork. After deciding on the focal point, select the other areas to blur, enhancing the focus on your chosen subject. Use **Gaussian Blur** in Procreate to soften those parts and complete the effect. **Gaussian Blur** is a tool that softens and smooths parts of your artwork by creating a gentle, out-of-focus effect. It's perfect for blending colors, adding depth, or creating a dreamy atmosphere in your illustrations. You can apply it to an entire layer or specific areas using your Apple Pencil.

To use it, tap the **Adjustments** menu (the magic wand icon), select **Gaussian Blur**, and then slide your finger across the screen to adjust the intensity. Ensure that the main focal point and the object you intend to blur are placed on separate layers. This way, adjusting or editing becomes much simpler and more flexible.

How to use the linear perspective built-in system

Linear perspective is a technique that creates an illusion of details and a sense of depth with parallel lines. It can be divided into three methods: **one-point perspective**, **two-point perspective**, and **three-point perspective**. With the help of Procreate's built-in settings, we can create a one-point perspective and a two-point perspective easily. Currently, Procreate does not offer a built-in feature for creating a three-point perspective. However, I will provide a step-by-step guide on how to manually apply this technique for background drawings in the Three-point perspective section. Let's take a look at how to create a one-point perspective easily using Procreate first.

One-point perspective

One-point perspective in art is a drawing technique that creates the illusion of depth and space on a flat surface by using a single vanishing point. This vanishing point is typically located on the horizon line, where all parallel lines in the scene appear to converge. In this walkthrough, we will learn how to use Procreate's built-in one-point perspective tool effectively.

Following the steps

Adding a one-point perspective with Procreate can be done as follows:

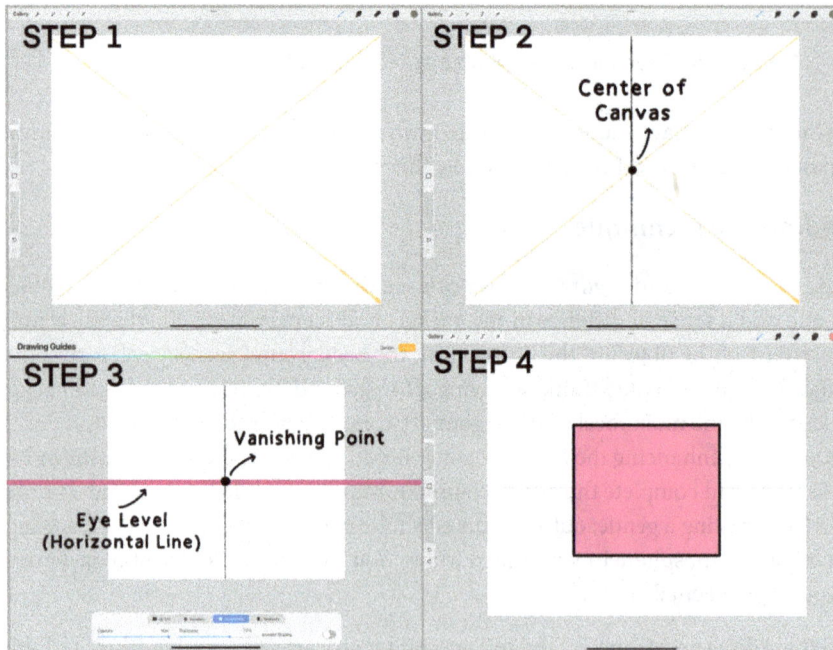

Figure 3.16 – Step-by-step process of creating one-point perspective using Procreate

> Tip
>
> 🔍 **Quick tip**: Need to see a high-resolution version of this image? Open this book in the next-gen Packt Reader or view it in the PDF/ePub copy.
>
> 🔒 **The next-gen Packt Reader** and a **free PDF/ePub copy** of this book are included with your purchase. Scan the QR code OR go to `packtpub.com/unlock`, then use the search bar to find this book by name. Double-check the edition shown to make sure you get the right one.
>
>

1. Firstly, find the center of the canvas by drawing two diagonal lines that stem from one corner of the canvas to the opposite, as shown in *STEP 1* in *Figure 3.16*.
2. Then, draw a vertical line in the middle of the canvas where the two lines cross.
3. Then, turn on **Drawing Guides** and select **Perspective**. Tap the center of the canvas and a horizontal line will appear. The center of the canvas works as the vanishing point.
4. Lastly, tap **Done**, and the one-point perspective is now available to use.

A one-point perspective has been created for you, and you can now use it as a guideline to create background scenery. Let us move forward with a two-point perspective. The two-point perspective is a little different from the one-point perspective. This technique is usually used to show different angles of an object.

> Tip
>
> The position of horizontal lines determines where objects are placed and how they relate to the viewer's perspective in terms of height and distance. It helps establish the overall viewpoint and depth of your artwork. In Procreate, the eye level (horizontal line) is automatically set when using perspective guides but can be manually adjusted.

Two-point perspective

A two-point perspective in art is another method for creating depth and dimension in a drawing. Unlike the one-point perspective, which uses a single vanishing point, the two-point perspective relies on two vanishing points placed on the horizon line. These two points are used to draw objects at an angle, showing two sides of an object as they recede into the distance. Now, we will learn how to use Procreate's two-point perspective tool easily by following the next steps.

Following the steps

Adding a two-point perspective using Procreate can be done as follows:

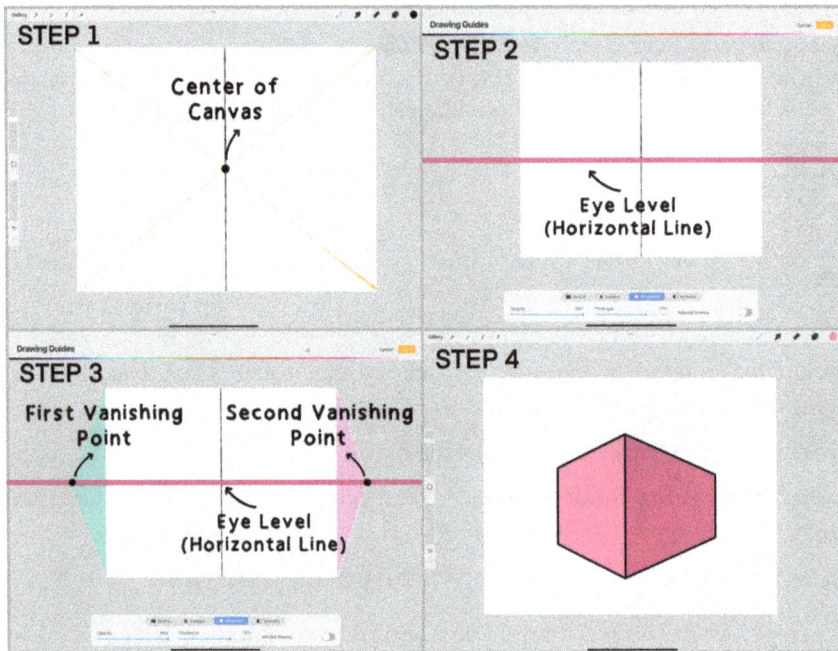

Figure 3.17 – Step-by-step process of creating a two-point perspective using Procreate

1. Firstly, go to Procreate's toolbar and turn on **Drawing Guides**. Determine the center of the canvas, as shown in *STEP 1* and *STEP 2* in *Figure 3.16*, and draw the extensive lines.

2. Then, tap **Edit Drawing Guide** and select the **Perspective** section.

3. Now, tap the center of the canvas, and a horizontal line will appear. Add another vanishing point for both the left and right sides of the horizontal line. It will look as shown in *STEP 3* in *Figure 3.17*.

4. Lastly, tap **Done**, and the two-point perspective is now available to use.

> **Important note**
>
> This horizontal line works as the eye level. The height of the horizontal line will decide the placement of an object.

A two-point perspective has been created for you, and you can now use it as a guideline to create a background.

Three-point perspective

Three-point perspective uses three vanishing points. These vanishing points create an illusion of depth in two-dimensional objects. The unique case in a three-point perspective is that the third vanishing point is nowhere near eye level. While two vanishing points are placed at eye level, the third vanishing point is placed outside of the canvas, and you will need to go a long way to find the end of the receding lines.

Following the steps

Creating a three-point perspective manually can be done as follows:

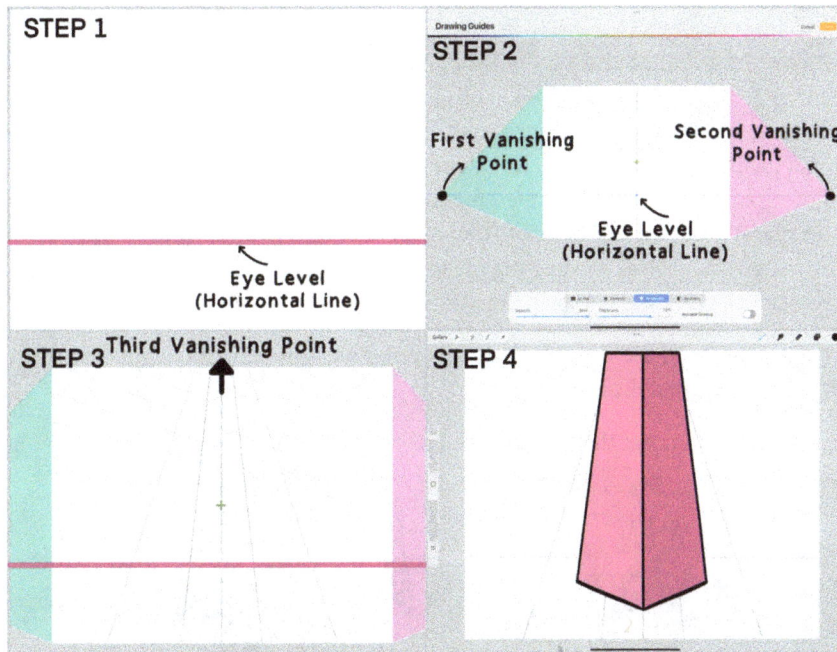

Figure 3.18 – Step-by-step process of creating a three-point perspective manually

1. Draw a straight line on a blank canvas. This line works as the eye-level line (horizontal line).

2. Find the center of the canvas, then add two vanishing points: one on the left and one on the right side of it.

3. Add a vanishing point above eye level. The lines should look as shown in *STEP 3* in *Figure 3.18*.

A three-point perspective has been created for you, and you can now use it as a guideline to create background scenery.

We have learned how to use one-point perspective, two-point perspective, and three-point perspective; now, let us learn how they work and when to use them in background scenery.

Understanding the technique

In a one-point perspective, you can freely decide where to place the eye level based on your preference. Procreate's built-in **Perspective** tools make it simple to create perspective guides without needing to draw them manually.

For a two-point perspective, the distance between the first and second vanishing points will determine the size of the objects in your drawing. If you move the vanishing points closer together, the perspective looks more extreme or stretched. If you place them farther apart, the perspective looks more natural and less dramatic. Keep this in mind as you plan and sketch out your ideas for accurate proportions and perspective.

Choosing between a one-point and two-point perspective depends on the composition and the effect you want to achieve. One-point perspective is ideal for scenes where the viewer is looking straight ahead, such as a hallway, street, or room. It uses a single vanishing point, creating a sense of simplicity and focus, which works well for symmetrical or straightforward designs. On the other hand, a two-point perspective is better suited for scenes viewed at an angle, such as the corner of a building or an expansive outdoor landscape. This perspective uses two vanishing points, allowing for more dynamic and realistic views by showing objects from multiple sides. By carefully selecting the perspective, you can enhance the depth and visual impact of your artwork.

A three-point perspective can be seen everywhere around us. It usually can be noticed when we are standing in front of a huge building or a tree.

For example, let us have a look at the following figure:

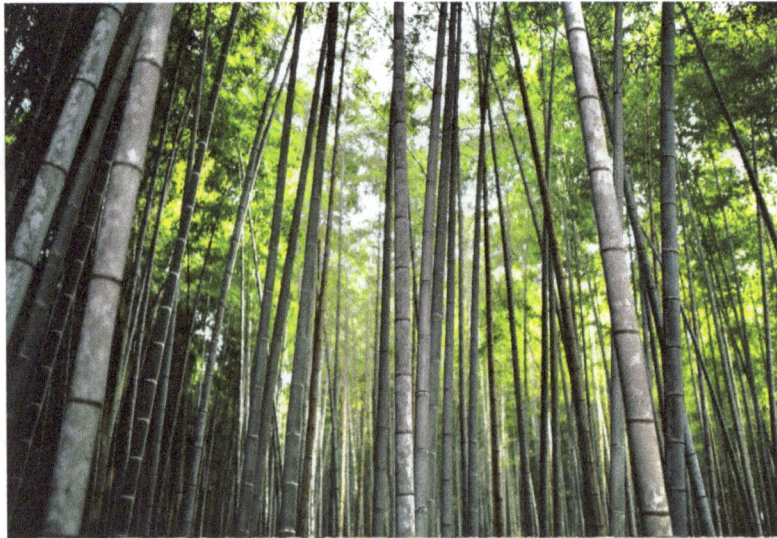

Figure 3.19 – Example of three-point perspective for background scenery (source: https://unsplash.com/photos/low-angle-photography-of-bamboo-trees-O7Fd4L72BkA)

The eye level is placed on the lower area of the bamboo; two vanishing points are placed on the eye-level line while the third vanishing point is placed somewhere above and away from the eye-level line. Using this method, we can create a three-dimensional object easily with a guide of the lines. Usually, objects drawn in a three-point perspective are placed either under or above eye level. It is as if we are looking at a tall building or standing in a higher place and looking down on the building lower than us. It is an easier way to differentiate between the two perspectives we learned earlier. Since Procreate does not have a feature to create a three-point perspective, we learned the manual way to do it.

As we learned previously, perspective techniques serve as a guideline to help you add depth to your background scenery. Do not depend too much on perspective guidelines. You can make your own adjustments to the guidelines based on what worked best for your background scenery.

> **Important note**
> The **vanishing point** is where parallel lines meet and disappear. **Eye level** is a horizontal line that is parallel to the ground.

How to identify linear perspective in real-life images

Linear perspective is a method used to create the illusion of depth and three-dimensionality on a flat surface. By utilizing vanishing points on a horizon line, it replicates how parallel lines appear to converge as they recede into the distance. This technique helps depict realistic spaces, such as landscapes, interiors, or cityscapes, making them appear more lifelike. Sometimes, it can be hard to figure out which perspective technique is used in a real-life image. This makes it tricky to find where the horizontal lines and vanishing points go. In this walkthrough, we will learn simple ways to spot one-point, two-point, and three-point perspectives in everyday pictures. We will begin with a one-point perspective and gradually move on to a two-point and three-point perspective as the chapter progresses. This will help build a solid foundation and make understanding each perspective easier.

Identifying a one-point perspective in a real-life image

You can recognize a one-point perspective in real life by observing situations where all parallel lines converge at a single point on the horizon. Examples include long hallways drawing your focus to the end, railway tracks seeming to meet in the distance, city streets framed by buildings heading toward a single spot, or tunnels curving toward a far-off point. Observing these elements can help you spot linear perspective in everyday scenes. The main problem with finding a one-point perspective in real-life images is figuring out where the eye level is. This walkthrough will show you a simple, step-by-step method to help you easily identify it and understand the one-point perspective better.

Understanding the technique

Figure 3.20 will be used for this walkthrough. You can use any image as long as it resembles the *Figure 3.20* composition.

Figure 3.20 – Example of a real-life image (source: https://unsplash.com/photos/white-wooden-house-on-snow-covered-ground-during-daytime-_hBBM5KEzdQ)

Let us learn together how to find the vanishing point and eye level (horizontal line) in one-point perspective:

1. Identify the eye level by locating where the sky meets the ground in the image. Draw a straight horizontal line across the image, as shown in *Figure 3.21*.

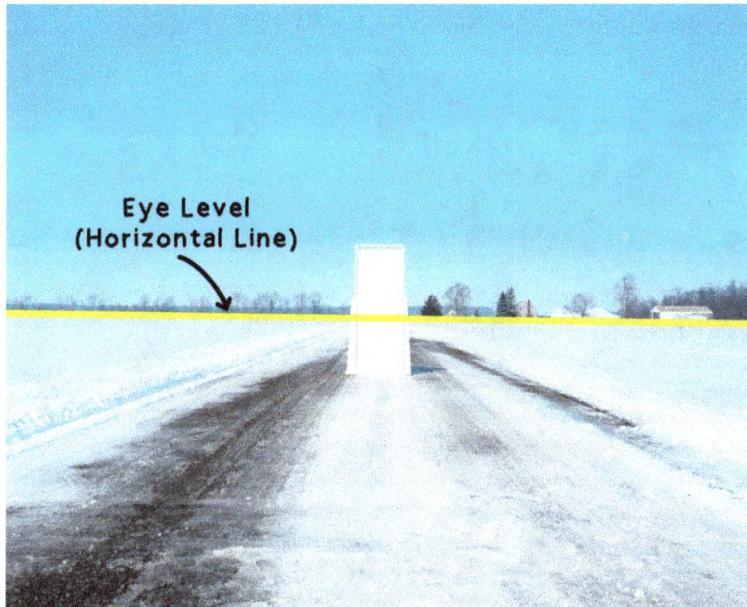

Figure 3.21 – Example of eye level in one-point perspective

2. Find the center of the image and mark the point where the eye level intersects this center. This is the vanishing point.

Figure 3.22 – Example of vanishing point in one-point perspective

3. Starting from the vanishing point, draw several straight lines radiating outward to create the perspective framework.

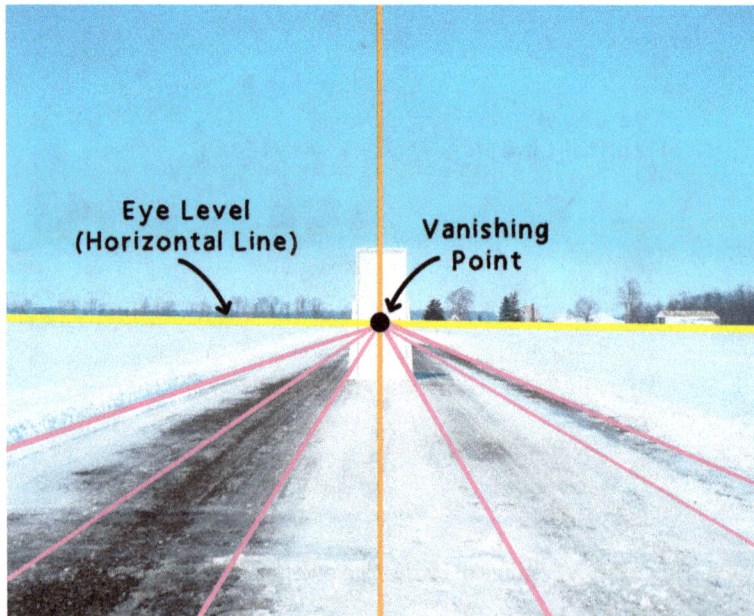

Figure 3.23 – Example of one-point perspective

Now, we have successfully identified the placement of the vanishing point and eye level (horizontal line) in a real-life image, as shown in *Figure 3.23*. Let us move forward to the next walkthrough, which identifies these in a two-point perspective.

Identifying a two-point perspective in a real-life image

You can identify a two-point perspective in real life by looking at scenes where two sets of parallel lines meet at two vanishing points on the horizon. For example, at the corner of a building, the edges appear to angle toward two distant points, creating depth and dimension. This technique is often found in angled streets or furniture positioned diagonally. The main problem with finding a two-point perspective in real-life images is figuring out where the second vanishing point is. In this walkthrough, you'll learn a simple, step-by-step method to easily identify it and make working with a two-point perspective much simpler.

Understanding the technique

Figure 3.24 will be used for this walkthrough. You can use any image as long as it resembles the *Figure 3.24* composition.

Figure 3.24 – Example of real-life image (source: https://unsplash.
com/photos/a-barn-with-a-red-roof-GlcG1J1CFEg)

Let us learn together how to find the vanishing point and eye level in two-point perspective:

1. Start by identifying the main object's shape in the image. Sketch the outline of this shape, as shown in *Figure 3.25*. Mark the corners of the shape by drawing small circles at each corner for better visualization.

2. Once the main shape is defined, resize the image (as illustrated in *Figure 3.25*) to ensure there is enough space to locate the vanishing points.

Figure 3.25 – Example of outlined main object and resized image

3.   Based on the shape you've outlined, draw two lines on one side of the object. These lines should converge at a single point on the horizon. This point is referred to as *Vanishing Point 1*.

Figure 3.26 – Example of the first vanishing point in two-point perspective

4.   Repeat the process for the other side of the object, drawing another set of lines that converge at a different point on the horizon. This second point is *Vanishing Point 2*, as shown in *Figure 3.27*.

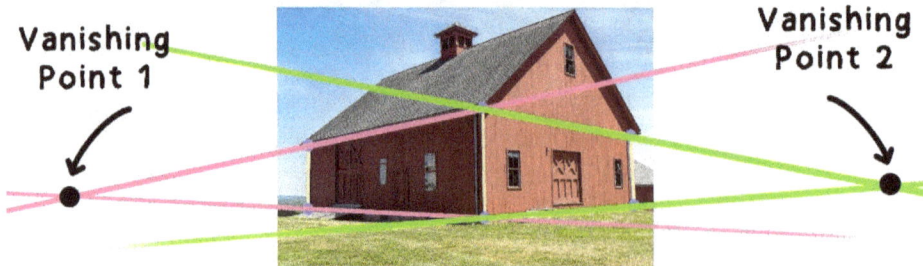

Figure 3.27 – Example of the second vanishing point in two-point perspective

5.   Finally, draw a straight horizontal line connecting *Vanishing Point 1* and *Vanishing Point 2*. This line represents the eye level, indicating the viewer's perspective.

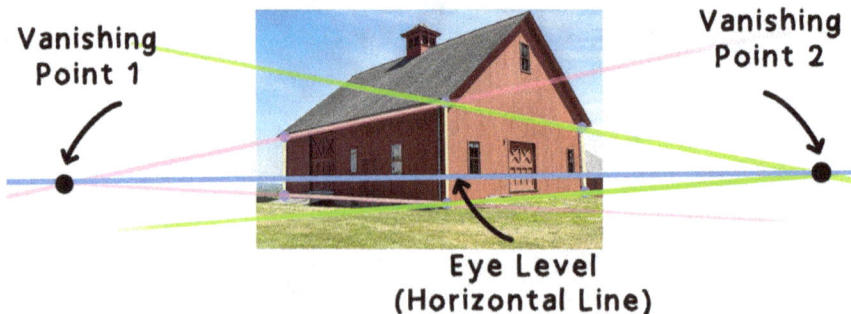

Figure 3.28 – Example of eye level in two-point perspective

We have successfully identified the vanishing points and eye level in a two-point perspective. Now, let's proceed to the next step, which involves identifying them in a three-point perspective.

Identifying a three-point perspective in a real-life image

A three-point perspective shows how we see objects from an extreme angle, such as looking up at tall buildings or down from a high place. It has three vanishing points: two for the sides of the object and one for its height. The lines of the object get closer and seem to meet at these points. This makes the object look more dramatic and realistic, especially with how big things look up close and how small they seem far away. The main challenge in identifying a three-point perspective in real-life images is figuring out where the eye level and the third vanishing point are located. In this walkthrough, we will explore a straightforward method to help you pinpoint these elements accurately and with ease.

Following the steps

Figure 3.29 will be used for this walkthrough. You can use any image as long as it resembles the *Figure 3.29* composition.

Figure 3.29 – Example of real-life image (source: https://unsplash.com/photos/a-stone-church-tower-rises-against-a-blue-sky-YagoqWNw0Pg)

Let us learn together how to find the vanishing point and eye level in a three-point-perspective:

1. Start by identifying the main object's shape in the image. Sketch the outline of this shape, as shown in *Figure 3.30*. Mark the corners of the shape by drawing small circles at each corner for better visualization.

2. Once the main shape is defined, resize the image (as illustrated in *Figure 3.30*) to ensure there is enough space to locate all three vanishing points.

Figure 3.30 – Example of outlined main object and resized image

3. Now, add vertical lines from the corners of the object that converge at a third vanishing point, located above the horizon. This point is referred to as *Vanishing Point 3*.

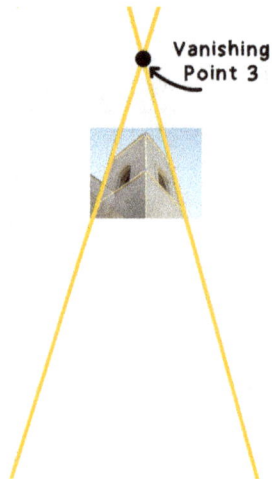

Figure 3.31 – Example of the third vanishing point in a three-point perspective

4. Based on the shape you've outlined, draw two lines on one side of the object that converge at a point on the horizon. This point is referred to as *Vanishing Point 1*.

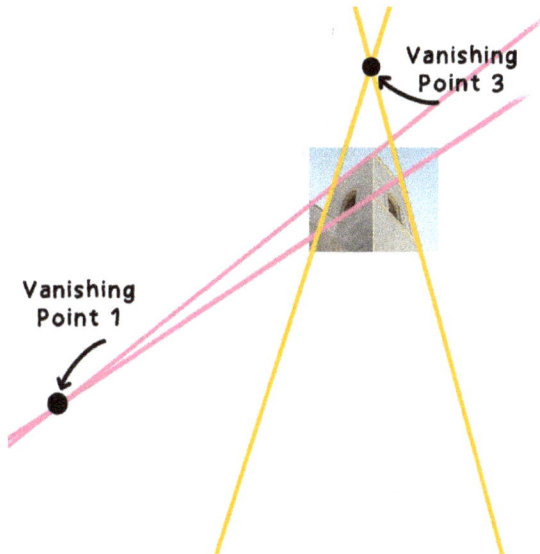

Figure 3.32 – Example of the first vanishing point in three-point perspective

5. Repeat the process for the other side of the object, drawing another set of lines that converge at a different point on the horizon. This point is *Vanishing Point 2*.

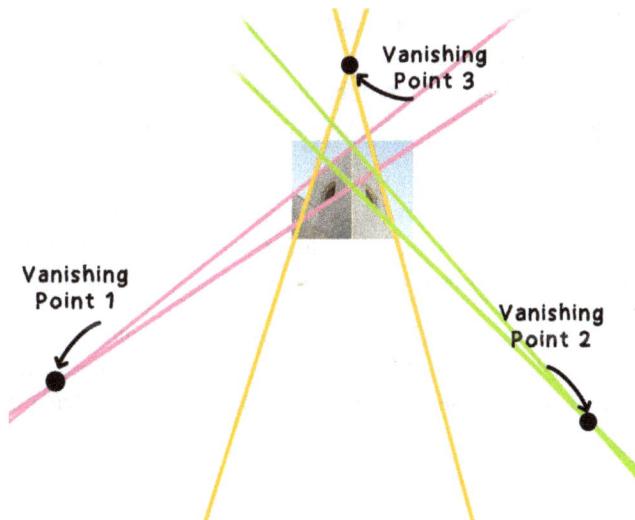

Figure 3.33 – Example of the second vanishing point in a three-point perspective

6. Finally, draw a straight horizontal line connecting *Vanishing Point 1* and *Vanishing Point 2* on the horizon. This line represents the eye level, indicating the viewer's perspective.

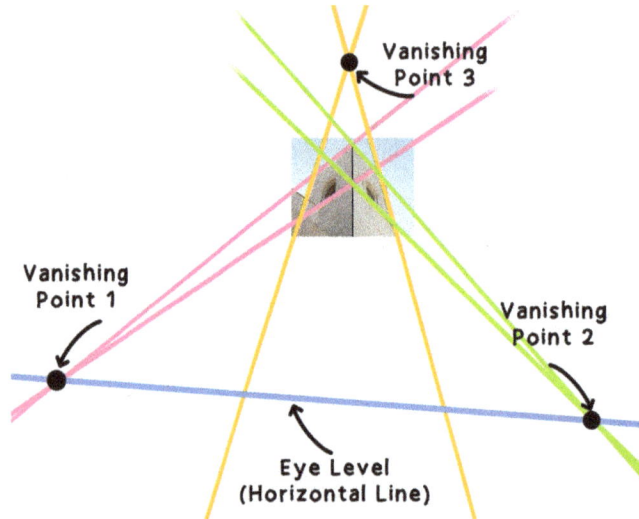

Figure 3.34 – Example of eye level in three-point perspective

We have successfully identified vanishing points and the eye level in a three-point perspective.

Understanding the technique

Knowing about vanishing points and eye levels in perspective drawing is key to making your drawings look realistic and accurate. Vanishing points are spots where lines in a drawing meet to show depth, such as how a road appears to be narrowing into the distance. Eye level is the horizon line, showing the viewer's position and guiding where objects sit – above or below that line.

In a one-point perspective, everything leads to a single vanishing point, which is great for straightforward views such as hallways. Two-point perspective uses two vanishing points for angled scenes, such as buildings. Three-point perspective adds drama, showing high or low views, with three points to keep it proportional. These tools help artists control depth and make their drawings professional and lifelike.

When we understand how to find vanishing points and eye levels in real-life pictures, it helps us create background scenery in our art that looks realistic and detailed. It also improves our understanding of perspective, allowing us to make illustrations that are more interesting and dynamic.

> **Important note**
>
> When working with multiple reference images for your artwork, it's crucial to ensure they all share the same eye level. This keeps your drawing consistent and prevents any mismatched perspectives that might make your composition look off or confusing.

How to implement linear perspective techniques in background illustration

In this walkthrough, we will try using all the linear perspective methods we have learned previously (one-point, two-point, and three-point perspective) to create scenery. By following the following step-by-step tutorials, we can gain a better understanding of linear perspective in our art and enhance our skill in adding depth to background scenery drawing.

Drawing background scenery using a one-point perspective

In this walkthrough, we will learn how to implement a one-point perspective effectively in our background drawing. By following these simple steps, we will be able to draw a one-point perspective easily.

Following the steps

The following steps will show you how to use a one-point perspective in railroad scenery:

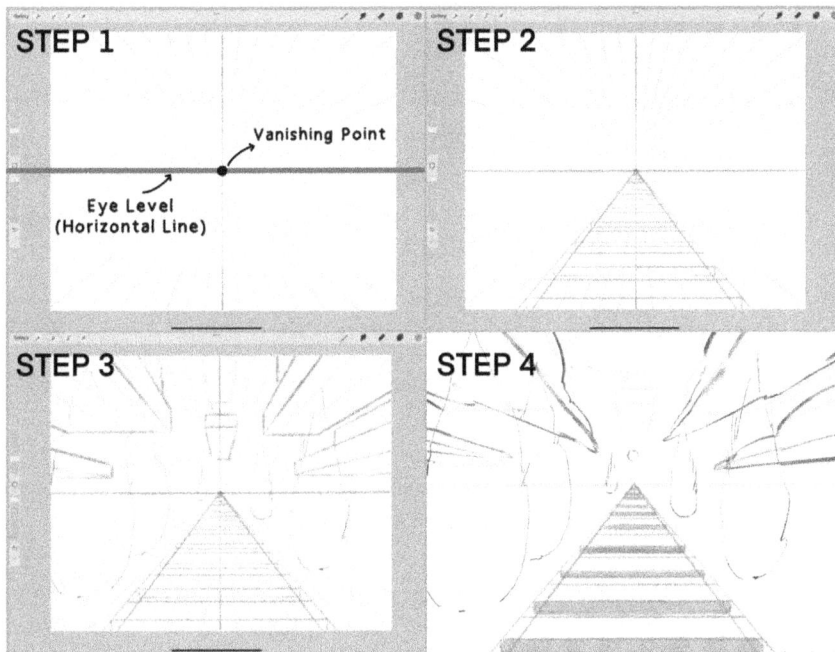

Figure 3.35 – Step-by-step process of drawing background scenery using a one-point perspective

1. Using perspective and line settings in Procreate, draw a straight horizontal line, as shown in *STEP 1* in *Figure 3.35*. The height placement of the line will decide the depth of the background scene. The higher the horizontal line, the further the depth will be, and vice versa.

2. Sketch out the railroad using the one-point perspective guideline provided by Procreate.

3. Draw several trees and clouds.

4. Turn off the guideline setting and add a new layer (`Clean Sketch layer`). In this layer, redraw and clean up the sketch.

This is the result we get from using the one-point perspective:

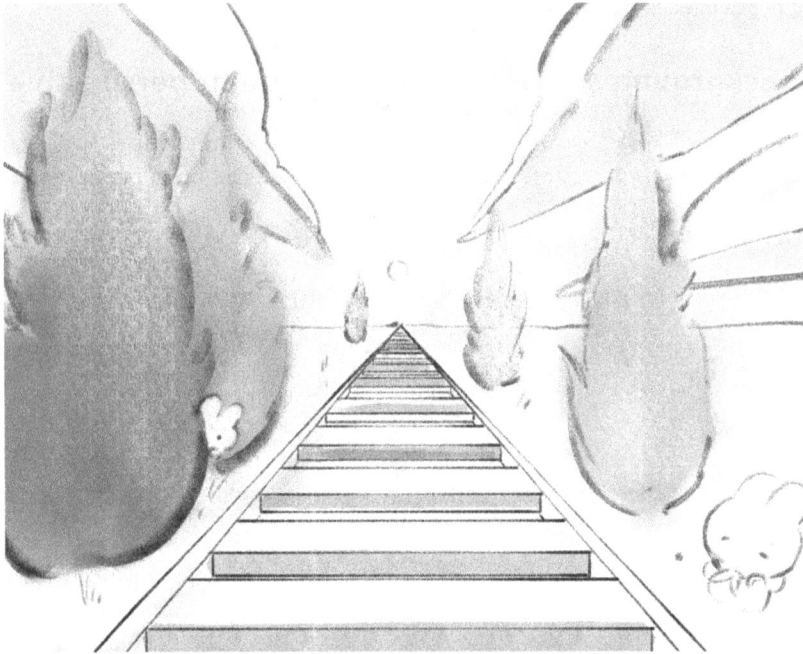

Figure 3.36 – Final result of using a one-point perspective

Using a one-point perspective is the easiest way to draw scenery due to its uncomplicated structure. It is important to keep in mind that you do not have to follow the line exactly; just use it as your guideline to draw out the details and placement of the object that you would like to draw.

Drawing background scenery using a two point-perspective

In this walkthrough, we will learn how to draw background scenery using a two-point perspective technique. By understanding how to use this technique, we can draw an eye-catching background drawing.

Following the steps

Here is how to use a two-point perspective to draw a house scene:

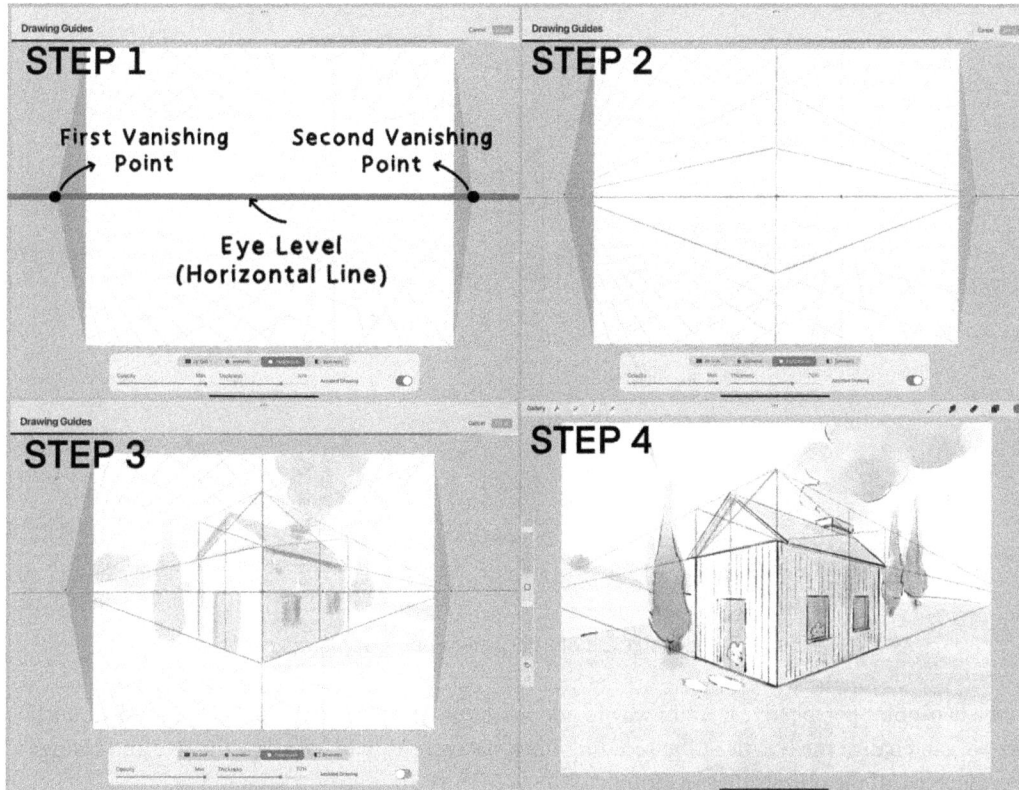

Figure 3.37 – Step-by-step process of drawing background scenery using two-point perspective

1. Using perspective and line settings in Procreate, draw a straight horizontal line and two vanishing points, as shown in *STEP 1* in *Figure 3.37*. The height placement of the line will decide the depth of the background scene.

2. Sketch out several lines coming from the two vanishing points, as shown in *STEP 2* in *Figure 3.37*. These lines should be drawn using Procreate's Assisted Drawing mode, which helps snap lines toward vanishing points accurately.

3. Draw several trees, clouds, and a house as the main focal point.

4. Turn off the guideline setting and add a new layer (`Clean Sketch layer`). In this layer, redraw and clean up the sketch.

This is the result we get from using the two-point perspective:

Figure 3.38 – Final result of using a two-point perspective

Using a two-point perspective is a fun way to add a unique perspective to the background scenery. Since we can change the length of the receding lines, we can easily manipulate the size and change the perspective of the objects that we draw.

Drawing background scenery using a three-point perspective

In this walkthrough, we will learn how to use a three-point perspective in background drawing. This technique can be confusing at first, but we will learn how to implement it into our art by following this step-by-step walkthrough.

Following the steps

Here is how to use a three-point perspective to draw a tree scene:

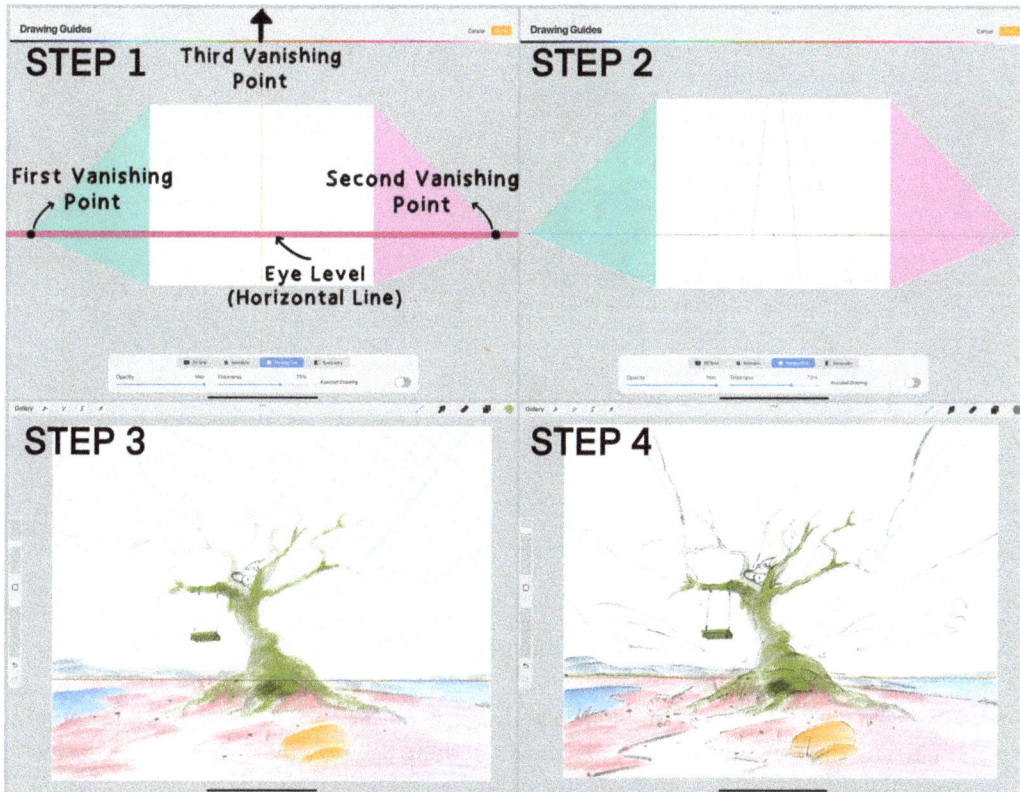

Figure 3.39 – Step-by-step process of drawing background scenery using a three-point perspective

1. Turn on the drawing guide and place two vanishing points as shown in *STEP 1* in *Figure 3.39*. The third vanishing point will be placed above eye level. Using line and perspective settings in Procreate, draw a straight horizontal line as shown in *STEP 1*.

2. Sketch out several lines pointing toward the third vanishing point, as shown in *STEP 2* in *Figure 3.39*.

3. Draw details such as a huge tree as the main focal point, grass, gravel, and stones.

4. Turn off the guideline and add a new layer. In this layer, redraw and clean up the sketch.

This is the result we get from using the three-point perspective:

Figure 3.40 – Final result of using a three-point perspective

In a three-point perspective, not all vanishing points are positioned along the eye level. While two of the points may still align with the eye level, the third vanishing point can be located above or below it. This creates the effect of looking up or down at an object, adding dramatic depth and making the perspective appear more dynamic and realistic. It is especially useful for drawing tall buildings or steep views!

Understanding the technique

When it comes to drawing and using perspective, there is no need to follow strict rules all the time. Most of the time, you can rely on your own eyes and draw what looks right to you. Perspective rules are helpful when you want to create accurate shapes, but sometimes they might not fit what you're trying to draw. Perspective techniques are used to help add depth and structure to your art – they don't have to capture every detail exactly as it is. Instead, they can guide your artistic approach while allowing room for creativity and interpretation. If the rules do not work for a specific situation, do not worry – you can skip them and just focus on drawing what you see. The most important thing is to express your vision and enjoy the process. Art does not have to be perfect; it just has to feel right to you!

Summary

In this chapter, we take a gentle step into learning how perspective helps bring depth and life to our artwork. We begin with natural perspective, where we focus on painting what we see. Techniques such as atmospheric perspective show us how distant objects can appear lighter and bluer, while size perspective teaches us to make faraway elements smaller to add depth. We also explore detail perspective, which teaches us how blurring certain areas with Gaussian Blur draws attention and adds a sense of distance.

Next, we explore linear perspective using Procreate's built-in tools. Through clear steps, we learn to use one-point perspective for scenes that look straight ahead, such as roads or hallways; two-point perspective for angled views, such as buildings and landscapes; and three-point perspective to add drama when looking up or down at tall objects.

We're also shown how to identify linear perspectives in real-life images, making it easier to understand vanishing points and eye levels. This helps us apply perspective naturally to our own drawings.

Finally, we practice using all three linear perspective techniques in background illustrations, drawing scenes with railroads, buildings, and trees to help confidently use these tools. With every walkthrough, the chapter reminds us that perspective isn't about strict rules—it's about using them as guidelines while trusting your eyes and drawing what feels right.

4

Enhancing Lighting to Elevate Your Artwork

Lighting and shadows are key elements in art that help create depth, dimension, and a well-composed piece. To make our artwork complete, we need to know how to add highlights and shadows to the background. These elements are crucial in drawing the viewer's attention. Good lighting can make our background more appealing. By understanding how light works with objects, we can create three-dimensional effects and guide the viewer's eye to important parts of the scene. Using highlights and shadows also helps show texture, emphasizes the shape of objects, and sets the mood or feeling of a scene. Mastering these techniques can make our art more visually appealing and eye-catching. In this chapter, we will learn how to improve our skills in using lighting and shadows for background scenery.

With the help of walkthroughs, we will cover the following topics:

- Observing lighting and shadows using real-life images and reference images
- Understanding lighting and shadow techniques
- Using light and shadow to illustrate a peaceful morning scene
- Using light and shadow to illustrate a bright afternoon scene
- Using light and shadow to illustrate a warm evening scene
- Using light and shadow to illustrate a calm night scene
- Mastering lighting and shading in the easiest way

Before beginning this chapter, please review the following important note to ensure that all steps can be followed smoothly. This will help maintain clarity and consistency throughout the process.

> **Important note**
>
> In this chapter, all illustrations will be created using separate layers to maintain flexibility for adjustments. The layers should be named as follows: *Sketch layer*, *Clean line art layer*, *Contrast layer*, *Base color layer*, and *Final details layer*. This structured approach ensures that each stage of the artwork remains editable, allowing for refinement without affecting previous steps. Keeping layers organized in this way makes the creative process smoother and more efficient.

Observing lighting and shadows using real-life images and reference images

Observing lighting and shadow in real-life images and reference photos can help us analyze how light interacts with different objects. We are also able to understand how lighting and shadow work, thus helping us paint more confidently.

We often encounter roadblocks when we are unsure how to add lighting to an object and determine where the object's shadow will be cast. By studying how light and shadow appear on different surfaces, we can create a realistic and visually appealing illustration, which is something we will learn from this walkthrough.

> **Tips**
>
> In Procreate, you can add a reference image to help with your artwork. Open the **Actions** menu by tapping the *wrench* icon at the top left, then go to the **Canvas** tab and turn on **Reference**. A small window will appear where you can import an image from your gallery. You can move and resize this window as needed while drawing. If you want to pick colors from your reference, use the **Eyedropper** tool. If you need multiple references, you can use **Split Screen** to view several images at once. This makes it easier to keep your artwork accurate and consistent.

Light and shadow on shiny surfaces

In this walkthrough, we'll learn how light and shadow work on shiny surfaces such as metal. Shiny surfaces reflect light in a special way, making them look bright and shiny in some areas and dark in others. When light hits metal, it creates bright highlights and deep shadows. The highlights and shadows change depending on where the light is coming from and how strong it is. To make metal look realistic in art, we need to understand how light bounces off the surface.

Following the steps

The following steps will show us how to introduce light and shadow on shiny surfaces:

1. Take a picture of your surroundings or an object near you. If you are unable to take pictures, you can choose a real-life image that you have chosen to study or use the following image, which I am using for this walkthrough:

Figure 4.1 – Reference image (source: https://unsplash.com/photos/a-yellow-light-house-sitting-on-top-of-a-pier-84vl7X58HMs)

2. In the image, find where the light is coming from. As we can see in *Figure 4.1*, the light is coming from the right side of the lighthouse. You can mark the relevant area as the light source.

3. Since the light came from the right side, the shadow was created on the left side of the lighthouse.

4. Circle the area where the light hit the object and where the shadow was cast from the lighthouse.

5. Then, identify the material and surface of the lighthouse. As we can see in *Figure 4.1*, the lighthouse is made from metal and the surface is shiny.

6.   Based on the information you get, write a description next to the reference image. You can write down the description like this:

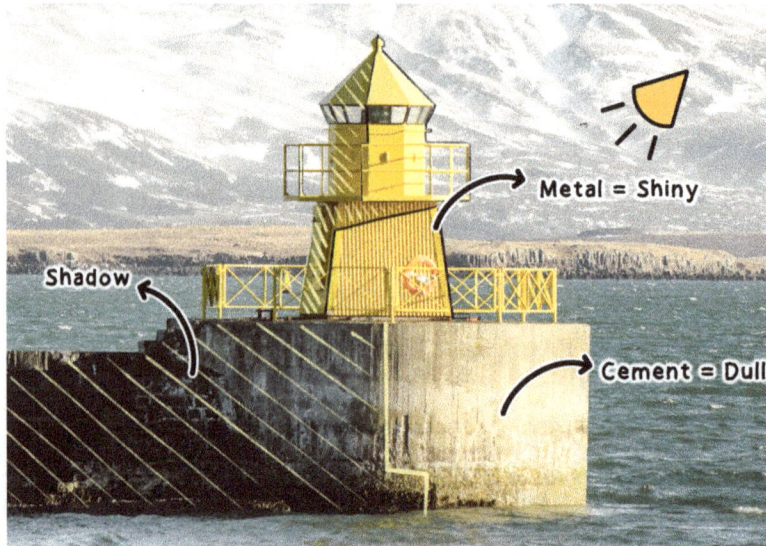

1) Metal creates shiny lighting due to its reflective surface
2) Cement creates dull lighting due to its rough surface
3) Light source coming from right side = Lighting created on right side
4) Shadow cast on left side, hidden from light source

Figure 4.2 – Example of a description on the reference image

We have learned from this walkthrough how light and shadow form on shiny surfaces. Different surfaces of an object will create a different way to paint the lighting. In the following walkthrough, we will learn about how light and shadow form on a rough surface object such as rocks.

Light and shadow on rough surfaces

In this walkthrough, we'll learn how light and shadow look on rough surfaces such as rocks. When light hits a rock, it creates bright spots and dark shadows. This happens because rocks have rough textures that make the light scatter in different directions.

To make rocks look real in art, we need to understand how light interacts with their rough surfaces. We'll learn how to add highlights to show the texture and use shadows to give depth and shape to the rocks. By getting these details right, we can make our drawings of rocks look more realistic.

Following the steps

The following steps will show us how to create light and shadow on rough surfaces such as rocks:

1. Take a picture of your surroundings or an object that has a different surface from the earlier photo. You can use the following image, which I am using for this walkthrough.

Figure 4.3 – Reference image; source: https://unsplash.com/photos/
shallow-focus-photo-gray-balance-stone-HWRAHxoBlpU

2. From the image, find where the light is coming from. As we can see in *Figure 4.3*, the light is coming from the right side of the rocks. Mark the area as a light source.

3. Since the light came from the right side, the shadow was created on the left side of the rocks.

4. Circle the area where the light hit the object and where the shadow was cast from the rocks.

5. Then, identify the material and surface of the rocks. As we can see from *Figure 4.3*, the rocks are made up of minerals, thus making the surface rougher and less reflective than the metal.

6.   Based on the information we get, write a description next to the reference image. You can write the description like this:

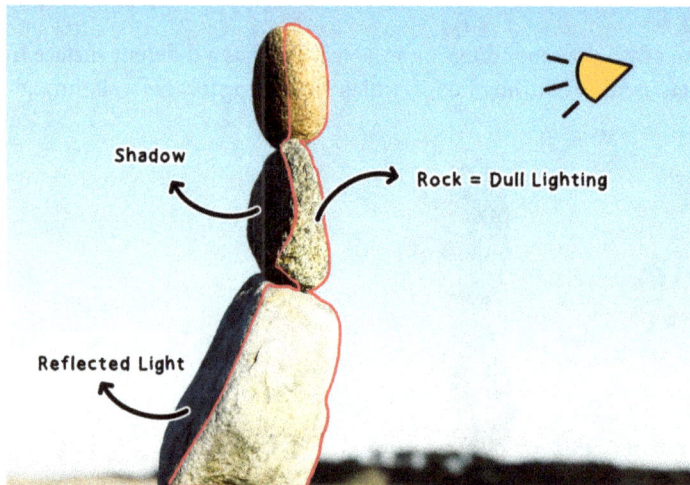

1) Rocks creates dull lighting due to their rough surface
2) Light source coming from right side = Lighting created on right side
3) Shadow cast on left side, hidden from light source

Figure 4.4 – Example of a description on the reference image

Understanding the technique

By following the preceding walkthrough, we can better understand how light appears on an object. At the same time, we can learn how shadows are cast from certain objects. In *Figure 4.1*, we can see that the metal surface of the lighthouse and the cement below it reflect the light differently. We can see that the lighting on a metal surface is more reflective compared to the cement surface. This is due to the differences in the surfaces. The smoother or shinier the surface is, the more reflective it is going to be.

Those two things are the main aspects we need to consider before continuing to add lighting to our illustration. However, the surface will not affect the density of the shadow cast from an object. It will only change the shape of the shadow; the darkness or opacity of the shadow will not be affected by the difference in surfaces. We will learn more about this in the next walkthrough.

Your description text can be as detailed as you wish, as it can help you understand when you decide to relearn what you have written before. To develop an in-depth understanding of how lighting and shadow are created, I would recommend that you make several versions of this walkthrough. Doing this will help you improve your ability to analyze the light and shadow in real images. The image and description can be kept in a folder so you can revisit it for future use. You can print it out as well for easy and quick access to it.

Understanding lighting and shadow techniques

Light affects how objects appear, shaping their form and texture. By watching how light falls on different surfaces, you can make your background drawings more interesting and natural. When you draw, knowing where the light is coming from and how strong it is helps bring your artwork to life. Bright spots show where the light hits, while shadows help define the shape of objects. Strong light creates sharp shadows, making things look bold and clear, while soft light creates gentle shadows, giving a calm and dreamy effect. For example, if you want to emphasize a character in a scene, you can make sure the brightest light falls on them while keeping the surroundings dim. This contrast will make the character stand out. Similarly, placing a strong light source near a key object will make it appear more important and capture attention immediately.

Using light and shadow correctly can turn a flat drawing into one that looks three-dimensional. It makes objects look more solid and realistic, helping them fit naturally into a scene. When adding lighting and shadows to our art, we often struggle with deciding how big the shadow should be, how dark it should look, how bright the lighting should be, and how the shadow is cast from an object. In this walkthrough, we'll learn how to add lighting and shadows more easily by using real-life photos as references. We'll also explore how the strength of a light source affects the way lighting and shadows appear in a drawing.

> **Lighting tips**
> We can use different lighting techniques to draw attention to important parts of a drawing. Rim lighting creates a glowing outline around an object, making it stand out from the background. Spotlighting focuses bright light on a subject, highlighting it as the main point of interest. Gradual shading helps blend light and shadow smoothly, creating a soft and natural look.

What you need

Prepare two real-life images: one showing a dull light source without intense or bright lighting, and another with a bright and intense light source. Refer to *Figure 4.5* for the soft light source and *Figure 4.7* for the bright light source.

Identifying a soft light source

In this walkthrough, we'll learn how to spot soft light sources and the shadows they create on objects. Soft light is gentle and even, making shadows with blurry edges. Soft light usually comes from big light sources, such as an overcast sky or light through a curtain. Using soft light in your drawings can make things look more natural and real. It's great for creating a calm and peaceful mood. By learning how soft light and shadows work, you can make your art look peaceful and soothing.

Following the steps

Identifying lighting and shadow from a soft light source through a real-life image can be done as follows:

1. Choose any real-life image that you prefer for this walkthrough. You can use this image as your reference:

Figure 4.5 – Reference image for a soft light source; source: https://unsplash.
com/photos/orange-fruit-on-white-textile-AKw62669WW0

2. From *Figure 4.5*, circle the lighting created on the oranges and mark it down as a lighting area.

3. Then, circle the shadow cast from the oranges and mark it down as a shadow area.

4. Take a look at the lighting and shadow cast from the oranges and write down a description and characteristics of the lighting and shadow.

5. Finalize it by adding the placement and strength level of the light source. You can finalize it as in the following example:

Figure 4.6 – Example description of soft light source

Now, we are able to identify and analyze soft light sources. Let us take a look at identifying a bright light source.

Identifying a bright light source

In this walkthrough, we will examine how to identify bright light sources and the resulting shadows they cast on objects. Understanding bright light is essential for creating vivid and dramatic illustrations that capture the viewer's attention.

Bright light, often referred to as hard light, is characterized by its intense and focused lighting. It creates sharp shadows and highlights, making the objects stand out with clear contrast against the background. This type of lighting is typically produced by direct light sources, such as the sun on a clear day, a spotlight, or strong artificial light.

Following the steps

Identifying lighting and shadow from a bright light source through a real-life image can be done as follows:

1. Choose any real-life image that you prefer for this walkthrough. You can use this image as your reference:

Figure 4.7 – Reference image for bright light source (source: https://unsplash. com/photos/orange-fruit-on-white-table-PUMfrQZQfFU)

2. From *Figure 4.7*, circle the lighting created on the orange and mark it down as a lighting area.

3. Then, circle the shadow cast from the orange and mark it down as a shadow area.

4. Take a look at the lighting and shadow cast from the orange and write down a description and characteristics of the lighting and shadow.

5. Finalize it by adding the placement and the strength level of the light source. You can finalize it as in the following example:

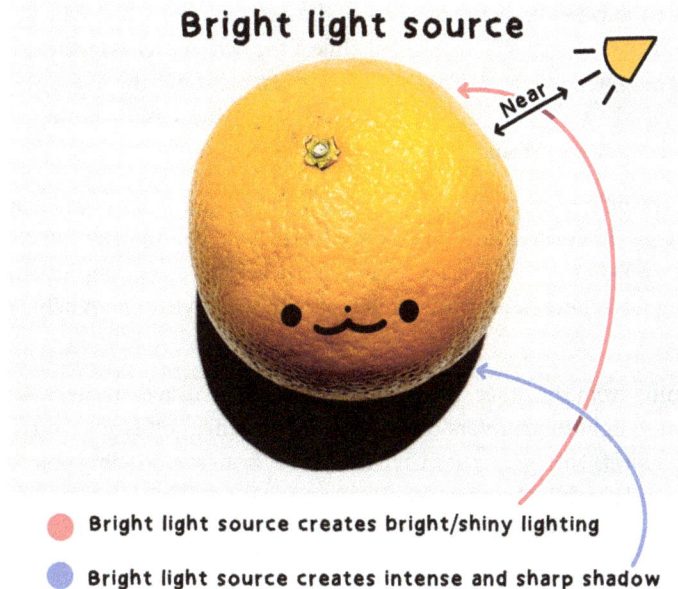

Figure 4.8 – Example description of a bright light source

With that, we now understand the effects of a bright light source on an object. We also know how to differentiate between soft and bright light sources.

Understanding the technique

In *Figure 4.6*, we can see that the lighting created and the shadows cast from the oranges are softer compared to *Figure 4.8*. This is because of the brightness and distance of the light source. The dull light source created soft lighting on the oranges, and the shadow was softer and less intense too. If we compare it with the bright light source, we can identify the shadow cast from the orange quickly due to the intensity of the shadow and the brightness of the light. *Figure 4.8* indicates that the light source is near the orange, and the level of brightness is higher than in *Figure 4.6*.

The easiest way we can remember it is as follows:

- Duller light source = softer lighting and shadow
- Brighter light source = intense lighting and shadow

Another thing we need to consider is the *distance* of the light source. If the light source is near the object, the lighting and shadow cast will be intense, while if the light source is farther away, the lighting and shadow cast will be softer. The farther the light source is, the softer the edges of the shadow cast from the object. Let us take a look at *Figure 4.8*; the nearest shadow cast from the orange is sharper compared to the shadow farthest from the orange.

Depending on what the light source is, the color of the lighting and shadow will change along with the overall color scheme. To create a natural-looking illustration, it's important to consider the light source. This could be sunlight or an artificial source such as a bonfire, stars, lamp, or other surrounding lights. Understanding how these light sources interact with the environment helps make the scene feel more realistic.

The light source coming from the other details in the background drawing will create reflected light on the object. Reflected light in art refers to the light that bounces off from a surface and hits the shadowed areas of an object. This happens when lights reflect from surrounding objects onto the main subject and create a subtle highlight within the shadow area. We will learn how to add reflected light in the last walkthrough of this chapter.

Using light and shadow to illustrate a peaceful morning scene

We need to learn how to recreate the soft hues, such as soft blue, pink, and yellow, typically seen at dawn to create a peaceful morning scene. Adding too many harsh colors such as dark blue, red, green, and so on can affect the morning atmosphere. However, the previously mentioned colors can be used for other settings, such as nighttime and evening atmospheres. By following this walkthrough, we can create a peaceful morning atmosphere easily.

Following the steps

Adding light and shadow for a peaceful morning scene can be done as follows:

1. Sketch out a background drawing and prepare a morning color palette.
2. Based on the morning color palette, paint a base color for the background scene.

Figure 4.9 – Example of base color and color palette for a peaceful morning

3. Decide where the light source is located for the morning setting. I will use the sunrise as the light source coming from the lower part of the background drawing.

4. Add lighting to the lower parts of the surrounding objects in the background drawing.

Figure 4.10 – Example of adding lighting

5.   Then, add shadows to the hidden side of the surrounding objects in the background drawing.

Figure 4.11 – Example of adding shadow

6.   Lastly, add reflected light on the main subject based on the surrounding objects and some details to finalize the morning background drawing. I will use **Oil Paint 3** and **Oil Paint 7** from the **Happyyu Brush Pack** to add texture to the background drawing.

Figure 4.12 – Finalized illustration of a peaceful morning

With this, your illustration of a peaceful morning is now complete. You can now grab a cup of tea and enjoy the effect of soft lighting in your work.

Understanding the technique

Choosing the right colors is crucial when painting an early morning scene, as they set the tone and mood of the artwork. The placement and intensity of the light source are equally important in creating a morning background. In the early morning, the light is typically soft and gentle, casting a warm glow over the landscape. To capture this atmosphere, you should use a color palette that includes shades of pale blue, soft pink, gentle oranges, and warm yellows. These colors mimic the natural hues of the morning light and evoke a sense of calm and freshness.

Where you put the light source is important too. In the morning, the light usually comes from a low angle, such as the rising sun. This creates long soft shadows that add depth to your drawing. By placing the light source carefully, you can highlight important parts of the scene such as the main focal point. Shadows usually look cooler because they don't get direct light, so they don't pick up as much warmth. A common mistake is making shadows too gray or black, which can make a drawing feel flat. Instead, adding hints of blue, purple, or soft green keeps the shadows looking natural.

Know more...

In Procreate, you can use the **Selection** tool to create precise shading effects. First, tap the **Selection** tool (S-shaped ribbon icon) in the top menu and choose either the **Freehand** or **Automatic** mode. Outline the area where you want to add shading, ensuring that only the selected part will be affected. After selecting the area, create a new layer above your base artwork to keep the shading separate, making it easier to adjust later. Then, using a soft brush such as an airbrush, gently apply shadows within the selected area. Adjust the opacity of your brush for smoother blending and use blend modes such as **Multiply** to achieve a more natural shadow effect. To refine your shading, use the **Eraser** tool to soften harsh edges.

Tip

In Procreate, you can save color palettes to keep your favorite colors organized. First, open the **Color** panel by tapping the color circle in the top-right corner. Then, go to the **Palettes** tab at the bottom of the panel. To create a new palette, tap the + icon and select **Create New**. You can add colors using the **Eyedropper** tool by picking a color and tapping an empty swatch in your palette to save it. If needed, rename your palette by tapping its name and rearrange colors for better organization. Additionally, Procreate allows you to export palettes by tapping the three dots next to a palette and selecting **Share**, which lets you save it to your files.

Using light and shadow to illustrate a bright afternoon scene

To create a bright afternoon scene, we need to focus on the placement of the light source and the intensity of the sunlight. Generally, the light source will be coming from upper and higher angles from the objects. We will have to use bright highlights for the lighting, but we must make sure we do not overdo it, as it will overshadow the main subject or focal point of the illustration. By following this walkthrough, we can learn how to maintain balanced lighting for an afternoon atmosphere and successfully illustrate a background scene.

Following the steps

Adding light and shadow for a bright afternoon scene can be done as follows:

1. Sketch out a background drawing and prepare an afternoon color palette.

2. Based on the afternoon color palette, paint a base color for the background scenery.

Figure 4.13 – Base color and color palette for a bright afternoon

3. Decide where the light source is located for the afternoon setting. I will use the bright sun as the light source coming from the upper part of the background drawing.

4. Add lighting on the upper sides of the surrounding objects in the background drawing.

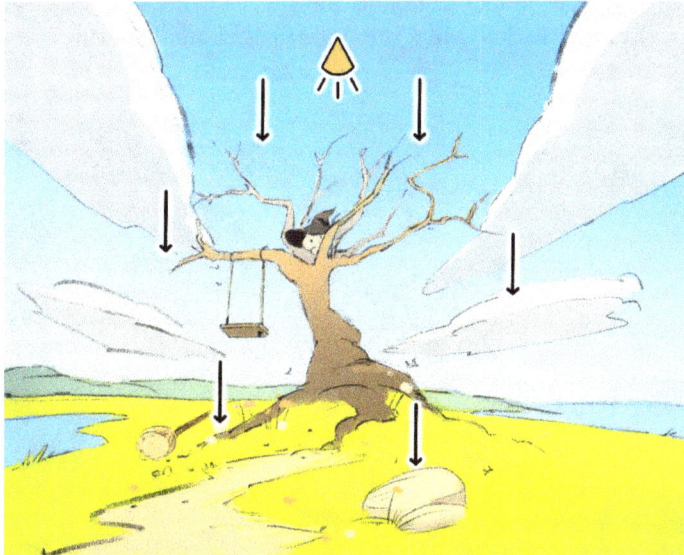

Figure 4.14 – Adding lighting

5. Then, add shadows on the hidden side of the surrounding objects in the background drawing. You can use a clipping mask and draw over the tree bark layer to make the shadow more customizable.

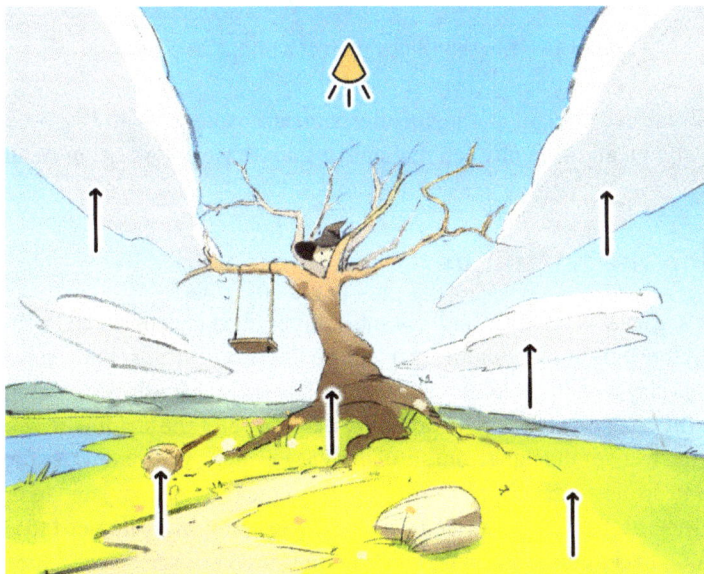

Figure 4.15 – Adding shadow

6. Lastly, add reflected light on the main subject based on the surrounding objects and add some details to finalize the afternoon background drawing. I will use **Oil Paint 3** and **Oil Paint 7** from the Happyyu Brush Pack to add texture to the background drawing.

Figure 4.16 – Finalized illustration of a bright afternoon

We have successfully created a bright and joyful afternoon atmosphere. With that, we can now draw afternoon scenery without any difficulty and maintain a smooth workflow. Let us move forward and explore the technique.

Understanding the technique

Afternoon scenery is usually very bright and vibrant. All the colors are enhanced by the natural light from sunlight. It's important to use *vibrant colors* for an afternoon atmosphere to create a realistic drawing. You can also play with the color temperature such as making it warmer by using more yellow or orange hues for the color palette. For shadows, we need to paint the shadow more intensely and sharper due to the intensity of the light from sunlight. For example, the shadow on the underside of the clouds is more intense as we can clearly see the outline of the shadow compared to the soft lighting from the previous walkthrough. These are some of the important things you need to consider when painting an afternoon background drawing, but you are free to use any colors to depict your own afternoon scene.

Using light and shadow to illustrate a warm evening scene

To create a warm evening scene, we need to use warm color tones such as yellow, orange, and soft red to evoke a cozy atmosphere. Adding several soft light sources can create a gentle evening atmosphere. Using darker shadows can create an intense atmosphere. It's a great way to create a complex atmosphere, but adding too much dark shadow can overshadow the overall atmosphere of the evening background drawing. By following this walkthrough, we can create a cozy evening background setting.

Following the steps

Adding light and shadow for a warm evening scene can be done as follows:

1. Sketch out a background drawing and prepare an evening color palette.
2. Based on the evening color palette, paint a base color for the background scenery.

Figure 4.17 – Base color and color palette for a warm evening

3. Decide where the light source is located for the evening setting. I will use the sunset as the light source coming from the left side of the background drawing.

4.   Add lighting on the left side of the surrounding objects in the background drawing.

Figure 4.18 – Adding lighting

5.   Then, add shadows on the hidden side of the surrounding objects in the background drawing.

Figure 4.19 – Adding shadow

6. Lastly, to complete the evening background, add reflected light to the main subject based on nearby objects. Then, refine details such as soft glows and textures to make the scene feel natural and complete. I will use **Oil Paint 3** and **Oil Paint 7** from the Happyyu Brush Pack to add texture to the background drawing.

Figure 4.20 – Finalized illustration of a warm evening

Now, we can effectively create a warm evening scene in our artwork. We can now sit back and enjoy the inviting scene we have created.

Understanding the technique

Using warm color hues, such as yellow and orange, and soft light can create a cozy atmosphere. We need to balance out these colors to prevent the scene from appearing too orange or too yellow. You can create gradients by using these colors, and this can be used as a background for the evening atmosphere. Remember to add a soft glow to create a relaxed and inviting scenery. To add a soft glow, you can use blending modes such as **Color Dodge** or **Soft Light**. You can use other colors too, as long as they represent the relaxing evening atmosphere, such as pink, purple, and soft yellow color hues. To adjust the colors in your artwork, go to **Adjustments | Hue, Saturation, Brightness** in Procreate. This tool lets you change how warm or cool the colors look, make them brighter or darker, and control how strong the colors appear. Increasing **Saturation** makes colors more vibrant, while lowering it softens them. Adjusting **Brightness** helps balance light and shadow so the background scenery looks more natural.

Using light and shadow to illustrate a calm night scene

To create a calm night scene, we need to maintain the balance of the overall light source on the surroundings to ensure that we can create a serene atmosphere. Adding too much light can turn the night background drawing a little harsh, thus losing the natural beauty of the nighttime setting. By following this walkthrough, we can create a calming night atmosphere by learning how to add light and shadow effectively.

Following the steps

Adding light and shadow for a calm night scene can be done as follows:

1. Sketch out a background drawing and prepare a nighttime color palette.

2. Based on the nighttime color palette, paint a base color for the background scenery.

Figure 4.21 – Base color and color palette for a calm night

3. Decide where the light source is located for the nighttime setting. I will use the moon as the light source coming from the upper part of the background drawing.

4.   Add lighting on the upper side of the surrounding objects in the background drawing.

Figure 4.22 – Adding lighting

5.   Then, add shadows on the hidden side of the surrounding objects in the background drawing.

Figure 4.23 – Adding shadow

6.   Lastly, to finalize the nighttime background drawing, add reflected light on the main subject by considering the surrounding objects and incorporating those details. I will use **Oil Paint 3** and **Oil Paint 7** from the Happyyu Brush Pack to add texture to the background drawing.

Figure 4.24 – Finalized calm night illustration

By following the techniques outlined previously, we are now capable of creating nighttime scenery with ease. Let us move forward to gain a deeper understanding of how nighttime illustrations work.

Understanding the technique

Creating a night atmosphere is the easiest as we only need to use two main color hues, such as blue and yellow. For the night atmosphere, we need to use cool color tones to depict a calm night. You can use warmer colors as well to create a warm night atmosphere, such as a camping night illustration. You can add subtle light sources such as stars and fireflies to create a serene environment. If you are not familiar with using blue and yellow color hues, you can use any color that represents night the best to you.

Mastering lighting and shading in the easiest way

The easiest way to master lighting and shading is by using blending modes such as **Add**, **Multiply**, and **Soft Light**. The **Add** blending mode can be used for lighting while **Multiply** can be used for shading purposes. The **Screen** blending mode can be used for adding reflected light. Usually, we will encounter a problem where we are unsure how to add the shadow and what colors we will need to use. By using this technique, we can easily add lighting, shadow, and reflected light to our drawing.

Following the steps

Adding lighting, shadow, and reflected light can be done as follows:

1. Draw out a character or any object using the base color that you prefer. I will draw a black cat for this walkthrough.

Figure 4.25 – Base color and line art for a black cat

2. Add three new layers and name them Highlight, Shadow, and Reflected Light.

3. Clip the three new layers into the main base color. The layers' order should be like this:

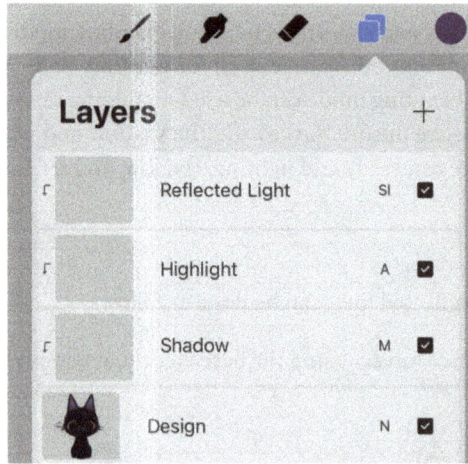

Figure 4.26 – The Highlight, Shadow, and Reflected Light layers

4. Then, change the blending modes as follows:

    - **Highlight**: The **Add** blending mode
    - **Shadow**: The **Multiply** blending mode
    - **Reflected Light**: The **Soft Light** blending mode

5. Decide where the light source is coming from for this drawing. My light source will be above the black cat. On the **Shadow** layer, add shadow to the area that is hidden from the light source.

Figure 4.27 – Adding shadow on the black cat

6. On the **Highlight** layer, add light to the area that is visible to the light source. Since the light is coming from above, the highlight will be on the upper part of the black cat.

Figure 4.28 – Adding highlight to the black cat

7. Observe the surroundings and add reflected light to the lower area of the black cat on the **Reflected Light** layer.

Figure 4.29 – Adding reflected light to the black cat

8.   Merge all the layers into one single layer to render it.

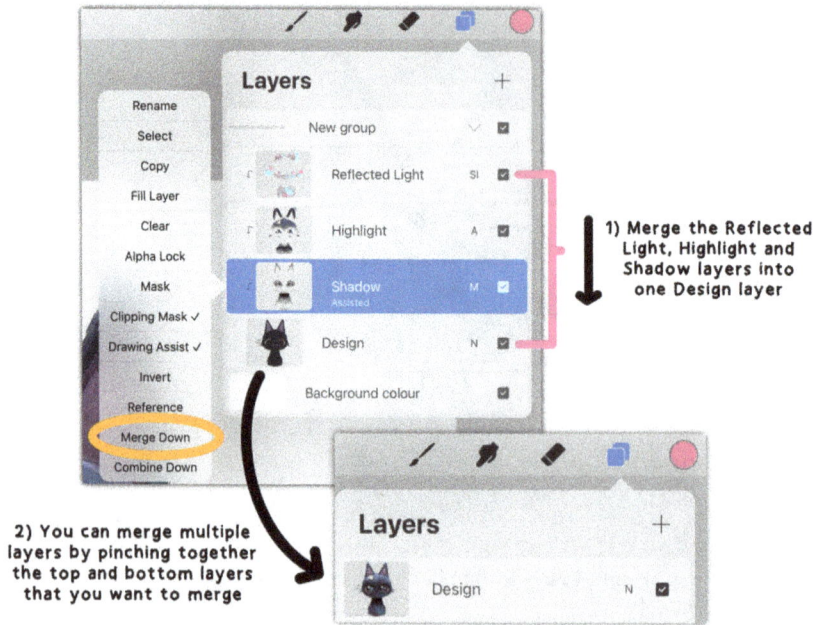

Figure 4.30 – Merging the layers

9.   Then, smooth out the highlight, shadow, and reflected light edges using the **Smudge** tool.

Figure 4.31 – Adding reflected light to the black cat

10. Lastly, add some final details such as white highlights and stars around the black cat. Here is the result of following this walkthrough:

Figure 4.32 – Softening the edges of the highlight, shadow, and reflected light

We have now successfully created a complete work with lighting and shadow using several blending modes, namely, **Add**, **Multiply**, and **Soft Light**. By using this technique, it will save more time and ensure a smooth workflow to complete an illustration.

Understanding the technique

The way light and shadow are cast varies depending on where the light source is located, while for reflected light, it depends on the surrounding objects. Let's have a look at *Figure 4.33*, *Figure 4.34*, and *Figure 4.35* as examples of how lighting works when it hits an object:

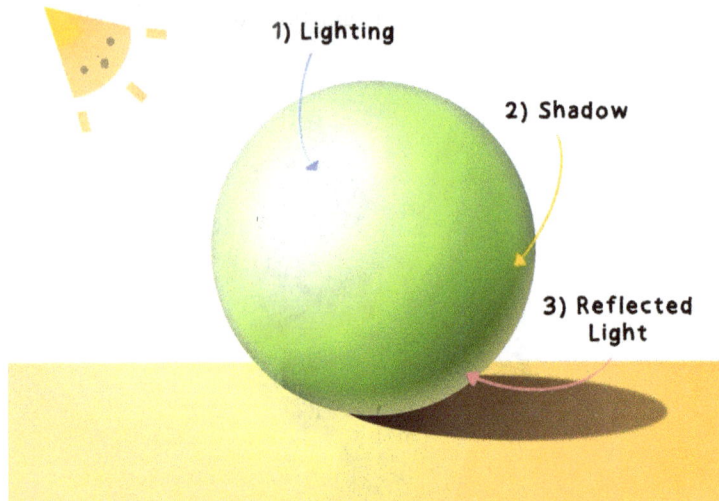

Figure 4.33 – Light coming from the left side of the sphere

The light source is on the left side thus the light is created on the surface of the sphere, and then a shadow is created on the area that the light does not hit. The shadow area that is close to the surrounding object or ground will create reflected light. Reflected light appears when a light meets an object and bounces back to another object near it. In this case, you can see that the reflected light is bright yellow because the surroundings are yellow. If we change the surroundings to purple, the reflected light will appear as bright purple:

Figure 4.34 – Changing the background affecting reflected light

Now,. back to the light source. No matter where the light source is located, highlight, shadow, and reflected light will appear in order. Once we understand this concept, we can add highlights, shadows, and reflected light easily. Shadows will always be created opposite where the lighting appears. It will never appear alongside or share the same area as the light.

Here are some examples of light sources above and to the right of the sphere:

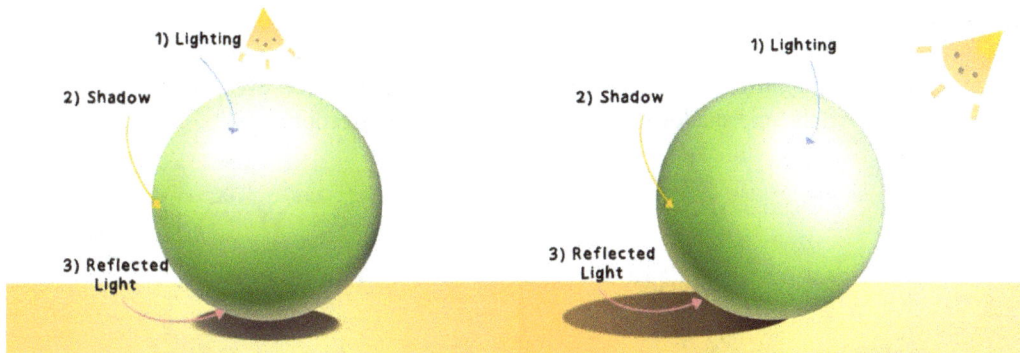

Figure 4.35 – Light coming from the upper and right sides of the sphere

With the help of blending modes, we can add lighting, shadow, and reflected light without spending too much time trying to find the right colors for them. If you are not familiar with using this method and prefer to manually find the colors, you are free to do so. It is best to use methods that you are comfortable with.

To draw complex shadows, look at real-life images to see how light interacts with objects. Shadows form based on the shape of the object blocking the light. For example, in *Figure 4.36*, the flowers create detailed shadows because flowers have complex shapes.

Figure 4.36 – Complex shadows cast from objects; source: https://unsplash.com/
photos/pink-and-yellow-flowers-on-white-background-6tmSqG9a1xE

To draw a shadow, simply follow the object's shape to define the shadow it casts. Shadows can change depending on how strong the light is and how far it is from the object. A bright, close light creates sharp shadows, while a soft, distant light makes them blurry. Understanding this makes drawing shadows easier. By understanding these principles, you can create natural and accurate shadows that enhance the realism of your artwork.

Know more...

To make shadows and lighting look natural, stick to one main light source. Everything in the scene (highlights, reflected light, and shadows) should follow that light direction.

Figure 4.37 – Light source coming from different directions and one main light source

This keeps your artwork looking realistic and helps objects feel like they belong in the same space.

Summary

In this chapter, we learn how light and shadow help bring life, mood, and realism to our backgrounds. We start by observing how lighting behaves on different surfaces, such as shiny metal and rough rock, and by using real-life photos to guide our understanding. These walkthroughs remind us that each surface reflects light differently, giving our scenes unique texture and depth.

We explore both soft and bright light sources: soft light creates calm, blurry shadows, while bright light casts bold, defined shapes. We learn how to recognize each type through observation and how they affect color, mood, and detail in our drawings.

Through step-by-step guides, we create four distinct moods: a peaceful morning scene with soft colors and gentle highlights, a bright afternoon filled with clear light and sharper shadows, a warm evening atmosphere using cozy tones, and, lastly, a calm night scene using cool colors and subtle lighting to reflect a quiet atmosphere.

Then we learn to master lighting easily by using Procreate's blending modes: Add for highlights, Multiply for shadows, and Soft Light for reflected light. By organizing layers and adjusting light direction thoughtfully, we simplify how light, shadow, and reflection work together to form a natural scene. This chapter shows us that lighting isn't just about technique; it's about feeling. Lighting helps make our drawings look more alive and full of emotion. You don't need to make it perfect—just draw what feels right for you.

In the next chapter, we'll explore color theory. We'll learn how color harmony, value, and contrast can help our art shine and stand out, using helpful tools and tips to build beautiful color palettes and, in the process, bring our imagination to life with confidence.

Unlock this book's exclusive benefits now

Scan this QR code or go to `packtpub.com/unlock`, then search this book by name.

5

Exploring Color Theory for Vibrant Illustrations

This chapter is all about color theory, which is important for taking your illustration to the next level. By learning how colors work together and understanding contrast, you can easily improve how you use colors in your art. Color theory helps artists pick the right colors to create beautiful and eye-catching pictures. There are many ways to do this, and in this chapter, I will show you some easy techniques. These tips will help you choose colors quickly and make a great color palette for your artwork. By the end of this chapter, you will know how to create your own color palette, adjust color values to make your art look better, and use contrast to add depth and interest to your illustrations.

You will learn about different color schemes, such as using one color with different shades of that color (monochromatic), colors that are next to each other on the color wheel (analogous), colors that are opposite each other (complementary), and three colors that are evenly spaced around the color wheel (triadic). By learning these techniques, you will be able to make your art more beautiful and save time when choosing colors. Let us get started and explore how to use color theory to create stunning illustrations.

With the help of walkthroughs, we will cover the following:

- Creating color harmony with Procreate
- The importance of color value and how to use it in art
- How and when to use warm and cool colors
- Improving contrast in art
- Choosing random colors to create a color palette
- Creating a color palette using Gradient Map
- Using color harmony, color value, and contrast in art

Before beginning this chapter, please review the following important note to ensure that all steps can be followed smoothly. This will help maintain clarity and consistency throughout the process.

> **Important note**
>
> In this chapter, illustrations will be drawn in separate layers to maintain flexibility for adjustments. The layers should be named as follows: *sketch layer, clean line art layer, contrast layer, base color layer*, and *final details layer*. This structured approach ensures that each stage of the artwork remains editable, allowing for refinement without affecting previous steps. Keeping layers organized in this way makes the creative process smoother and more efficient. You can refer back to *Chapter 1* for the brushes used for this book.

Creating color harmony with Procreate

Color harmony is crucial in art because it makes an illustration visually pleasing and captivating. When we look at a piece of art, color is often the first thing that catches our eye. This is why achieving color harmony is so important. As illustrators, we frequently struggle to choose the right colors for our sketches, which can leave us feeling stuck and unsure about how to move forward. In this walkthrough, we will explore how to find a good color scheme with ease. Understanding color harmony can significantly enhance the quality of your artwork and make it more enjoyable for viewers. There are several effective methods to achieve color harmony, each offering unique benefits and aesthetics. In this chapter, we will learn four popular methods: monochromatic, analogous, complementary, and triadic color schemes.

> **Note**
>
> Color harmony can evoke different feelings and moods. For example, complementary colors can create an exciting and bold atmosphere, while analogous colors are often calming and harmonious.

Creating monochromatic schemes

We will now learn how to manually use monochromatic schemes to easily create a color palette.

Following the steps

Using monochromatic schemes can be done as follows:

1. Firstly, create a new canvas on Procreate and choose a single base color. I will use yellow for this walkthrough:

Figure 5.1 – Yellow base color

2. Create variations of the color, from light to dark:

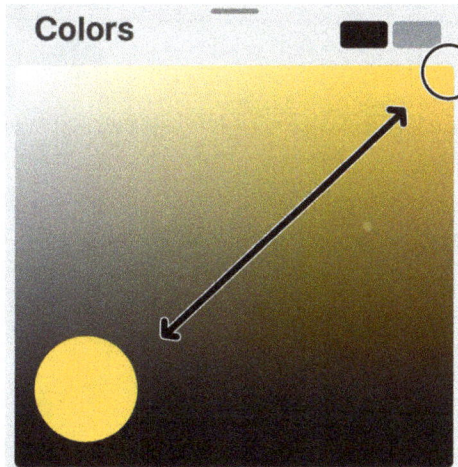

Figure 5.2 – Yellow color in different color values

3. Use these variations to create a serene color palette:

Figure 5.3 – Monochromatic color palette for yellow

A monochromatic color palette for yellow has now been created. Let us move forward to learn how to create analogous color schemes.

Creating analogous schemes

Now, we will learn how to use analogous schemes with Procreate's tool to easily create a color palette.

Following the steps

Using analogous schemes can be done as follows:

1. Firstly, create a new canvas on Procreate and choose one base color. I will use light blue for this walkthrough.

Figure 5.4 – Light blue base color

2. Using Procreate's color wheel system, tap **Harmony** in the color wheel section. Then, change the setting to **Analogous**:

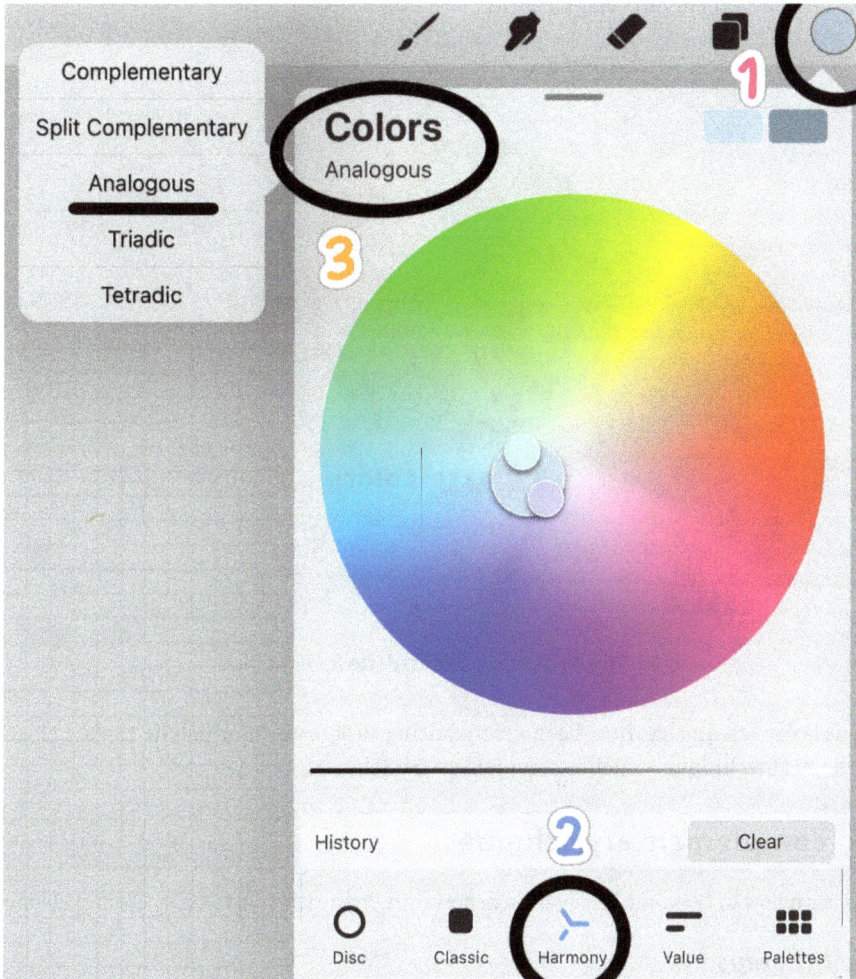

Figure 5.5 – Example of using Procreate tools to change color scheme settings

3. Move around the base color and you will notice that the other two colors will automatically create and follow around the light blue base color. Save the three colors created using a color picker and paste them on a blank canvas:

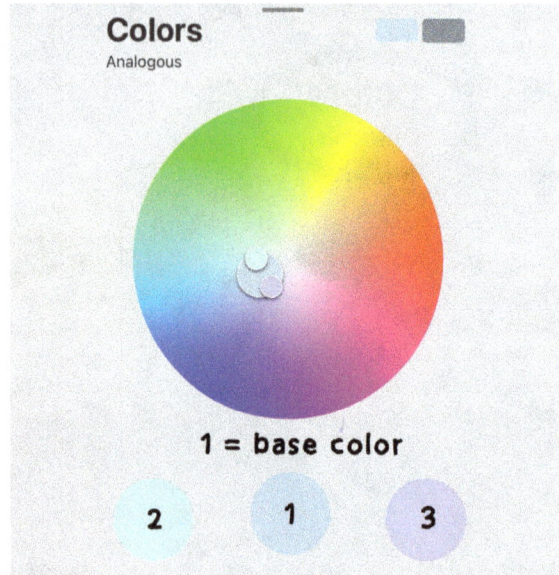

Figure 5.6 – Analogous color palette for light blue

An analogous color scheme has now been created using Procreate color palette tools. Let us move forward to the next technique, which is complementary schemes.

Creating complementary schemes

Next, we will learn how to use complementary schemes with Procreate's tool to easily create a color palette.

Following the steps

Using complementary schemes can be done as follows:

1. Firstly, create a new canvas in Procreate and choose one base color. I will use vibrant blue for this walkthrough:

Figure 5.7 – Blue base colour

2. Using Procreate's color wheel system, tap **Harmony** in the color wheel section. Then, change the setting to **Complementary**:

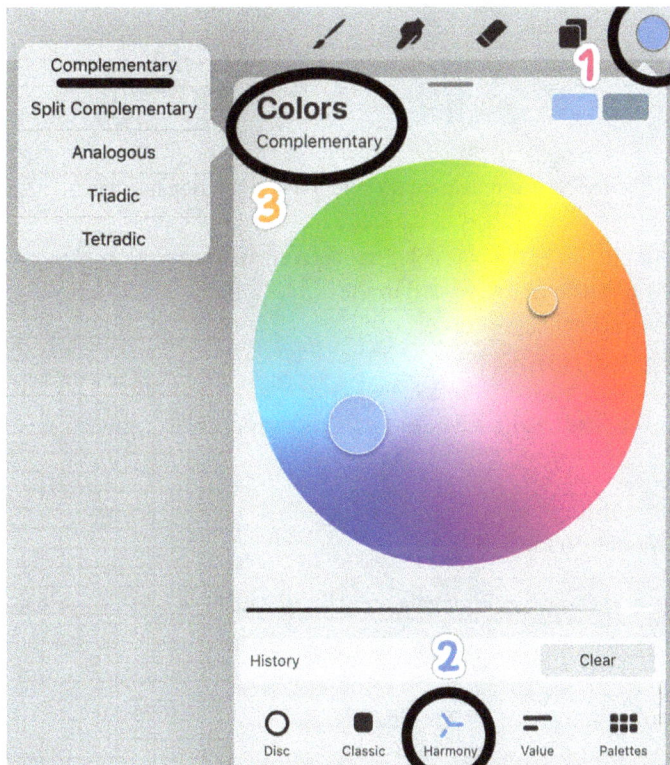

Figure 5.8 – Example of using Procreate tools to change color scheme settings

3. Move around the base color and you will notice that the other color will automatically create and follow around the vibrant blue base color. Save the two colors created using the color picker and paste them on a blank canvas:

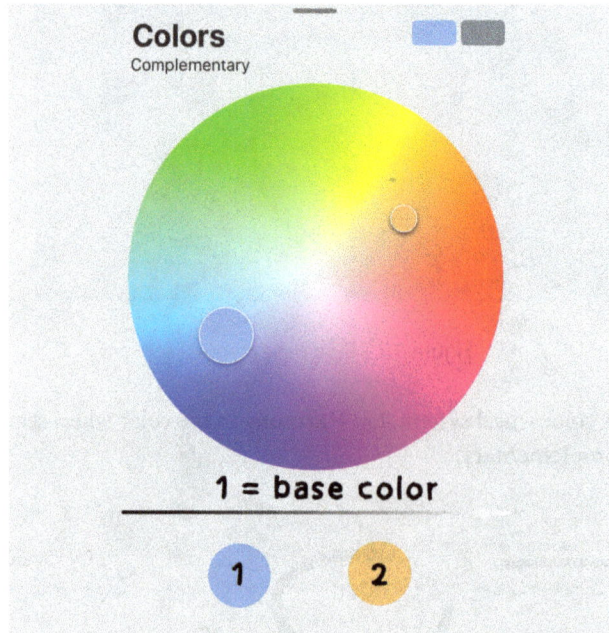

Figure 5.9 – Complementary color palette for the blue color

A complementary color palette for the blue color has been created for you. You can now use it for your design illustrations. Now, let us move forward to the last technique, triadic schemes.

Creating triadic schemes

Here, we will learn how to use triadic schemes with Procreate's tool to easily create a color palette.

Following the steps

Using triadic schemes can be done as follows:

1. Firstly, create a new canvas in Procreate and choose one base color. I will use light brown for this walkthrough:

Figure 5.10 – Light brown base color

2. Using Procreate's color wheel system, tap **Harmony** in the color wheel section. Then, change the setting to **Triadic**.

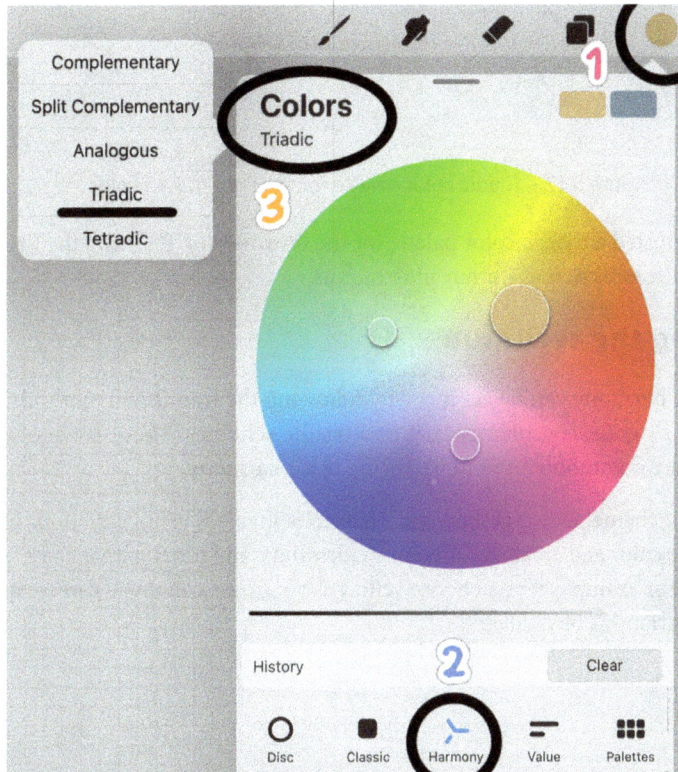

Figure 5.11 – Example of using Procreate tools to change color scheme settings

3. Move around the base color and you will notice that the other color will automatically create and follow around the light brown base color. Save the two colors created using a color picker and paste them onto a blank canvas:

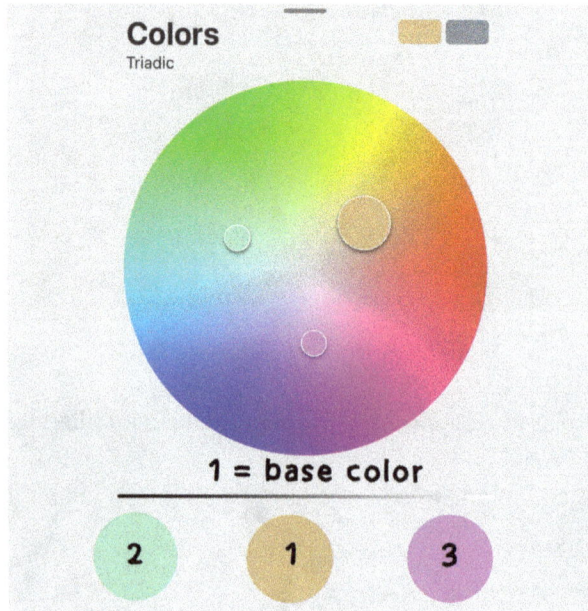

Figure 5.12 – Triadic color palette for the light brown color

With that, we have created a triadic color palette for the brown color. By using the Procreate tool, we can create unlimited color schemes for our illustrations.

Understanding the technique

Creating good color harmony can be achieved by following the traditional methods, which are the monochromatic, analogous, complementary, and triadic schemes. There are a lot more methods available, but these are commonly used in balancing color harmony.

The monochromatic scheme, which is shown in *Figure 5.3*, involves using variations of a single color. By choosing one base color and creating different shades, tints, and tones of that color, you can achieve a harmonious look. For example, if you choose yellow as your base color, you can create a palette with lighter and darker variations of yellow.

The analogous scheme, which is shown in *Figure 5.6*, uses colors that are next to each other on the color wheel. These colors usually match well and create serene and comfortable designs. For example, if you choose light blue as your base color, you can create a color palette such as light turquoise and light purple.

The complementary scheme, which is shown in *Figure 5.9*, involves using colors that are opposite each other on the color wheel. These colors create a high contrast and vibrant look. For example, if you choose vibrant blue as your base color, you can pair it with its complementary color, which is orange.

Lastly, the triadic scheme, which is shown in *Figure 5.12*, uses three colors that are evenly spaced around the color wheel. This creates a balanced and vibrant color palette. For example, if you choose light brown as your base color, you can create a palette with colors such as turquoise and purple.

These methods are commonly used to create color harmony in art and design, helping to improve your coloring skills. These are some examples of how to create a color palette traditionally but if you find it difficult to use, you are free to use your own way to find a good color combination. In choosing colors, it is important to trust what you see. If you find a color combination that is perfect for you but it goes against the traditional methods, then you do not have to follow the traditional rules.

The importance of color value and how to use it in art

Color value in art refers to the lightness or darkness of a color. It is an important aspect of color theory because it helps create depth and contrast in an artwork. By adjusting the color values, we can highlight certain areas, thus helping to catch the viewer's attention to look at your art. We are often scared to add a little bit of dark color to our art fearing it might affect the overall scenery. Adding a little darkness and highlight to our art will enable us to create a dynamic and mysterious illustration. In this walkthrough, we will learn how to apply color value effectively to our art.

Following the steps

For this walkthrough, we will learn how color value can affect the overall mood and atmosphere of the background scenery. Often, we are not sure how to do it, but by following this walkthrough, we can improve our color value technique easily.

Applying color value to our art can be done as follows:

1.   Sketch out a background scenery illustration, as in the following figure:

Figure 5.13 – Background scenery sketch

2.   Prepare a simple base color for the sketch:

Figure 5.14 – Example of base color without color value

3. To add depth to the illustration, paint the closest and farthest objects in darker colors while keeping the middle area lighter due to the center placement of the lighting. Paint a black-toned background color to create a sense of depth and distance in the scenery:

Figure 5.15 – Example of adding color value on background scenery

4. Lastly, add shadow to the upper part of the trees, as shown in *Figure 5.16*, using the **Multiply** blending mode:

Figure 5.16 – Example of adding shadow to the background scenery

By following this step-by-step walkthrough, we can now easily add color value to our art. Let us take a look at how color value works.

Understanding the technique

In Figure 5.14, we can see that the illustration looks plainer and flatter compared to Figure 5.15. This is due to the limited colors that we used for the background scenery. This type of coloring is often used in children's illustrations to make the viewer easily understand the storyline. Sometimes, it is used for aesthetic purposes that are favored in simple and minimal design.

Since we want to create dynamic background scenery, we have to use the color value technique. Using color value, we can add depth and improve the atmosphere. If using colors directly is a little difficult for you, you can practice using different tones of gray as a guideline for the coloring. You can refer to Figure 5.34 for an example of that.

How and when to use warm and cool colors

Warm and cool color tones play a significant role in art. Warm colors, such as reds, oranges, and yellows, are often associated with energy, passion, and warmth. They tend to stand out as vibrant, making them ideal for drawing attention to certain areas. On the other hand, cool colors, such as blues, greens, and purples, evoke calmness, tranquility, and distance. They provide a sense of depth and balance. Understanding how and when to use warm and cool colors can enhance the mood and impact of your artwork.

Applying warm tones

In this walkthrough, we will learn how to use and apply warm color tones to enhance our background scenery. By following this walkthrough, we will learn how to use these warm hues in our backgrounds to create an inviting atmosphere.

Following the steps

Using warm color tones can be done as follows:

1. Start by sketching out the background scenery:

Figure 5.17 – Background scenery sketch

2. Create a palette of warm colors that includes shades of yellow, orange, and brown:

Figure 5.18 – Example of warm color tones palette

3. Paint the background scenery using a warm color palette, and the background scenery will appear as follows:

Figure 5.19 – Result of using warm color tones

We have successfully created warm and cozy scenery using warm color tones. Let us move forward to the next walkthrough to create a calm background scenery using cool color tones.

Applying cool tones

In this walkthrough, we will learn how to use and apply cool color tones to our background scenery. Cool color tones, such as blues, greens, and purples, are great for creating a calm and soothing atmosphere in our artwork. By following these steps, we can easily use these colors and enhance our background scenes for serene scenery.

Following the steps

Using cool color tones can be done as follows:

1. Start by sketching out the background scenery:

Figure 5.20 – Background scenery sketch

2.   Create a palette of cool colors that includes shades of pink, blue, turquoise, and gray:

Figure 5.21 – Example of cool color tones palette

3. Paint the background scenery using a cool color palette, and the background scenery will appear as follows:

Figure 5.22 – Result of using cool color tones

With that, we have created a calming and serene scenery using cool color tones such as blue and turquoise. Let us move forward to understand more about how cool and cool tones affect the atmosphere and how they can evoke emotion.

Understanding the technique

Warm and cool color tones play important roles in portraying certain emotions. Warm color tones can be used to create a welcoming and cozy atmosphere while blue color tones can evoke a calming and serene feeling. The color wheel can be divided into two sections, where the upper part is for warm color tones while the lower part is for cool color tones. Let us have a look at the following example for a better understanding:

Figure 5.23 – Example of warm and cool color tones on the color wheel

If we look at *Figure 5.19*, the atmosphere looks warmer than *Figure 5.22*. All colors play important roles in creating a unique atmosphere. Mixing warm and cool color tones will also create a wonderful atmosphere. We can see examples of that around us, such as green land with blue sky. The blue sky is a cool color tone while the green land is a warm color tone. Let us see an example here:

Figure 5.24 – Example of warm and cool color tones in one image; source: https://
unsplash.com/photos/a-grassy-hill-with-a-fence-in-the-distance-ZZAHHbqqAv4

When both warm and cool color tones are combined, these colors can create a visually appealing contrast that adds depth and a serene atmosphere to your art. If you want to get used to painting backgrounds, you can try painting using both color tones to improve your background scenery coloring.

Improving contrast in art

Contrast in art refers to the difference between elements in a composition, such as color, value, size, and texture. It is used to create visual interest, draw attention to certain areas, and enhance the overall impact of the artwork. To improve contrast in art, you can use several techniques, such as **color contrast**. Use colors that are opposite each other on the color wheel, such as the complementary scheme method, to create a good contrast. For **value contrast**, incorporate a range of light and dark values to create depth and highlight important areas. Vary the size of elements to create a sense of scale and importance. This technique is called **size contrast**. Lastly, a **texture contrast** can be achieved by combining different textures to add interest and complexity to the artwork. By effectively using these techniques, you can add contrast to improve your illustrations.

Following the steps

In this walkthrough, we're going to learn how to add contrast to our background art. Adding contrast helps make your artwork more dynamic and visually interesting. By following these steps, you'll improve your skills and create a more engaging environment. Adding contrast means using differences in light and dark colors and textures to make different parts of your artwork stand out.

Here's how to add contrast to the background drawing:

1.   Prepare a clean line art drawing that's ready for base coloring:

Figure 5.25 – Background drawing sketch

2.   Then, fill the background with a dark gray color:

Figure 5.26 – Example of filling out the background with a dark gray color

3.   Lastly, decide the main subject and focal point of the background drawing. Using white color, highlight the main subject area. I will paint it in the center of the background illustration. It should look like this:

Figure 5.27 – Results of adding highlight to the main subject to add contrast

By following this tutorial, we can now create a good contrast in our art. Let us move forward to have a better understanding of the techniques.

Understanding the technique

Contrast relates to the differences in background art composition, such as color, value, size, and texture. To enhance contrast in your artwork, you can use varying light and dark color values to create depth, change the sizes of elements for a sense of scale, and mix different textures to draw attention to your art.

In *Figure 5.27*, our eyes are immediately drawn to the center of the illustration because that area is highlighted. The darker colors at the front and back give the illustration depth, making it seem as if the room is longer and divided into three sections. If we compare *Figure 5.25* with *Figure 5.27*, we can see that *Figure 5.27* has a better atmosphere and composition. Changing the position of the highlight will also alter the illustration's atmosphere. Let us look at an example here showing different highlight placements:

Figure 5.28 – Example of different placements of the highlight

As illustrated in *Figure 5.28*, altering the highlight placement or focus of the illustration generates a more mysterious effect compared to *Figure 5.27*. The darker areas evoke a sense of hidden meaning, creating an eerie atmosphere. This approach captures the viewer's attention, encouraging them to delve deeper into the artwork's story, thereby enhancing storytelling in art. Before going ahead with coloring, it is advisable to decide on the contrast first for a smoother workflow in the coloring process.

Choosing random colors to create a color palette

Choosing colors in art involves understanding color theory and applying it to create visually appealing and harmonious compositions. We often struggle with choosing colors and worry whether they complement each other. Usually, we will use traditional methods such as using monochromatic schemes, triadic schemes, and so on to create a harmonious color palette. In this walkthrough, we will learn how to create our own color palette without using the traditional methods. By following this walkthrough, we can have more freedom in creating a color palette.

Following the steps

For this walkthrough, we will discover how to create our own color palette without relying on traditional methods for finding suitable color combinations for our artwork. By following these steps, we will have a better understanding of color theory and be more confident in creating palettes.

Creating a color palette by selecting random colors can be done as follows:

1. Draw a shape or character silhouette; it can be anything you like. I will draw a bunny for this walkthrough (*STEP 1* in *Figure 5.29*).

2. Choose one color to start creating your palette. I will use pink for the first color (*STEP 2*).

3. Then, choose the second color. I will use a blue color, as shown in *STEP 3*.

4. Start mixing up random colors until you are satisfied with the overall color results (*STEP 4*).

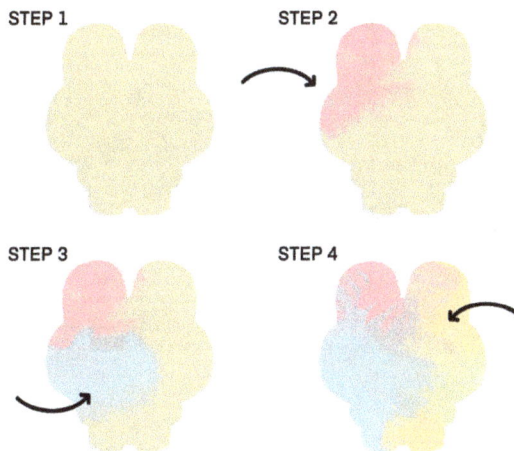

Figure 5.29 – Color palette created from this method

5. Arranged the colors as shown in *Figure 5.30*, ensuring they are ready to import into a Procreate palette.

Figure 5.30 – Color palette created from this method

6. Finally, import it into **Palettes** in Procreate. For detailed instructions on accessing the **Palettes** tool, refer to *Figure 5.31*:

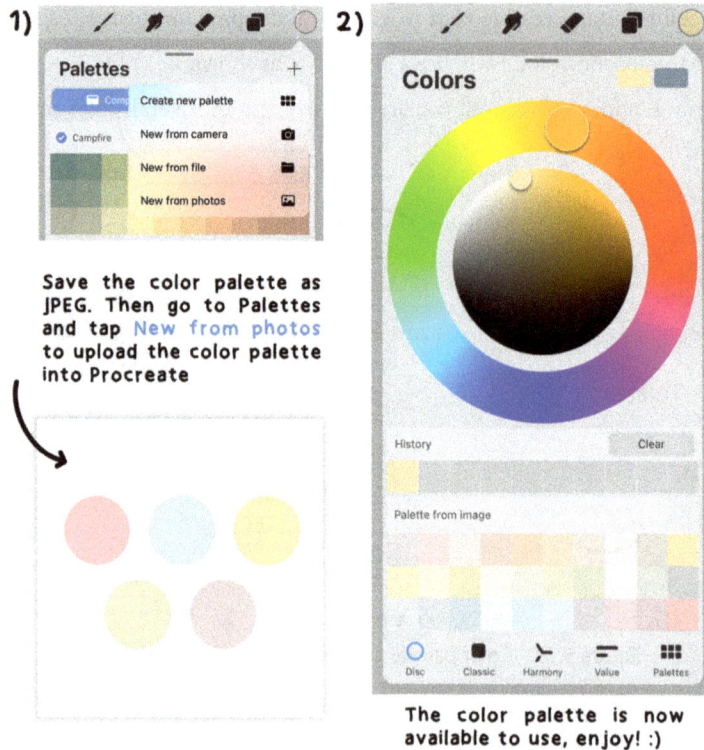

Figure 5.31 – Color palette created from this method

> **Tip**
>
> 🔍 **Quick tip**: Need to see a high-resolution version of this image? Open this book in the next-gen Packt Reader or view it in the PDF/ePub copy.
>
> 🔒 **The next-gen Packt Reader** and a **free PDF/ePub copy** of this book are included with your purchase. Scan the QR code OR go to `packtpub.com/unlock`, then use the search bar to find this book by name. Double-check the edition shown to make sure you get the right one.

A new and unique color palette has been created for you. We can now use it to create a one-of-a-kind design illustration.

Understanding the technique

Randomly selecting colors and experimenting with them can lead to unexpected and unique color combinations. This approach allows for a more intuitive and creative process, where you can trust your instincts and see where it will take you. By stepping away from traditional color schemes and methods, you open yourself up to more possibilities in discovering new and exciting ways to use color in your artwork.

When you choose colors randomly, you might stumble upon combinations that you would not have considered before. This can add a fresh and new element to your work, making it stand out. Additionally, this method encourages you to think creatively. It can be a fun experience since it allows you to explore and experiment without the need to follow the traditional way of color theory.

Trust your instincts, mix the colors freely, and do not be afraid to play around with colors. You might be surprised at the unique results you can achieve through random selection and experimentation.

Know more...

To create a color palette from an image in Procreate, first, import the image into the app. Then, open the **Colors** panel and tap the + button. Select **New from photos** and choose your image, allowing Procreate to automatically generate a palette based on the colors detected in the image. This is a quick and effective way to get a color scheme from a reference.

Creating a color palette using Gradient Map

In an earlier walkthrough, we learned about how to create color palettes by selecting random colors. Some might find the previous technique more difficult. In this walkthrough, we will learn how to create color palettes easily and quickly by using the **Gradient Map** tool.

Following the steps

For this walkthrough, we will learn how to create a color palette using the **Gradient** tool in Procreate. Creating a color palette using gradients in Procreate can be a fun and creative process. By following this step-by-step walkthrough, we can easily create endless color palettes for our art.

Creating a color palette using the Procreate **Gradient Map** tool can be done as follows:

1. Sketch out the background scenery and fill the background with different tones of gray:

Figure 5.32 – Example background art with added color value

2.   Then, go to the **Gradient** tool and you will see the **Gradient Library** panel pop up on the screen. Tap the + symbol and a set of gray sections will appear.

3.   Then, on every gray square section, change it to a new color to suit your own preference. You can add a gray section for more color palette choices.

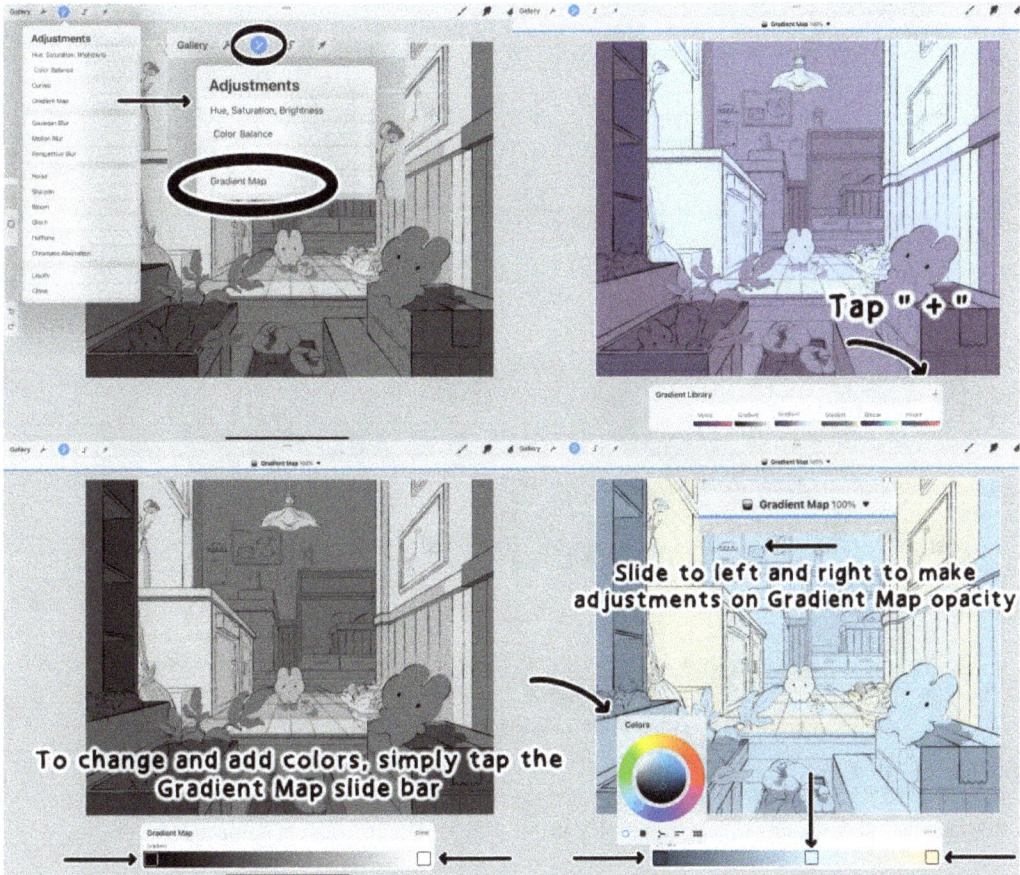

Figure 5.33 – Example of using the Gradient Map tool in Procreate

4. After modifying the colors, finalize it by clicking on **Done**. This will save your gradient settings.

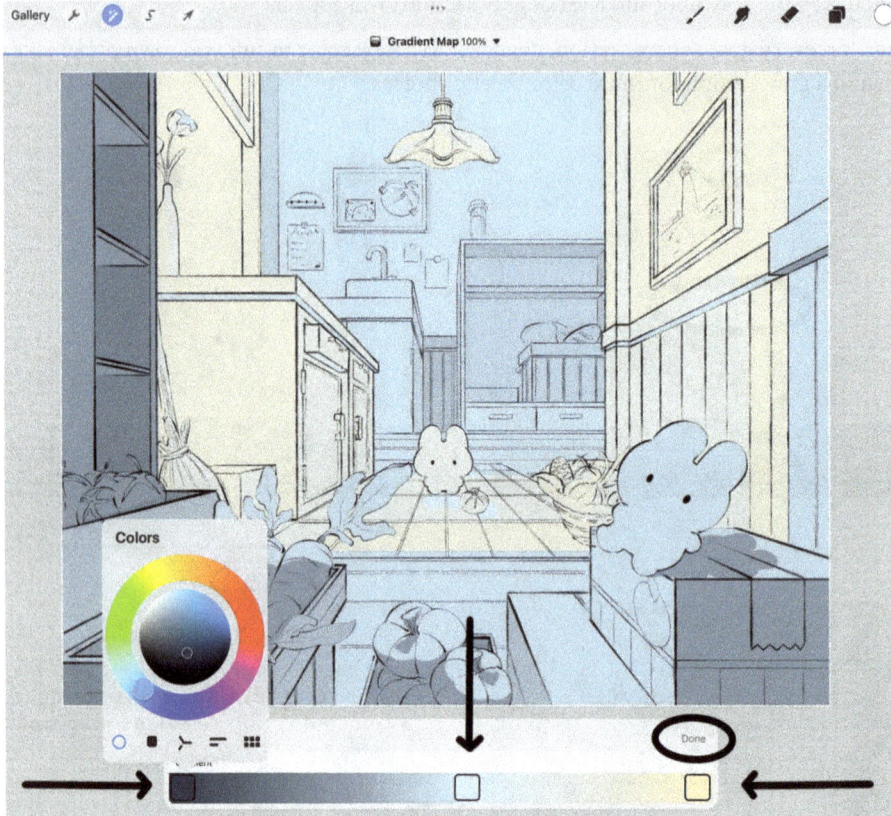

Figure 5.34 – Final result from using the Gradient Map tool

With the help of the **Gradient Map** tool in Procreate, we can create an unlimited color palette for our art. We can now sit back and enjoy this cool feature in Procreate to create a color palette.

Understanding the technique

Using the **Gradient Map** tool in Procreate allows you to efficiently create a wide variety of color palettes, making the process quicker and more convenient. This approach saves time because it eliminates the need for manual color mixing. To use this method, start by filling your background with different shades of gray. Once you have your grayscale background, apply the **Gradient Map** tool.

The **Gradient Map** tool will transform the shades of gray into a diverse range of colors, based on the gradient you choose. This technique allows you to experiment with various color schemes and find the perfect palette for your artwork without the hassle of mixing colors manually. By using the **Gradient Map** tool, you can improve your workflow and create a color palette easily.

Using color harmony, color value, and contrast in art

Understanding and applying color harmony, color value, and contrast can significantly enhance your artwork. Color harmony refers to the pleasing arrangement of colors in an artwork, while color value is the lightness or darkness of a color. Contrast refers to the difference between elements in a composition, such as color, value, size, and texture. Applying all these techniques to our art can create a dynamic and appealing background. We learned about all these methods in previous walkthroughs, but we may face a problem with how to apply them all to our art. In this walkthrough, we will learn how to use them to create a simple and quick background scene that can be used for portfolio purposes.

Following the steps

For this walkthrough, we will learn how to add contrast, balance color value, and make sure we have a harmonious color scheme. By understanding and applying these methods, you can create vibrant and wonderful background art.

Applying color harmony, color value, and contrast can be done as follows:

1. Begin by drawing a background outline and shading it using various tones of gray in two separate layers. Next, highlight the main subject (bunny) with lighter and brighter shades of gray:

Figure 5.35 – Example of background art with color value added

2. Next, open the **Gradient Map** tool in Procreate and modify the color according to your preference. You can refer to *Figure 5.33* for a guide on how to access the **Gradient Map** tool. After modifying the colors, finalize it by tapping **Done**:

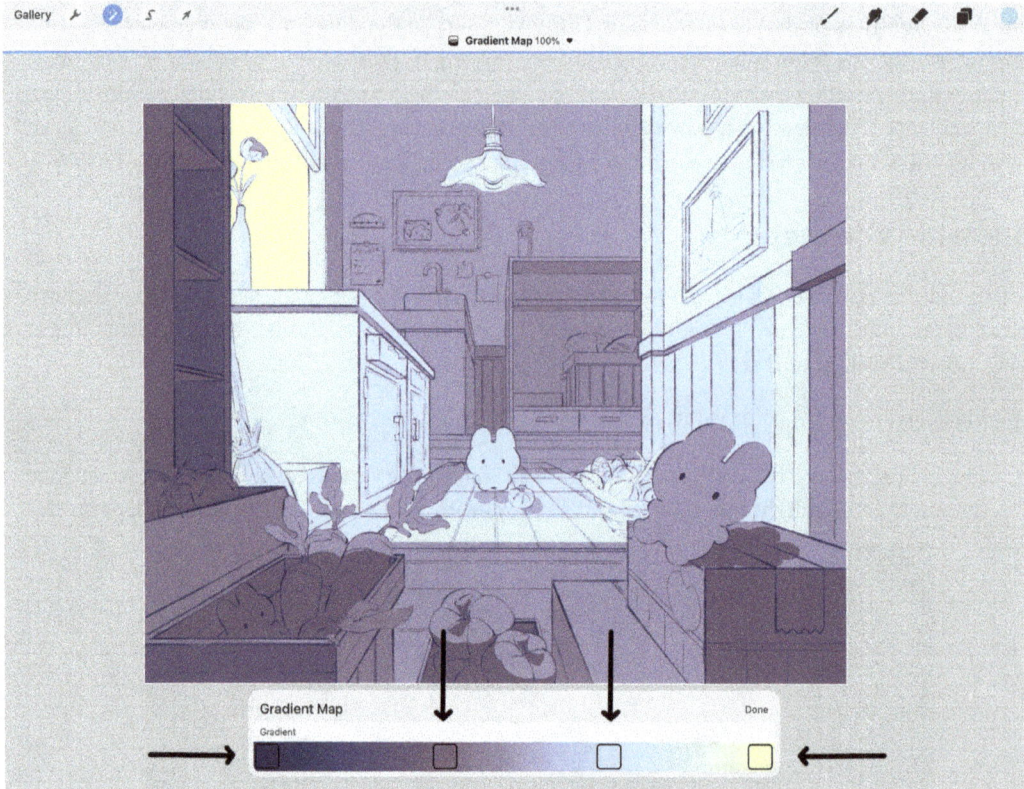

Figure 5.36 – Color palette generated using Gradient Map

3. Paint over the objects in the background illustration using a **Darken** blending mode layer. This will help you paint without affecting the shadow and color scheme created before. You can refer to *Figure 5.40* for layers and blending mode guidelines.

Figure 5.37 – Example of painting over the base color using a Darken blending mode layer

4. Next, modify the line art layers by blurring the second line art and adjusting the colors according to *Figure 5.38*:

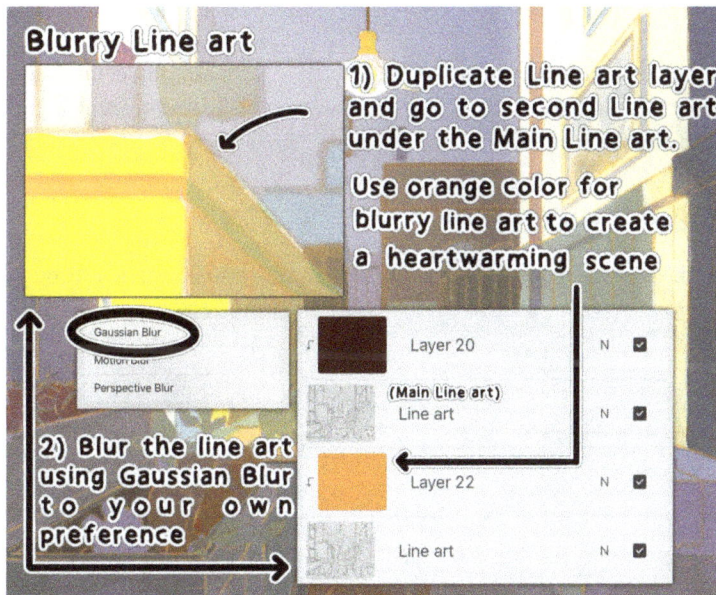

Figure 5.38 – Example of Line art layers setting

5. Lastly, add lighting using **Add** and **Overlay** blending modes to recreate the warm lighting. You can refer to *Figure 5.40* for the layer placement.

Figure 5.39 – Final result of the illustration

With this approach, we can now create illustrations with good color harmony, color value, and contrast. By understanding how this method works, we can enhance our background scenery and improve our drawing skills to create a masterpiece.

Understanding the technique

Figure 5.40 displays the arrangement of layers and the blending modes applied throughout this walkthrough:

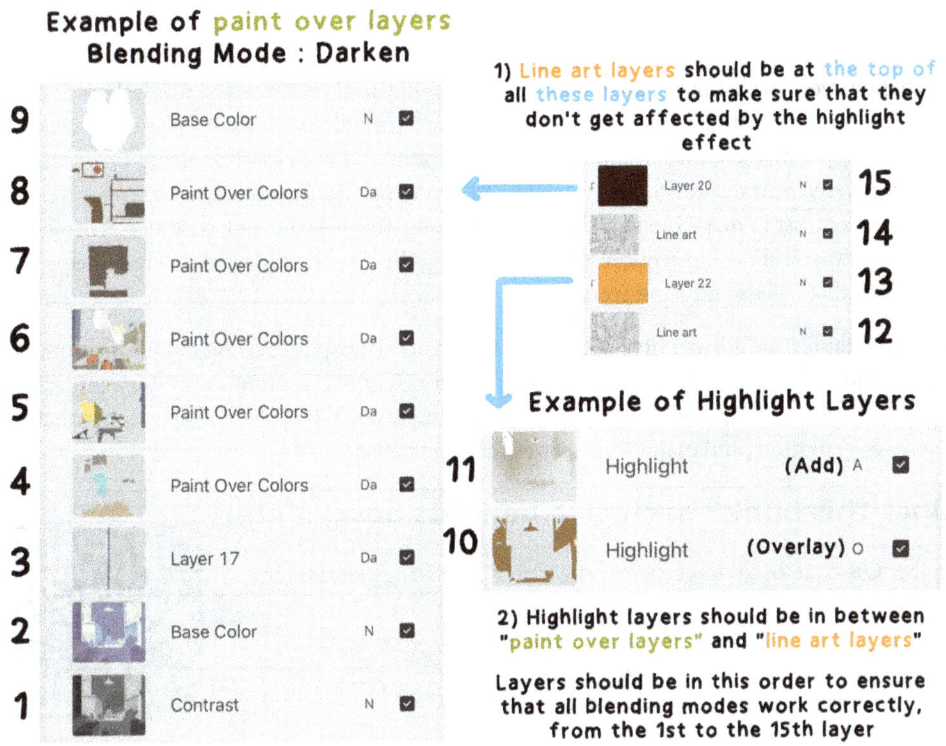

Example of paint over layers
Blending Mode : Darken

9 — Base Color — N ☑

8 — Paint Over Colors — Da ☑

7 — Paint Over Colors — Da ☑

6 — Paint Over Colors — Da ☑

5 — Paint Over Colors — Da ☑

4 — Paint Over Colors — Da ☑

3 — Layer 17 — Da ☑

2 — Base Color — N ☑

1 — Contrast — N ☑

1) Line art layers should be at the top of all these layers to make sure that they don't get affected by the highlight effect

Layer 20 — N ☑ **15**

Line art — N ☑ **14**

Layer 22 — N ☑ **13**

Line art — N ☑ **12**

Example of Highlight Layers

11 — Highlight — (Add) A ☑

10 — Highlight — (Overlay) o ☑

2) Highlight layers should be in between "paint over layers" and "line art layers"

Layers should be in this order to ensure that all blending modes work correctly, from the 1st to the 15th layer

Figure 5.40 – Layer settings

In art, having good contrast is crucial for a dynamic view. Before coloring, decide on the contrast by adding highlights to the main focal point, then create a color palette and paint according to the contrast and color value. We can use gray tones as shown in *Figure 5.35* to help create contrast in artwork and make lighting and shadows easier to plan. They act as a guide, showing where the light hits and where shadows fall before adding colors. This makes the final image look more balanced and realistic. You can use traditional methods, select random colors, or use the **Gradient Map** tool in Procreate for a smooth coloring process. Finalize with lighting and clean up the coloring.

Mastering the use of color harmony, color value, and contrast can significantly elevate your artwork. By understanding how to create a pleasing arrangement of colors, adjust the lightness and darkness of colors to add depth, and use contrast to draw attention to key areas, you can create dynamic and engaging illustrations. These techniques not only enhance the visual appeal of your art but also help convey the intended mood and message more effectively.

Let us keep on practicing and experimenting with these techniques to become better at background coloring.

Summary

In this chapter, we learned how to use color to make our illustrations more beautiful, clear, and full of emotion. We explored different ways to pick and choose harmonious colors, such as monochromatic, analogous, complementary, and triadic schemes, and practiced each method using Procreate tools. We also discovered how to adjust color value to add depth, use warm and cool tones to set the mood, and improve contrast to make the main subject stand out. Towards the end, we had fun creating our own color palette by choosing random colors and using the Gradient Map tool, which helps us find combinations that feel exciting and fresh.

In the next chapter, we'll learn how to create mood and atmosphere using color emotions. We'll explore how to choose colors that evoke emotions such as happiness, sadness, mystery, intensity, and warmth. By understanding how colors connect to feelings, you'll be able to shape scenes that speak to the viewer's emotions and make your stories more relatable.

Unlock this book's exclusive benefits now

Scan this QR code or go to `packtpub.com/unlock`, then search this book by name.

6

Crafting a Mood and Atmosphere with Useful Techniques

Using color to create mood and atmosphere helps your art stand out as meaningful and makes a deep emotional impact. Different colors can make people experience different emotions; for example, yellow tends to create a sense of happiness, and blue can make people feel calm or sad. At the same time, how people feel about colors can change depending on their own experiences, so it's good to explore what works best for your story.

In this chapter, you'll learn how to pick colors that match the feeling you want to convey in your artwork. Whether you want your drawing to feel joyful, mysterious, or cozy, the colors you choose will help your viewers feel the emotion you intend to show. As you can imagine, understanding this can make your art more powerful and easier to connect with.

With the help of walkthroughs, we'll cover the following:

- Color emotions and how to apply them to our art
- Learning which colors create a happy atmosphere
- Learning which colors create a sad atmosphere
- Learning which colors create a mysterious atmosphere
- Learning which colors create an intense atmosphere
- Learning which colors create a heartwarming atmosphere
- Discovering the connection between colors and composition

Before beginning this chapter, please review the following important note to ensure that all of the steps can be followed smoothly. This will help maintain clarity and consistency throughout the process.

> **Important note**
>
> In this chapter, illustrations will be drawn in separate layers to maintain flexibility for adjustments. The layers should be named as follows: *Sketch layer*, *Clean line art layer*, *Contrast layer*, *Base color layer*, and *Final details layer*. This structured approach ensures that each stage of the artwork remains editable, allowing for refinement without affecting previous steps. Keeping layers organized like this makes the creative process smoother and more efficient. You can refer back to *Chapter 1* to learn about the brushes used for this book.

Color emotions and how to apply them to our art

Color emotion refers to the emotional responses that colors can evoke and how they connect with individuals. Certain colors can trigger psychological reactions, which can influence the color schemes we choose for our art. By mastering the use of color emotions, we can effectively engage the right audience. For example, to create a calming and therapeutic illustration, blue and green can be used. Each color has a unique purpose, but deciding on the right colors to convey specific emotions in art can sometimes be challenging. With a deep understanding of color emotions, we can enhance both the visual impact and storytelling of our art. Let us look at an example of color emotion next.

Breaking down color emotions

Figure 6.1 is a diagram of color emotions that can be used for your reference when choosing colors for your art. You can import this or any other color emotion diagram into Procreate using the **Reference** tool.

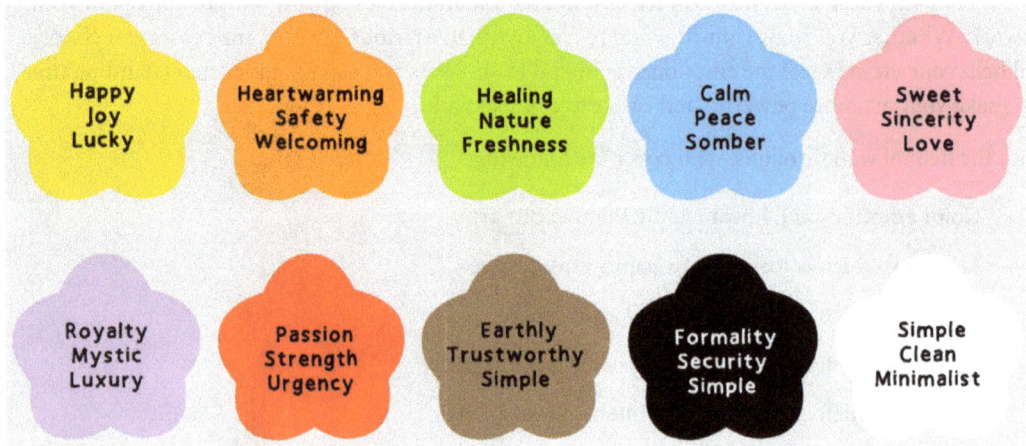

Figure 6.1 – Guidance for color emotion

Different color tones are often associated with specific feelings or moods, and they can influence how people perceive and connect with your art or branding.

Take the following examples:

- Yellow may inspire happiness, joy, or luck

- Green is associated with nature, growth, and serenity

- Blue is often linked to calmness, peace, and somberness

- Pink is associated with sweetness, sincerity, and love

- Red can evoke strength, passion, or urgency

- Black conveys a formality, security, or a simple vibe

Understanding color emotion allows artists and designers to intentionally use colors to enhance storytelling, convey certain emotions, or attract specific audiences. It plays a crucial role in visual communication and how messages are perceived. Refer to *Chapter 5, Creating Color Harmony with Procreate*, for more guidance.

The relevance of color emotion

Adding specific color emotions to our art is not only useful for branding purposes but also for storytelling. For instance, if we want to create a heartwarming scene, we can use orange as the dominant color tone. By choosing the right colors for our art, we can ensure our viewers connect with and understand the message we want to convey. It is crucial to know when and which color emotions to use in our art.

For example, if we want to color a panel for a comic of the mystery genre, we should use darker and less saturated color tones to create a suspenseful atmosphere. If we use bright colors instead, it might diminish the sense of mystery in the story, making the illustration look confusing or unclear to the audience.

Now that we have familiarized ourselves with the concept of color emotion, let's dive into some walkthroughs.

Learning which colors create a happy atmosphere

As discussed, to convey a **happy atmosphere** in art, we need to use bright and warm colors, such as yellows, oranges, vibrant blues, and soft pinks. These colors can help to evoke a sense of joy and a feeling of optimism. Yellow, for instance, is often used for children's toys, cartoon characters, and playgrounds, as it is associated with happiness and positivity, while blue is often used for a calm and serene atmosphere. As artists, we may be unsure about the choice of colors for a happy atmosphere because there are so many colors to choose from. In this walkthrough, you will be guided through finding the right colors for a happy atmosphere.

Following the steps

Now, let us explore how to choose colors for a happy atmosphere. After this, we will learn how to apply these colors in our artwork:

1.   Firstly, draw some background scenery. It can be a sketch or clean line art. Next, add shades of gray with varying values to the *Contrast* layer as shown in *Figure 6.2*.

Figure 6.2 – Background scenery sketch

2.   Use yellow as the main color. Then, mix and match colors based on your preference to create a color palette. The following is my color palette for a happy atmosphere. You can add this color palette to Procreate's **Reference** tool for easy access while working on your artwork.

Figure 6.3 – Happy atmosphere color palette

3. Lastly, paint the rest of the background scenery using the color palette and finalize it by adding details. I used **Color Curve** to adjust the contrast. This is the final look of my happy atmosphere background scenery.

Figure 6.4 – Example of a happy atmosphere

Understanding the technique

In *Figure 6.4*, you can see how using a mix of warm and cool colors, such as bright yellow, vibrant green, and light blue, can create a cheerful vibe. The blue sky, combined with the yellow and green grass, gives a happy feeling. Just make sure to balance the colors so the overall mood you want to share is conveyed. Feel free to select colors that resonate with you; just make sure they evoke a sense of warmth and vibrancy!

Know more...

Using too much blue can create a cool, heavy mood. It's perfect if you're aiming for something somber or melancholic. But if you're going for a more vibrant and uplifting feel, consider balancing the palette with warm hues such as warm pinks, oranges, or golden yellows. These can soften the coolness and brighten up the scene.

You can also use the **Curve** tool to adjust and tweak the color values for shadows, midtones, and highlights for better balance.

> **Coloring tips**
>
> **ColorDrop** in Procreate lets you quickly fill an area with a color. Just pick a color, then drag it from the top-right color circle onto the spot you want to fill. If the color doesn't spread how you want, hold down the drop to adjust the **Threshold** slider – this controls how much of the space gets filled. It's a super-quick way to color large sections without painting everything manually.

Learning which colors create a sad atmosphere

To design a color palette for a sad atmosphere, focus on muted and cool tones, such as deep blues, desaturated greens, and grays. To simplify the process, you can choose from any desaturated shades to create a sense of heaviness and a somber mood in your artwork. There is often the tendency to stick to blue when creating a sad theme. In this walkthrough, we'll explore how to include other colors to craft a striking and somber illustration.

Following the steps

Now, let us take a look at how to create a sad atmosphere using a specific color palette:

1. Firstly, draw some background scenery. It can be a sketch or clean line art. Next, add shades of gray with varying values to the *Contrast* layer as shown in *Figure 6.5*.

Figure 6.5 – Background scenery sketch

2. Use blue as the main color. Then, mix and match colors based on your preference to create a color palette. This is my color palette for a sad atmosphere. You can add this color palette to Procreate's **Reference** tool for easy access while working on your artwork.

Figure 6.6 – Sad atmosphere color palette

3. Lastly, paint the rest of the background scenery using the color palette and finalize it by adding details. I used the **Color Curve** to adjust the contrast. This is the final look of the sad atmosphere background scenery.

Figure 6.7 – Example of a sad atmosphere

Understanding the technique

To create a sad atmosphere, blue stands out as an excellent choice due to its association with feelings of melancholy. We can use monochromatic color theory where varying shades, tints, and tones of a blue hue to create a sad mood. If the artwork feels a bit plain, adding a touch of warmer tones can enhance its visual appeal. When using warm colors, desaturated tones are ideal to ensure they don't overpower the cool tones. You can use blending modes such as **Overlay** and **Soft Light** to create a soft and warm glow in the background scenery, such as the moon and shooting stars. For instance, in *Figure 6.7*, I used a muted yellow for the moon to maintain the somber mood of the background. It's best to avoid vibrant colors, as they can shift the mood to other emotions, such as happiness. I drew the bunny with a semi-transparent effect, paired with falling rain, to create the impression that it is fading away while waving goodbye. This is to convey a farewell and melancholic atmosphere. I changed the expression as well to evoke a sad feeling.

Learning which colors create a mysterious atmosphere

To create a color palette for a mysterious atmosphere, focus on deep, rich colors, such as dark blues, purples, blacks, and muted greens, with a hint of metallic tones such as gold or silver. Adding shades of foggy gray and desaturated purple can evoke an eerie yet elegant atmosphere. Darker colors can be tricky to work with since they might overpower the whole design. In this walkthrough, we will learn together how to find the perfect colors for a mysterious atmosphere.

Following the steps

Let us learn how to choose colors for a mysterious atmosphere and apply it to our background drawing:

1. First, draw some background scenery. It can be a sketch or clean line art. Next, add shades of gray with varying values to the *Contrast* layer as shown in *Figure 6.8*.

Figure 6.8 – Background scenery sketch

2. Use gray as the main color. Then, mix and match colors based on your preference to create a color palette. This is my color palette for a mysterious atmosphere. You can add this color palette to Procreate's **Reference** tool for easy access while working on your artwork.

Figure 6.9 – Mysterious color palette

3. Lastly, paint the rest of the background scenery using the color palette and finalize it by adding details. I used the **Color Curve** to adjust the contrast. This is the final look of the mysterious atmosphere background scenery.

Figure 6.10 – Example of a mysterious atmosphere

Understanding the technique

To create a mysterious atmosphere, we need to incorporate specific elements such as moody lighting, shadow, and a foggy atmosphere. We can use darker shades of colors and muted green tones to evoke mysterious feelings in the viewer. Adding a hint of red can also evoke an eerie feeling. If we compare *Figure 6.7* and *Figure 6.10*, we can see that by using different color hues, we can change the overall atmosphere regardless of using the same sketch base or design concept. This shows that color emotion plays a key role in telling stories and sharing your vision. Even though the bunny is seen smiling, by using different color schemes, we can create a whole new story and atmosphere.

Learning which colors create an intense atmosphere

An intense atmosphere is created by using strong lighting and bold contrasts to make your artwork dynamic and eye-catching. Adding textures can help add depth and make the composition look even better. You can use colors such as red, vibrant purple, and black to create this effect, as they're often tied to feelings of passion and urgency. Bright red tones can be hard to work with since they are tricky to mix into a balanced color scheme. In this walkthrough, we will focus on using red and darker shades to create an intense and dramatic look.

Following the steps

Choosing colors for an intense atmosphere and how to apply them to our art is explained as follows:

1. Firstly, draw some background scenery. It can be a sketch or clean line art. Next, add shades of gray with varying values to the *Contrast* layer as shown in *Figure 6.11*.

Figure 6.11 – Background scenery sketch

2. Use red as the main color. Then, mix and match colors based on your preference to create a color palette. This is my color palette for an intense atmosphere. You can add this color palette to Procreate's **Reference** tool for easy access while working on your artwork.

Figure 6.12 – Intense atmosphere color palette

3. Lastly, paint the rest of the background scenery using the color palette and finalize it by adding details. I used **Color Curve** to adjust the contrast. This is the final look of the intense atmosphere background scenery.

Figure 6.13 – Example of an intense atmosphere

Understanding the technique

As you can see in *Figure 6.13*, we can create an intense atmosphere by using red, blue, and deep purple with a hint of vibrant purple. To create a good contrast, I painted the character with a desaturated blue color to make it stand out more. If we paint everything with intense and vibrant colors, it will overwhelm the overall scenery and design. The drawing will lose its contrast, making it harder to focus on the main subject of the drawing. It is important to keep the overall color hue balanced and harmonious. We can balance the color hue for an intense atmosphere by mixing high saturation and desaturated color tones. I used warm and cool color tones to create a good contrast, as shown in *Figure 6.13*.

Learning which colors create a heartwarming atmosphere

To create a heartwarming atmosphere, we can use warm colors such as yellow, orange, and soft red. Adding warm lighting to the background scenery will create a soft and welcoming atmosphere. We usually use warm colors for heartwarming scenery, such as cozy and nostalgic environments. Using warm colors can be limiting due to the limited available hues for it. In this walkthrough, we will learn how we can create an eye-catching, heartwarming atmosphere using limited color hues.

Following the steps

Let us learn which colors are suitable for a heartwarming atmosphere. Then, we will learn how to apply it to our background drawing:

1. Firstly, draw some background scenery. It can be a sketch or clean line art. Next, add shades of gray with varying values to the *Contrast* layer as shown in *Figure 6.14*.

Figure 6.14 – Background sketch

2. Use orange as the main color. Then, mix and match colors based on your preference to create a color palette. This is my color palette for a heartwarming atmosphere. You can add this color palette to Procreate's **Reference** tool for easy access while working on your artwork.

Figure 6.15 – Heartwarming atmosphere color palette

3. Lastly, paint the rest of the background scenery using the color palette and finalize it by adding details. I used the **Color Curve** to adjust the contrast. This is the final look of the heartwarming atmosphere background scenery.

Figure 6.16 – Example of a heartwarming atmosphere

Understanding the technique

As we can see in *Figure 6.16*, we are using only warm colors to create a heartwarming atmosphere. I avoided using cool color tones for a heartwarming atmosphere because I would like to keep the atmosphere warm and inviting. If we look closely at *Figure 6.16*, the scenery appears to be glowing even though we didn't use the blending mode to add lighting. This means that by using colors that blend well with each other, we can create a glowing effect naturally. We can achieve this by practicing and experimenting with colors. We can also use blending modes such as **Add** and **Overlay** in separate layers to recreate the warm and glowing lighting.

Happy atmosphere   Sad atmosphere   Mysterious atmosphere

Intense atmosphere   Heartwarming atmosphere

Figure 6.17 – Compiled color emotions added to the background scenery

Figure 6.17 shows the different background scenes placed next to each other. Looking at them, we can see how colors change the mood and feel of a drawing. This proves how important it is to choose colors that match the story or artistic style we want to create.

Know more...

After you have completed these color emotion illustrations, you can save the color palettes on Procreate for future use. To create a color palette from an image in Procreate, first import the image into the app. Then, open the Color Panel and tap the + button. Select **New from Photos** and choose your image, allowing Procreate to automatically generate a palette based on the colors detected in the image. This is a quick and effective way to get a color scheme from a reference.

Discovering the connection between colors and composition

Colors and composition play important roles in art. Colors can evoke and influence the emotional impact of the illustration on the viewer. Contrast can guide the viewer's eye and enhance the overall composition of the illustration by adding depth. For example, warm colors can evoke a cozy feeling, and adding a highlight on the main subject can create a good contrast. Color composition refers to the way colors are arranged and combined in an artwork to create a visually appealing and harmonious design. It involves understanding how different colors interact with each other and their contrast, balance, and overall effect on the mood or story of the piece. However, applying them to your artwork can feel a bit overwhelming at first. In this walkthrough, we'll explore simple ways to seamlessly integrate a harmonious color scheme and effective composition into your art.

Following the steps

Now we will learn how to implement both color and composition into our background drawing to create an eye-catching illustration:

1. Firstly, prepare a background scenery with different gray color values. You can refer to this background scenery as guidance.

Figure 6.18 – Background scenery sketch using gray tones

2. Choose a base color based on your preference. The base color value must be following the gray color value. You can use **ColorDrop** to fill in a specific area of the drawing.

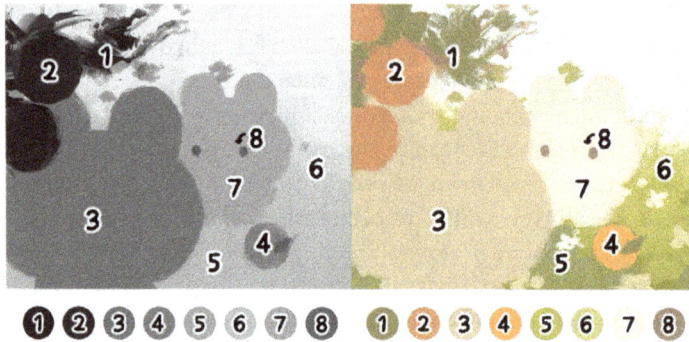

Figure 6.19 – Example of a base color for a background sketch

3. Add shadow on the nearest subject to add depth and create contrast. To darken the color of the nearest object, open the Adjustments menu by tapping the Magic Wand icon on the left side of your screen. Then select **Hue**, **Saturation**, **Brightness (HSB)** and lower the **Brightness** slider to achieve a darker tone. To adjust specific details in your illustration, use the Selections tool. I used Freehand to draw around the area I wanted. It's an easy way to make changes to a specific part of your drawing.

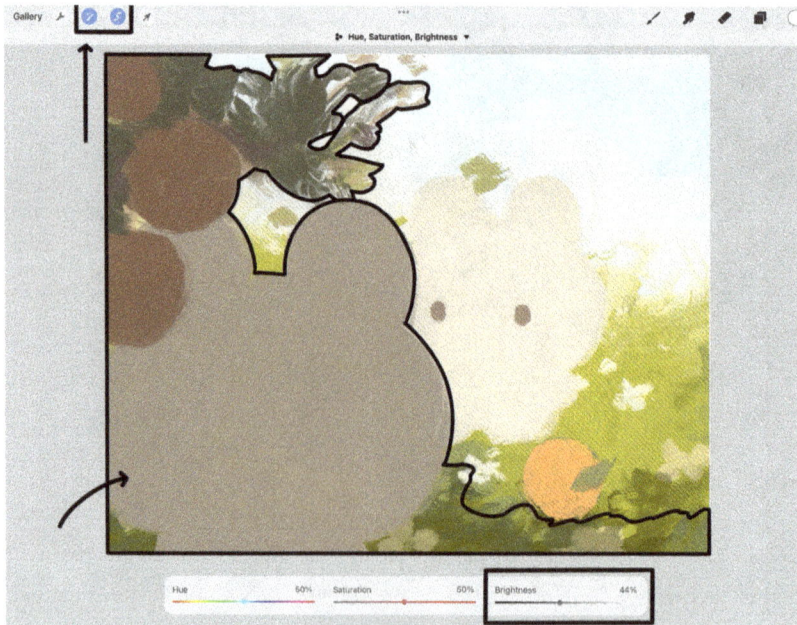

Figure 6.20 – Example of adding shadow to the background scenery

4. Lastly, to complete the background scenery, refine the rendering by smoothing out the colors, adjusting the lighting, and enhancing the depth. Then, add final details, such as highlights and reflected lights, to add charm.

Figure 6.21 – Final results of the background scenery

Understanding the technique

In *Step 1*, we are using a gray color value to paint the background. This is to ensure that we get the perspective and composition correct. By making the nearest object darker and the main subject highlighted, we can create a good contrast.

Figure 6.22 – Example of how eye movement is guided through background scenery

If we look closely at *Figure 6.22*, the gray color value gradually decreases as we get further away from the nearest object, which is the branch with the oranges. If you need a quick reminder about **atmospheric perspective**, you can refer to *Chapter 3*. This technique helps make things look farther away by using softer edges and lighter colors. It's a great way to add depth to your artwork.

By adding a good composition and contrast to our background drawing, we can guide the viewer's eyes from looking at the branch with the oranges, to the nearest bunny, to the orange on the ground, to the bunny in the middle, and, lastly, to the sky background. This will draw the interest of your viewers and help them understand the story that you wish to convey through your art. As shown in *Figure 6.19*, please use the gray color values as guidance for choosing a color. You can add your grayscale layer to Procreate's **Reference** tool to use as a guide while painting. This helps you keep in mind values and composition without disrupting your color scheme. Just enable the **Reference** tool from the **Canvas** settings, then upload the grayscale version to check as you work. It's a great way to ensure the lighting and depth remain consistent throughout the painting. To create better contrast, you can make the nearest objects darker to create a dynamic scene. Lastly, render the illustration and add details to the objects in it.

As you can see in *Figure 6.21*, I purposely made the branch with the oranges more detailed since I wanted the viewer to focus on that area first, then slowly move their view to the nearest bunny, and lastly to the main subject, which is the highlighted bunny. In *Figure 6.21*, I have used the golden spiral method to create a good composition and harmonious scene. We will learn more about this technique in *Chapter 9*. By using this technique, you can create a dynamic scene and help viewers to understand what you wish to convey in your art. From this illustration, we can see that the bunny encountered a new friend while plucking some oranges. In *Figure 6.23*, you can see how I used the golden spiral to shape the illustration. By resizing the spiral, it becomes easier to guide the scene in a more natural, balanced way.

Figure 6.23 – Example of the golden spiral

To share a story through art, you can use these methods and implement them into your art. It can be hard at first, but with consistent practice, you can get better at it and successfully create a masterpiece.

Summary

In this chapter, we learned how to use colors and composition to set the mood and atmosphere in our illustrations. We explored how different colors can express feelings such as joy, sadness, mystery, intensity, and warmth, and how these emotional tones help tell a story. With simple walkthroughs, we learned how to create color palettes for different moods and apply them step by step. We also looked at how composition plays a role in guiding the viewer's eye, using contrast, lighting, and helpful methods such as the Golden Spiral. We learned that by combining color choices with composition techniques, we can create scenes that not only look beautiful but also connect emotionally with our audience.

In the next chapter, we'll start turning ideas into stories with sketches, colors, and emotion to bring everything in your artwork to life. You'll be gently guided through each step, from brainstorming your first idea to creating the final illustration. Together, we'll explore how to build a mood board, sketch out your storyline, make changes as you go, and add color that supports the feeling you want to share.

Unlock this book's exclusive benefits now

Scan this QR code or go to `packtpub.com/unlock`, then search this book by name.

7

Storytelling Through Art: Creating Visual Narratives

When your art tells a story, it becomes more emotionally engaging, meaningful, and expressive. Just as colors create mood, your storyline gives the viewer something to connect with—whether it's a brave little character, a peaceful green field, or a whimsical scene. When all the parts of your drawing fit together with a clear story, your artwork becomes more interesting and complete.

In this chapter, we'll learn how to turn our ideas into a simple story that flows naturally through our illustration. At the same time, we'll learn how to seamlessly blend our character into the background scenery. From sketching main scenes and characters to adding details and emotions through colors, you'll see how visual storytelling brings everything in your artwork to life. Whether your story feels heartwarming, adventurous, or mysterious, the steps in this chapter will help guide your creative choices and make your artwork more relatable and memorable.

With the help of walkthrough examples, we will cover the following:

- Brainstorming and writing down ideas
- Creating a mood board for references
- Sketching out the storyline
- Improvising the story and sketch
- Integrating color emotion into the sketch
- Finalizing the story and illustration

Before beginning this chapter, please review the following important note to ensure that all steps can be followed smoothly. This will help maintain clarity and consistency throughout the process.

> **Important note**
>
> In this chapter, illustrations will be drawn in separate layers to maintain flexibility for adjustments. The layers should be named as follows: *Sketch* layer, *Clean line art* layer, *Contrast* layer, *Base color* layer, and *Final details* layer. This structured approach ensures that each stage of the artwork remains editable, allowing for refinement without affecting previous steps. Keeping layers organized in this way makes the creative process smoother and more efficient. You can refer back to *Chapter 1* for the brushes used in this book.

Brainstorming and writing down ideas

Brainstorming ideas is a great way to generate creative concepts and solutions. It involves writing down all the ideas that come to mind, no matter how random or unstructured they may seem. This process helps in organizing thoughts and can lead to innovative and unique ideas. Thinking of new ideas on the spot may be difficult, and you may feel overwhelmed by the pressure to be creative. Additionally, writing down all the ideas and trying to connect them all can be challenging, as we do not know how and where to start. In this walkthrough, I will share the quickest and easiest way to generate ideas.

Following the steps

Let us learn together how to brainstorm and write down our ideas:

1. Firstly, create a template with three empty boxes. The template should look like this:

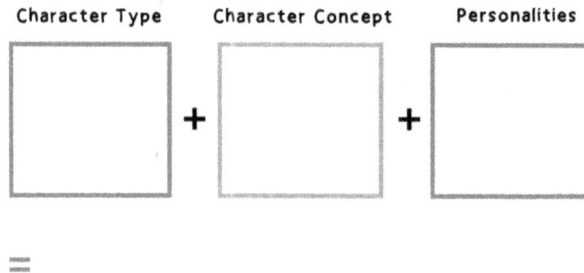

Figure 7.1 – Template example

2. Fill in the **Character**, **Environment**, and **Theme** boxes.

3. Write down any ideas that come to mind based on the template you have created.

4. Lastly, choose one from the ideas you have written and complete it. The complete version will look like this:

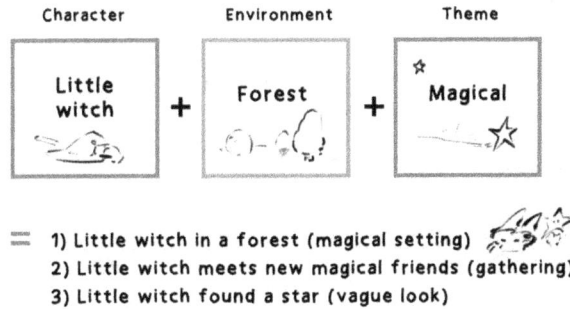

Figure 7.2 – Example of filled-in template

Understanding the technique

The three-box method helps generate a lot of fresh ideas while keeping the storyline consistent. Remember, the ideas from each box are important, so make sure the final storyline stays true to them. Otherwise, our storyline will become unclear and inconsistent as it develops.

Creating a mood board for references

Creating a **mood board** is the easiest way to help you visualize your ideas and gather inspiration for your project. Drawing from imagination requires a strong understanding of anatomy, perspective, and composition skills. Without using references, it can be difficult to visualize and create detailed and exact drawings. This can lead to a lack of inspiration to complete our drawings. If we force ourselves to draw by relying solely on imagination, it can be mentally exhausting and will result in burnout. Without references, it can be difficult to maintain consistency in our drawings, especially when working on a series of connected storylines such as a comic or storybook. Creating a mood board at the beginning of a project is a great way to establish a clear direction. Since all creativity stems from real-life experiences, using references allows you to incorporate authentic elements into your work while adding your own imaginative touch. It is like a collection of ideas and inspiration that you can look at whenever you need a reference and to stay on track. In this walkthrough, we will learn how to create a mood board step by step.

Following the steps

Now, let us learn how to create an appealing and informative mood board:

1. Firstly, search for several images to use as a reference for your idea based on the idea created in the previous walkthrough.

2. Then, go to Procreate and design a mood board. You can design your own mood board based on your preference. This is my mood board design:

Figure 7.3 – Mood board example; source: https://unsplash.com/
photos/brown-textile-on-white-background-IggtliOpeFU

3. Import all the images on the mood board. A quick way to bring in reference images is by using **Actions** > **Add** > **Insert a photo**, which allows you to pull images directly from your device into your canvas.

4. Lastly, write down notes and draw some sketches related to your idea in different layers to keep the mood board editable and organized.

Figure 7.4 – Mood board with reference images example; source: https://unsplash.com/photos/sunflower-CeSpMyxqKl4; https://unsplash.com/photos/sunflower-CeSpMyxqKl4https://unsplash.com/photos/white-rabbit-on-green-grass-u_kMWN-BWyU; https://unsplash.com/photos/black-leafed-tree-near-gazebo-6uEtb1fLX7E; https://unsplash.com/photos/raccoon-walking-on-lawn-grass-6GMq7AGxNbE; https://unsplash.com/photos/multicolored-abstract-painting-QwoNAhbmLLo; https://unsplash.com/photos/a-woman-in-a-blue-dress-holding-a-piece-of-paper-0LSV9wTjNRc; https://unsplash.com/photos/red-fox-standing-on-grass-field-7TGVEgcTKlY; https://unsplash.com/photos/brown-star-decor-r82HiTMi8eM

Understanding the technique

Creating a mood board is a fantastic way to organize and visualize your creative ideas in a single place. It acts as a reference point throughout your project, helping you stay aligned with your original concepts and themes. By having a clear visual guide, you can avoid drifting away from your initial ideas, reducing the risk of reworking or second-guessing later. This makes it easier to stay consistent with your vision, ensuring that all elements of the project work together harmoniously. A mood board makes the creative process smoother by keeping everything neat and easy to follow. It helps you stay organized, saving time and effort as you work. It's more than just a planning tool; it's also a great way to stay inspired and visualize the design concept because you can see all your ideas come together in one place.

Know more...

Some illustrators are more comfortable having a physical mood board to keep everything in place. Here is the method to create a fun and informative physical mood board for your project:

1. Design your mood board in any way that suits you, whether based on your art's storyline or project theme, by preparing a large cardboard box or simply just a notebook.

2. Arrange the elements you have collected (such as photographs, materials, printed images, and so on) onto your mood board.

3. Look for a common theme or style among your elements to ensure your mood board clearly represents your vision and storyline.

4. Write down notes next to your elements to explain why you selected them and how they connect to your storyline.

5. Once all the elements are in place, carefully review the mood board.

6. Remove any images or references that do not fit or align with your overall vision.

7. Lastly, ensure that everything on your mood board supports your desired storyline and artistic direction.

The physical mood board is now ready for use, serving as a helpful reference that you have next to you while drawing in Procreate. You can glance at it throughout the process to maintain consistency in colors, themes, and overall artistic direction.

> **Important note**
>
> A well-designed mood board reflects your artistic style and can be used to present your ideas to clients or collaborators in an appealing way. The mood board is meant to guide your artwork, but you don't have to incorporate every element from it. Seeing your collected references together can surely inspire new ideas for your work.

Sketching out the storyline

Sketching out a story is a process that represents the storyline. This method allows for the translation of ideas into visual form, making it easier to see the overall structure and understand how different details of the story fit together. By outlining the main scenes, characters, and settings, we can create a clearer and more detailed storyline for an illustration. This practice not only improves storytelling skills but also helps in refining ideas. Creating exact and detailed sketches of the settings and backgrounds where your story takes place can be challenging. In this walkthrough, we will learn how to sketch out our ideas better.

Following the steps

Now, we will sketch out our storyline by following these simple steps:

1. Firstly, think about the key scenes in your story and how you want to visualize them.

2. Then, sketch the settings and backgrounds for your story based on the idea in *Figure 7.4*. To achieve natural sketch strokes, you can reduce the **Opacity** value of your brush or adjust the **Pressure & Smoothing** settings in Procreate, especially if you're using an **Apple Pencil**. These adjustments will help make your sketch feel more natural and expressive.

Figure 7.5 – Environment sketch

3. Draw rough sketches of your main character and a few items that are associated with your character.

Figure 7.6 – Main character sketches

4. Lastly, draw other details such as other characters, decorations, and anything else connected with the storyline.

Figure 7.7 – Side character and details sketch

Understanding the technique

When sketching out a storyline, it's important not to get caught up in the details at this stage. Instead, focus on freely drawing the ideas that come to mind, as long as they align with the storyline you're developing. This early phase is all about exploring concepts and translating your vision into rough sketches without worrying too much about perfection or precision. To stay organized, you can draw the background, main character, and side characters on separate canvases, as shown in *Figure 7.5*, *Figure 7.6*, and *Figure 7.7*. This way, you can work on each part one at a time and keep things clear. For example, sketching the background alone lets you try out different settings and moods without distractions. Similarly, drawing the characters separately gives you space to adjust their poses, expressions, and details without worrying about how everything fits together just yet. It makes the process simpler and more focused. This step-by-step process allows you to explore ideas and build a visual story while keeping everything balanced and harmonious.

> Tip
> At this stage, we will let the sketches be drawn separately. Then, we will mix and match. This will make our workflow easier as we can make as many changes as we want. Sketching all the details together without completing the storyline will lead to many changes occurring during the project.

Improvising the story and sketch

Improvising a story and improving sketches is an important part of the creative process. It helps your first ideas grow into a clearer and better story. This method means being flexible, trying new things, and being open to making changes as you work on your storyline and drawings. Improvising also lets you look at your work in different ways, which can lead to fresh and exciting ideas that make your story even better.

When starting with rough sketches, there is often a tendency to aim for perfection right away. However, this can make the sketches feel unnatural, limiting the creative flow. Rough sketches are meant to be free and expressive, serving as a foundation to build on rather than the final product. Embracing their imperfections allows for more creative results. In this walkthrough, we will learn how to improvise our storyline and sketch naturally.

Following the steps

Now, let us improvise our story and sketch out the storyline:

1. Firstly, based on the sketches created in the previous walkthrough, refine your storyline by making changes and editing. Write down or type the improvised storyline using Procreate's **Add Text** tool.

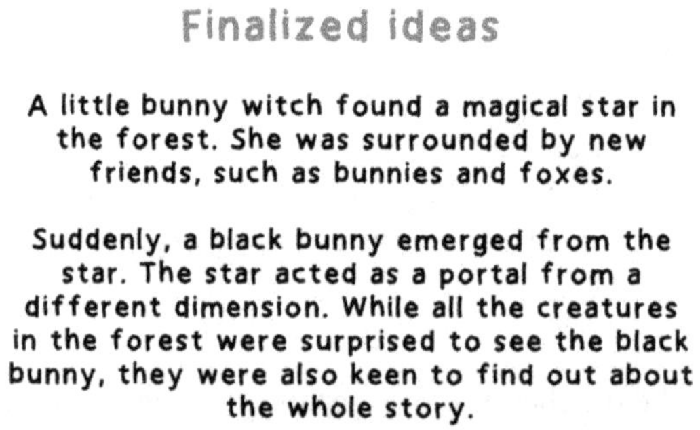

Finalized ideas

A little bunny witch found a magical star in the forest. She was surrounded by new friends, such as bunnies and foxes.

Suddenly, a black bunny emerged from the star. The star acted as a portal from a different dimension. While all the creatures in the forest were surprised to see the black bunny, they were also keen to find out about the whole story.

Figure 7.8 – Finalized storyline

2. Then, mix and match the sketches we created in the previous walkthrough (*Figure 7.5*, *Figure 7.6*, and *Figure 7.7*) to create several compositions. We can copy the elements across canvases or duplicate layers using **Actions** > **Add** > **Copy** > **Paste**. Additionally, adjusting Procreate's **layer opacity** and **transform tools** allows for non-destructive adjustments, making it easier to experiment with different layout options while preserving the original idea.

Figure 7.9 – Background scenery sketches

3. Lastly, redraw the elements to develop a new background concept and bring the idea to completion. At this stage, don't worry about the sketch looking rough. Focus on ensuring that the composition is correctly structured and aligned with the intended art direction.

Figure 7.10 – Chosen background illustration sketch

Understanding the technique

As shown in *Figure 7.10*, the background scenery was created based on the improvised ideas in *Figure 7.8* and *Figure 7.9*. Do not hesitate to revise and refine your ideas and storyline as you work through the process. If the initial idea does not feel quite right, you can always change and improve it. For example, I improvised the ideas in *Figure 7.2* into a better and clearer storyline, as shown in *Figure 7.9*. *Figure 7.10* was chosen based on the storyline as it fits better than the other sketch. Striving for perfection can sometimes lead to a lack of variety and uniqueness, resulting in a less engaging storyline. Remember, the best ideas are often created from imperfections and spontaneously. Feel free to experiment with different concepts. For example, introducing an element of suspense can add a thrilling plot twist to your storyline and artwork. Once your ideas feel more polished, take the time to write down the updated version of your storyline. This will help you stay organized and ensure all changes are well documented.

Integrating color emotion into the sketch

As discussed in *Chapter 6*, different colors evoke different emotions and feelings. For example, red can signify passion or anger, blue can represent calmness or sadness, and yellow can convey happiness or energy. By using different color palettes, we can express certain emotions in our art.

We can also use colors to draw attention to important scenes in our storyline and art. The problem we usually face in coloring is choosing colors that work well with each other. The illustration and storyline could become confusing if the colors used do not complement or harmonize with one another. In this walkthrough, we will learn how to choose a color palette that aligns with our storyline and art atmosphere.

Following the steps

We will now add color emotion based on a mysterious atmosphere, which we learned about in *Chapter 6*:

1. Firstly, create a color palette that aligns with the emotions that you want to convey in your storyline and art.

2. Then, try different color combinations to see how they affect the mood of your artwork. You can refer to *Chapter 6* to find the perfect color palette for a mysterious atmosphere.

3. Finalize the color palette that will be used for your storyline. I will use the color palette shown in *Figure 7.11* for the background scenery.

Figure 7.11 – Base color palette

4. Lastly, do a rough coloring under the sketch's layer to complete it.

Figure 7.12 – Example of rough coloring

Understanding the technique

Creating a color palette can be challenging when we are unsure about the atmosphere or vibe we want to express through our art. However, having a clear vision of the illustration's mood and storyline can make the process much easier. For instance, as shown in *Figure 7.2*, if the theme of the background scenery is focused on discovery and magic, visualizing a magical setting may lead us to choose blue and purple tones, as these colors best represent the feeling of wonder and enchantment associated with those themes.

To keep the project on track, it's important to stay focused and stick to the storyline. Changing ideas halfway through is okay, but making major changes, especially when working with a team, can be inconvenient since others have already put effort into creating the original concept. Thus, it is important to keep a clear direction from the start to help everything run smoothly and save more time.

> **Tips**
>
> Inspiration can pop up at any time, so stay open to adding fresh ideas that can make your illustration even better while still sticking to your main vision. Keep a *Color Test* layer at the top of your layer stack to freely experiment with swatches, blend modes, and other effects without altering your main artwork. This allows you to test colors and adjustments while keeping your composition intact. It's a simple yet effective way to refine your palette before committing to final changes.
>
> Creating a clear and detailed illustration takes time, so give yourself room to think and improve as you go. It is all part of the creative process, so allow yourself the freedom to explore and experiment without holding back too much.

Finalizing the story and illustration

Through art, you can tell stories and connect with people emotionally. By illustrating important scenes, characters, and settings, you can turn a storyline into something people can visually experience and connect with. It allows you to show emotions, ideas, and themes in a way that words alone might not fully capture. This is why creating visual narratives can bring so much life and depth to your story.

Sharing your storyline with others for feedback is an important part of the process, even though it might feel intimidating at first. Getting input from others can help you spot areas to improve and give you fresh ideas. It also allows you to see your story from a new perspective, which can be incredibly valuable as you refine your work. Feedback can highlight strengths you might not have noticed and uncover ways to enhance your storytelling and art.

Finalizing a storyline and its illustration can be challenging. Sometimes it's hard to know how to make an illustration feel complete and polished. You might worry that something is missing or feel unsure about what finishing touches to add. This is a common struggle that we face in finalizing illustrations. In this walkthrough, we'll explore simple steps to help you successfully complete your storyline and illustration with confidence and clarity.

Following the steps

We have reached the final art process; we will now finalize the storyline and illustration by following these simple steps:

1. Firstly, refine your sketch and add some final details such as clouds, the moon, and flowers. For symmetrical elements such as the star, you can use **Drawing Assist** to help you draw it easily.

Figure 7.13 – Refined sketch

2. Then, clean up the base coloring that we did earlier in *Figure 7.12* to make it clearer and ready for rendering.

Figure 7.14 – Base color cleaned-up version

3. Add lighting and shadows to your illustration based on the techniques we learned about in *Chapter 4*.

Figure 7.15 – Example of adding lighting

4. Lastly, render your illustration and complete it by adjusting the contrast in the background to enhance the overall atmosphere. Refine the details of the characters to ensure they blend harmoniously with the scene while standing out where needed. These final touches will add depth and a polished look to your artwork.

Figure 7.16 – Rendered and finalized illustration

Understanding the technique

To finalize our storyline and illustration, start by reviewing your first sketch and making any necessary adjustments. This might involve refining the lines, adding details, or correcting any mistakes, as shown in *Figure 7.15*. The goal is to create a clean and precise sketch that serves as the foundation for your illustration, so it is easier for you to do base coloring. Once your sketch is refined, focus on cleaning up the base colors. This involves filling in the areas of your illustration with the color palette we created previously in *Figure 7.11*, ensuring that they are fully colored. To give your illustration depth and dimension, add lighting and shadow. For *Figure 7.16*, I used a darker shade of the base color for shadows instead of the **Multiply** blending mode. This approach helps maintain a natural look and ensures the colors blend smoothly. However, if you're looking to speed up your workflow, using the **Multiply** blending mode can be a great shortcut for adding shadows. Feel free to choose the method that best suits your process. Then, consider the light source in your scene and how it affects the different elements of your illustration.

In *Figure 7.15*, the light source is on the left, so the light comes from the left side of the illustration and the fallen star. Add shadow and highlight to create a good contrast, as shown in *Figure 7.15*. The last step is to render your illustration, which involves adding the finishing touches and details. This includes refining the textures of the brush, adding small details, and ensuring that all elements are well balanced. You can enhance your artwork by adding texture using texture materials.

Pay attention to the tiny details, such as small flowers, stars, and details on the character that can enhance the overall quality of your artwork. By following these steps, you can effectively complete your story and illustration, creating a complete and visually unique piece.

Finalizing an illustration means cleaning up the rough sketches and base colors to make them look clearer and more polished. For example, in *Figure 7.13*, the rough draft from *Figure 7.10* was cleaned up, making it easier to add colors and complete the illustration. This cleaned-up version is an important step as it helps your illustration look clearer and more ready for the final touches. As you can see in Figure 7.17, I added final touches such as the stars and the soft highlights to draw attention to the black bunny, which is the main focus of the illustration. I also included texture and small details to make the background scenery feel more magical and full of charm.

Figure 7.17 – Close-up details

When coloring, you have choices: you can combine all layers into one to improve brush strokes and create smoother textures, or you can keep the layers separate if that works better for you. Adding textures, as mentioned in *Chapter 1*, is another great way to give the illustration a unique, finished touch. Wrapping up your illustration and blending everything together can feel a bit intimidating at first, but do not let that worry you. Just trust the process, take it step by step, and you will be amazed at how it all comes together in the end. Sometimes, magic happens when you least expect it!

Summary

In this chapter, we learned how to tell a story through drawing. We started by using the three-box method to come up with fun ideas, then created a mood board to collect helpful reference images. After that, we sketched the main scenes and characters, gradually building up our illustration. We refined our ideas along the way, using color to convey emotion, adding light and texture for depth, and finishing the artwork with vibrant colors and final details.

In the next chapter, we'll explore, through some simple steps, the process of creating characters with unique personalities and backstories. We'll also learn how to create a character sheet that clearly shows your character's appearance, expressions, and unique traits. Then, we'll look at how to place your character into a background that supports their story and makes the entire scene feel connected and alive.

Whether you're creating just for fun or assembling work for a portfolio, this chapter will help you present your characters with confidence and joy.

Unlock this book's exclusive benefits now

Scan this QR code or go to `packtpub.com/unlock`, then search this book by name.

8

Designing Characters That Blend Seamlessly into Backgrounds

Drawing character designs is important in the art industry, especially for animation, gaming, physical art such as 3D figurines, merchandise, and so on. It also helps in defining a character's role in the story by displaying their personality through their appearance. For example, mysterious characters look gloomy, and we tend to find them in darker or pale-colored outfits. Physical traits, such as unique features (for example, a birthmark or pattern), can reflect their personality and identity. Clothing and color schemes also play significant roles in evoking specific emotions and matching the character's traits as well. Along with this, various other factors make designing characters challenging, such as our concerns that we may inadvertently end up copying someone else's style and maintaining consistency for the character sizes and at different angles.

In this chapter, I will guide you through the process of creating characters that fit naturally into their environments, enhancing the overall composition and storytelling of your illustrations.

With the help of walkthroughs, we'll cover the following:

- Brainstorming and sketching out character designs
- Finalizing character designs
- Drawing character designs from different perspectives
- Drawing facial expressions
- Preparing a character sheet for a portfolio
- Adding a character to a background drawing
- Perfectly blending a character into the background drawing

Brainstorming and sketching out character designs

When designing a character, it is important to think about several important aspects that represent the character. Start by defining the character's role in the story and design the character based on it. It is important to consider the character's concept and motives to show their personalities in their appearance. For example, a villain character might have a scary appearance or scars, while cheerful characters look happy and wear brightly colored outfits. Physical traits such as body type and unique features should show their personality and identity.

The unique feature can be a birthmark or symbol on the character. Clothing should match the character's personality as well. As mentioned earlier, color plays an important role in character design, so please make sure that you are using the correct colors to evoke specific emotions and match the character's traits. Coming up with original and unique character concepts can be difficult. It is easy to fall into a cycle of creating characters that are too similar to existing ones. In this easy, step-by-step walkthrough, we will learn how to create unique original characters without any worries.

Following the steps

Here's how you can approach brainstorming and sketching for character design:

1. Firstly, create a template with three empty boxes following the same method we learned previously in *Chapter 7*. To do it, activate **Drawing Guide** (via **Actions** > **Canvas** > **Drawing Guide**) and select **Grid**. Then, draw three evenly spaced boxes labeled Character Type, Character Concept, and Personalities. Add notes using the **Add Text** tool for clarity. The template should look like this:

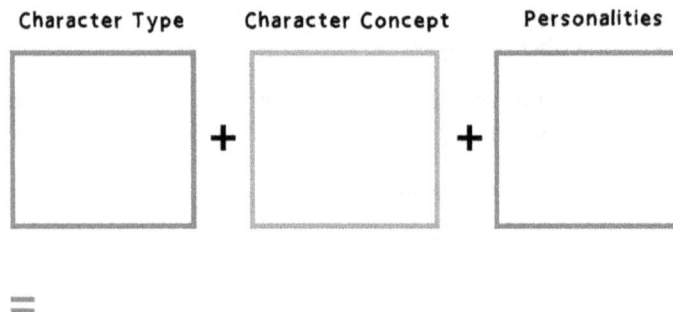

Figure 8.1 – Template for organizing ideas into character type, concept, and personality

2. Fill in the **Character Type**, **Character Concept**, and **Personalities** boxes by writing down any ideas that come to mind based on the template you have created:

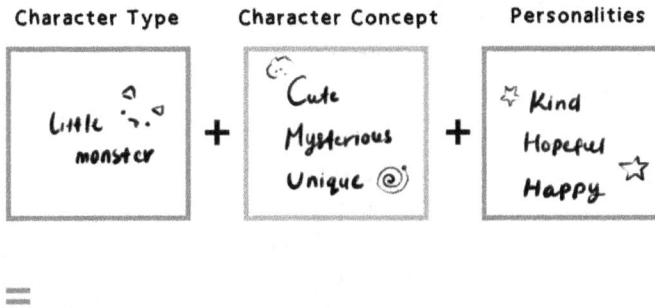

Figure 8.2 – Example filled-in template with traits for designing a little monster character

3. Lastly, sketch several character designs by mixing and matching the **Character Type**, **Character Concept**, and **Personalities** ideas. Replace handwritten words with typed text inside each box. This makes the layout easier to read and more visually clear.

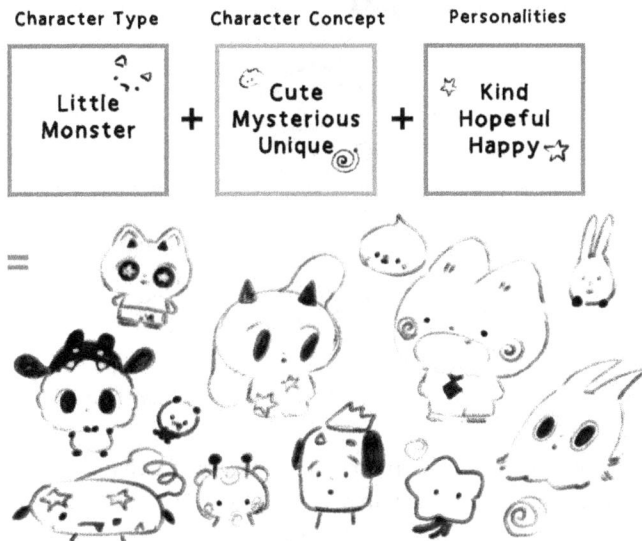

Figure 8.3 – Sketches showing how different traits are mixed and matched into unique designs

Now that you've finished the brainstorming steps, let's take a closer look at how this method helps shape your character in a more meaningful way.

Understanding the technique

The purpose of the three boxes is to help organize your ideas efficiently. Once we have listed the information for each box, we can mix and match the details to create a character design. For example, as shown in *Figure 8.2*, for **Character Type**, I chose *Little Monster*, then I chose *Unique* for **Character Concept** and *Kind* for **Personalities**. The result of the character design from the mix and match is shown in *Figure 8.3*.

Let's look at another example in *Figure 8.4*. In this design, I wanted the character to feel soft and round, so I chose a fluffy, circular shape. The concept was inspired by fruit, with big, wide eyes to make the character feel expressive and cute. For the personality, I focused on traits such as being sweet and shy. To show that clearly, I drew gentle blush marks on their cheeks and gave them a soft, quiet look. These small details help the design match the character's feelings, making them feel kind and approachable.

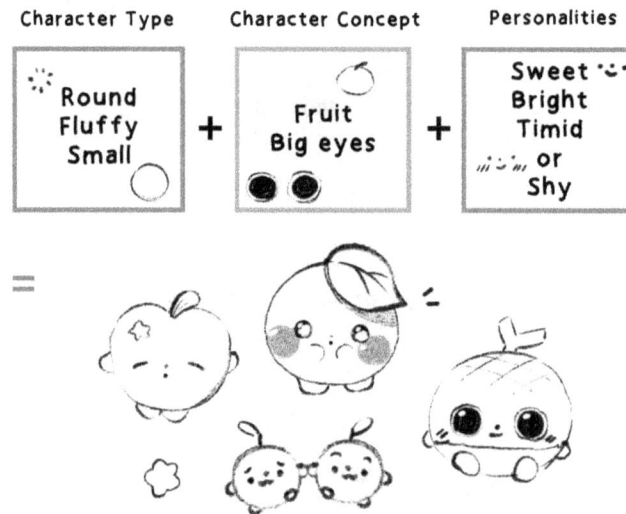

Figure 8.4 – Sketches showing how different traits are mixed and matched into unique designs

Here's another example shown in *Figure 8.5*. This character was designed to feel soft and sleepy, with a clumsy personality that adds charm. To match this idea, I drew them with a round and squishy shape to make them look extra cute and cozy. Their soft form emphasizes the sleepy feeling, like a character who's always just about to doze off, which helps bring out their gentle and clumsy traits.

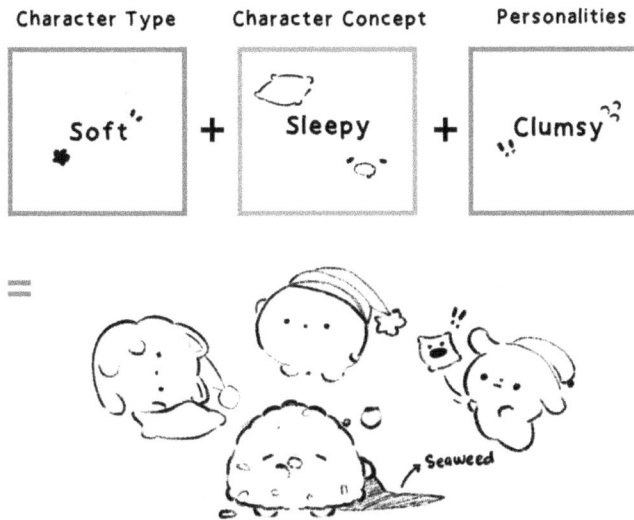

Figure 8.5 – Sketches showing how different traits are mixed and matched into unique designs

By mixing personality traits with concept elements, we can give our character emotional depth. This makes them feel alive in the viewer's mind and makes the viewer want to know more about your character.

> **Tips**
>
> Other than the method previously, we can also create a character design by referencing a mood board, as shown in *Chapter 7Storytelling Through Art: Creating Visual Narratives*. Some artists prefer this method as they get to visualize how the character will look based on the images we have on the mood board. Feel free to choose the method that works best for you.

Now that our ideas are starting to take shape, it's time to bring one of them to life with clean lines and colors.

Finalizing character designs

Finalizing a character design involves creating a polished design that represents the character's role, background, and personality traits. It is important to create physical appearance, clothing, and color schemes that reflect their story and personality. Developing a detailed character sheet with various angles and expressions helps to maintain consistency in design elements. We will understand this better as we progress through this chapter. Once satisfied, we can finalize the character design while remaining open to adjustments as ideas evolve throughout the storytelling process.

While creating a character design, it is easy to get carried away with details, which can overwhelm the initial design and make it harder to finalize. In this walkthrough, we will learn how to finalize a character design efficiently without becoming trapped in an endless cycle of adding excessive details.

Following the steps

Now, we will learn how to finalize our character design and add color to it:

Firstly, choose one of the character design sketches in *Figure 8.3* and create a clean line art version of it. You can use a brush such as **Studio Pen** to create smooth line art:

Figure 8.6 – Clean line art created from the selected sketch

1. Prepare a color palette for the character. Make sure the color palette matches the character's personality and concept:

Figure 8.7 – Color palette matching the character's personality and concept

2. Lastly, color your character using the color palette from *Figure 8.7*. To ensure clean and efficient coloring, you can use either **Alpha Lock** or **Clipping Mask** in Procreate. These techniques help preserve your line art while allowing you to color underneath or on top of it.

> **Tips**
>
> Using **Clipping Mask**: First, create a base color layer beneath your line art. Then, add a new layer above it, tap once on the layer, and select **Clipping Mask**. Any brush strokes you apply will now stay within the base color range.
>
> Using **Alpha Lock**: Alternatively, tap on the base color layer and enable **Alpha Lock**. This locks the transparent pixels, letting you paint only within the colored area. Feel free to choose the method that fits your workflow best.

Figure 8.8 – Finalized character design

You've brought your sketch to life with clean lines and color. Let's explore why each part of this process helps with your workflow and the connection between colors and your character.

Understanding the technique

Creating a color palette before starting to color a character helps save time and makes the workflow smoother. If the color palette is chosen during the rendering process, it can lead to delaying your progress, as you might need to make frequent changes. It's also important to ensure the colors match the character's personality and theme. For example, in *Figure 8.8*, I used a palette with purple and muted colors to keep the design aligned with the character's mysterious concept.

> **Tips**
>
> Colors carry feelings. Use warm tones for friendly characters, cool tones for calm personalities, and bold colors such as bright red for energetic ones.

Cleaning up your design helps people focus on your character's story, not just the details. A nice line art and the base colors show you've thought carefully about who your character is, and that makes it easier for others to understand them too.

Now that your character has a polished look, let's see how it appears from different angles.

Drawing character designs from different perspectives

As you know, regarding characters, it is extremely important to know how they appear from different angles. This method helps artists understand how a character looks in different scenarios and interacts with their surroundings. By drawing the character from various angles, such as front, sides, and back, you can easily see the details of their design, including their posture, expressions, and proportions, making the character look more realistic and lively. Drawing from different perspectives also allows for creative poses and a better understanding of the character's overall shape, making it simpler to draw them in different situations. Keeping the character's appearance, clothing, and color scheme consistent across a storyline or series of illustrations can be difficult, but with this walkthrough, you'll learn how to draw characters from different angles while maintaining their form and design details throughout.

Following the steps

We finalized and colored the character in the previous walkthrough. Now, let us draw the character from different angles:

1. Firstly, draw several parallel lines behind the character design for shaping and size guidelines. Use **Perspective Grid** in **Drawing Guide** to draw out the straight line for consistent proportions:

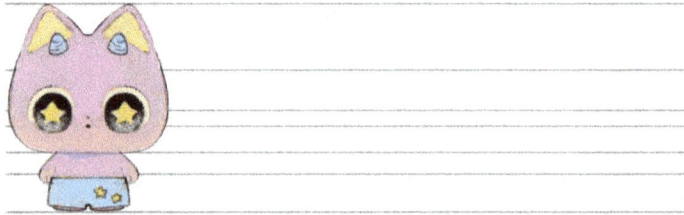

Figure 8.9 – Character design guidelines

2. Draw the left side of the character by following the guidelines:

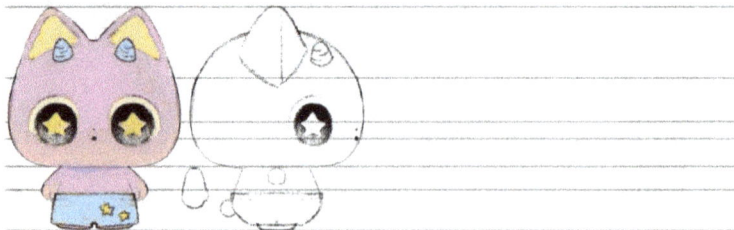

Figure 8.10 – Left view of the character

3.   Then, draw the right and back views of the character. For the right view, you can flip and mirror the previous left view of the character to guide symmetrical poses. To do this, duplicate your layer and use **Transform** > **Flip Horizontal/Flip Vertical**:

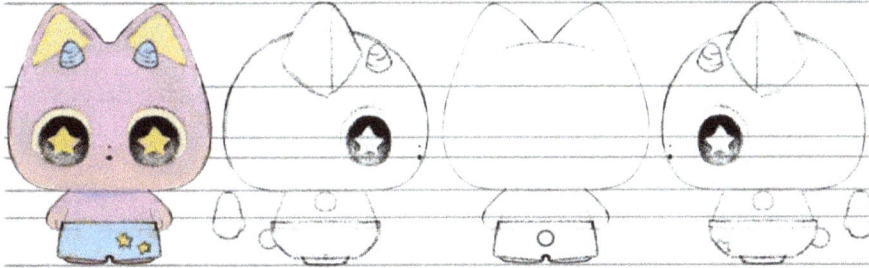

Figure 8.11 – All angles of the character

4.   Finally, color the character design to finalize it:

Figure 8.12 – Fully colored character shown from different angles

Understanding the technique

Once your character is finalized, it's time to explore how it looks from different angles: front, sides, and back. To maintain design consistency and keep your workspace tidy in Procreate, group each perspective into separate layers or folders. For each view (front, sides, and back), create a dedicated group folder in the **Layers** panel. Name each folder clearly, such as *Front View*, *Left Side View*, *Right Side View*, and *Back View*. Inside each folder, include layers for line art, base color, shading, and highlights. This makes it easier to adjust elements from an angle without mixing things up.

You can use **Perspective Grid** in **Drawing Guide** to maintain proportions and alignment. Access it via **Actions** > **Canvas** > **Drawing Guide**. Consider duplicating your front view sketch and flipping it horizontally (via **Transform** > **Flip Horizontal**) as a starting point for the side or back view. Showing your character from every side proves they're real in your world, as the audience can visualize them. Grouping the views into folders keeps things tidy, and it also saves you time finding all the designs in one folder.

With your character's views now complete, let's explore their emotions through facial expressions.

Drawing facial expressions

Facial expressions are a powerful way to convey emotions, thoughts, and personality in art and character design. They play an important role in storytelling, as they allow the audience to connect with characters on a deeper, emotional level. By knowing how facial expressions work, we can show different emotions using features such as the eyes and mouth. Some key techniques include making features bigger to show emotions clearly, changing the facial features' shape, and adding additional details such as lines and shading. These elements can help audiences relate and understand how the characters feel.

Drawing facial expressions can also be quite tricky for many, but studying and using reference images of real people can greatly improve your understanding. By observing real-life examples, we can better capture the details needed to create more accurate and expressive characters. One of the main difficulties is understanding and accurately conveying a wide range of emotions through facial features such as the eyes, eyebrows, and mouth, which requires a deep understanding of how these features change with different emotions. In this walkthrough, we will learn how to draw facial expressions for our character.

Following the steps

Now, let's draw several different facial expressions to make the character look lively and full of personality:

1. First, decide on 5–9 facial expressions that suit your character. For this walkthrough, I'll go with shy, cheerful, scared, excited, calm, happy, sad, and shocked. If drawing too many at once feels overwhelming, feel free to start smaller, with just 3–5 expressions.

2. Then, start sketching the character's facial expressions based on the ones you've chosen. Feel free to use reference images too. They're really helpful for understanding how each emotion looks and how facial features change:

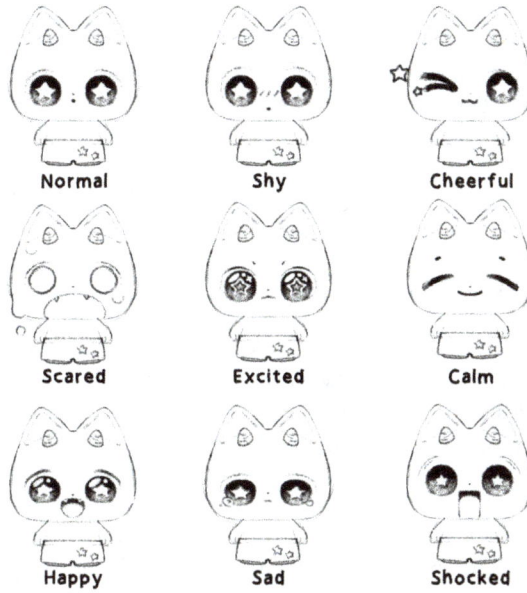

Figure 8.13 – Examples of facial expressions

3. Lastly, finalize it and add color to it:

Figure 8.14 – Final colored expressions to bring the character to life

> **Tips**
> You can use **Liquify** (in **Adjustments**) to subtly modify expressions non-destructively. Keep each expression on a separate layer or group them into folders for easy edits later.

With all those wonderful expressions complete, let's look at why showing a range of emotions brings your character to life.

Understanding the technique

Expressions are how your character talks without words. When you draw their emotions, such as joy or surprise, viewers can understand how the character feels at that time. It makes your character feel like someone they know and helps bring out their personality. Thus, creating different facial expressions will help the character look more attractive and lively as it gets to portray different emotions.

We start by deciding on 5–9 facial expressions for the character. These could include emotions such as happiness, sadness, anger, surprise, and more. Next, sketch the character's face with each of these expressions. Focus on the eyes, eyebrows, mouth, and other facial features to accurately depict the emotions. The eyes, eyebrows, and mouth are key aspects in creating a facial expression. By changing the placement and shape of the eyebrows, we can create different expressions. For example, by changing the eyebrow angle to point toward the eye, the character will appear angry, whereas pointing it downward toward the end of the corner of the eye makes the character appear calm.

Once you are satisfied with the expression sketches, finalize them by refining the lines and adding color. This will bring the expressions to life and make them more visually appealing.

Each expression tells a part of their story, so let's organize it all into a character sheet you can proudly share.

> **Try this**
> Imagine your character has just arrived in a place they've never been. How would they react? Would they be curious, anxious, or excited? Sketch their expression in that moment.

Preparing a character sheet for a portfolio

Making a **character sheet** is a great way to show your skills in character design. It helps you organize and display your character's unique features, personality, and flexibility. A good character sheet can make your portfolio stand out and show that you can create consistent and interesting designs. It also shows how the character looks, their story, and their personality, helping employers or clients understand them better. This is your chance to show your skills in areas such as character design, colors, facial expressions, and storytelling, which are important for jobs in animation, gaming, and illustration. By combining visuals and story, you can create a portfolio that highlights your style and creative process. This walkthrough will show simple steps to make a portfolio that works well and is helpful for art-related jobs.

Following the steps

Now we have everything ready, let us learn how to organize the character sheet and turn it into a portfolio:

1. Firstly, create a file specifically for your character design on Procreate by creating a folder in an empty canvas.

2. Then, design the first interface to introduce your character design:

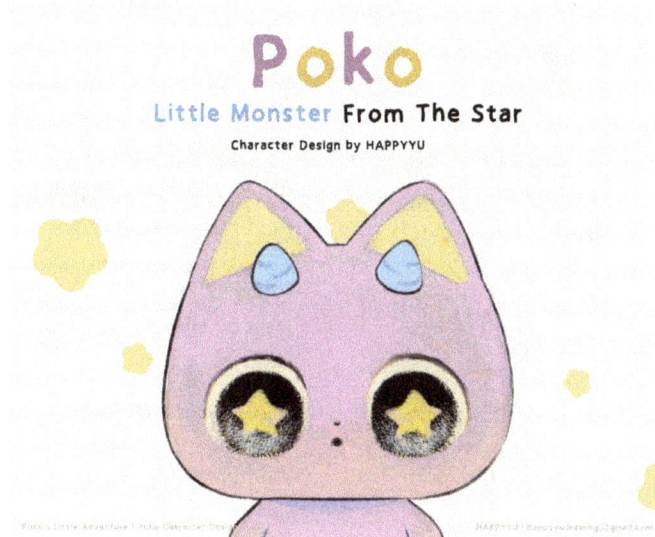

Figure 8.15 – Example of a character design interface for the portfolio

3. Prepare a backstory for your character. You can write it down in paragraphs or keep the backstory simple. If you're going for a simplified version, aim for 3–5 sentences that capture the character's motivation and personality:

Figure 8.16 – Example of character design background story

4.   Now, you can display your character design from a different perspective:

Figure 8.17 – Character views from different angles arranged on one sheet

5.   Add the character's facial expressions:

Figure 8.18 – Facial expression sheet showing full range of emotions.

6.   Lastly, export the images into a separate JPEG file or PDF to share them as a portfolio. For exporting, use the **Actions** > **Share** > **PDF** or **JPEG**, depending on your portfolio's format:

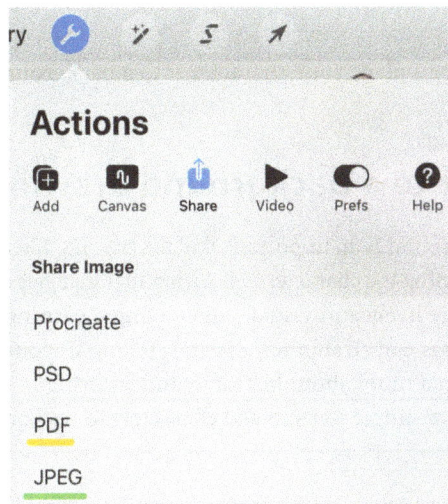

Figure 8.19 – Example of how to export the images to create a portfolio

Now that your character sheet is ready, let's reflect on how each element helps others connect with your character and your creativity, which eventually can be turned into a portfolio.

Understanding the technique

Your character sheet is like telling a story on one page. A short, clear backstory shows who the character is and what they care about. That helps others feel curious and interested in the world you've created. It's also a great way to share your creative voice.

Creating multiple character sheets allows clients to see a variety of your work and assess your ability to handle their projects. Don't stress too much about perfecting every detail of your character; the key is to keep your portfolio neat and well organized, making it easy for clients to focus on your designs. You can add small decorative elements in the background of the character sheets, but ensure they do not overshadow the character itself. Once everything is finalized, you can export your work as JPEG or PDF files. PDFs are often preferred as they keep everything in one organized document. After preparing the file, upload it to your website. Free platforms such as Carrd, Behance, Issuu, and Google Sites are excellent options for showcasing your portfolio online for free. You can also send your portfolio to potential clients via email if they are seeking illustrators to hire.

> **Links**
>
> Carrd: `https://carrd.co/`
>
> Behance: `https://www.behance.net/`
>
> Issuu: `https://issuu.com/`
>
> Google Sites: `https://sites.google.com/`

Once your sheet is set, it's time to place your character into a background that tells even more of their story.

Adding a character to a background drawing

Placing a character into a background is an important skill for creating illustrations that feel complete and engaging. It involves positioning the character in a setting that matches their story and personality, making the whole artwork more lively and visually interesting. Learning how to blend characters naturally into their surroundings can strengthen the storytelling in your art and make the scenes more eye-catching. We will learn more about blending and coloring in the next walkthrough. In this walkthrough, we will explore simple steps to add characters to backgrounds in a way that looks natural to the viewer.

Following the steps

Here's a simple guide to drawing a background with the character as the main focus:

1. Firstly, add your character design to a blank canvas:

Figure 8.20 – Example of adding character design to a blank canvas

2. Draw a background scenery that matches the main character's design concept:

Figure 8.21 – Background scenery sketch

3.   Lastly, clean up the rough sketch by making the sketch clearer and neater to finalize it:

Figure 8.22 – Finalized background scenery for the character

You've placed your character into their world. Let's take a moment to understand how backgrounds support the storytelling of your character.

Understanding the technique

When creating background scenery, it's important to make sure it matches the character's overall vibe. Placing your character in a scene shows they belong there. It helps people understand where they came from and what kind of story they're part of. When everything fits together, the colors, lighting, and feeling make the picture feel complete and exciting. For example, in *Figure 8.21*, I drew the character emerging from a portal to suggest it came from another world, making the viewer eager to know more about the character's backstory. In *Figure 8.3*, I decided that the character has a mysterious concept, so the background drawing needs to enhance that mysterious feeling. By doing this, we help viewers understand the character's story and learn more about the character that we are showcasing through the art. In addition to matching color schemes, make sure the character's lighting matches the environment. Use highlights to make the character stand out, and place your character according to background composition, placement, or depth that can attract the viewer's attention.

With the background added, let's blend everything together so it feels like one complete and magical illustration.

Perfectly blending a character into the background drawing

Adding a character to a background drawing is an essential skill for creating an engaging illustration. This process involves placing your character within a setting that matches their story and personality, making the overall composition more natural and interesting. By learning how to blend characters perfectly into environments, we can enhance the storytelling of our artwork and create more unique scenes. Blending a character into a background drawing can be quite challenging for several reasons. One of the main difficulties is ensuring that the character and the background look natural together. This involves matching the lighting, color palette, and perspective of the character with the background. In this walkthrough, we will learn how to blend our character into the background drawing.

Following the steps

We have reached the end of the character design process. Now, let us learn how to blend a character with a background scenery:

1. Firstly, prepare a base color for your background drawing:

Figure 8.23 – Color palette for background scenery

2.   Color the background using the color palette created in *Figure 8.23*:

Figure 8.24 – Color base for background scenery

3.   Render the character and background drawing:

Figure 8.25 – Rendering the character and background to blend them

4. Lastly, add the final details and enhance the color using the **Hue**, **Saturation**, **Brightness**, and **Curves** tools in Procreate:

Figure 8.26 – Finalized illustration

You've completed your scene! Let's see how this blending technique can create a finished look that feels magical.

> **Tips**
>
> When blending illustrations, I usually combine all the layers into one. This improves the brushwork and texture and makes it easier to blend the character naturally with the background. However, it is not necessary to merge all the layers to achieve this—just go with the blending method that suits your workflow best.

Understanding the technique

To blend a character into a background, make sure the background colors work well with the character's colors. This step helps your illustration feel smooth and natural, as if the character and background were always meant to be together. Good blending makes it easier for people to focus on your story. It also brings out the best in your artwork by adding a story that people can follow and feel connected to.

For example, in *Figure 8.24*, since the character's main colors are purple and blue, I picked background colors such as blue, purple, and yellow using triadic schemes. As we learned in *Chapter 5*, you can use any color-picking method to create the color palette. Just make sure the background colors don't overpower the character. You can add highlights to the character to make it stand out as the focal point of the artwork.

Remember, your goal isn't perfection, it's storytelling. Procreate gives you tools such as layer settings, reference images, and drawing guides to build your character gradually. Have fun, experiment, and trust your vision. You've completed your character design, where everything comes together in one beautiful story. In the next chapter, we'll move forward and explore how composition can guide your viewers' attention and make your illustrations even more powerful.

Summary

In this chapter, we learned how to create characters that truly feel like they belong in their world. From brainstorming unique traits using the three-box method to sketching expressive designs and finalizing them with color, we built characters with emotion and backstory. We also practiced drawing characters from multiple angles to ensure consistency, captured their personalities through facial expressions, and organized the designs into a completed character sheet for portfolios. Lastly, we learned how to blend these characters into background illustrations by harmonizing lighting, color palettes, and mood, resulting in scenes that feel more alive.

In the next chapter, we'll explore the power of composition and how it helps guide the viewer's eye across your illustration using techniques such as the Golden Spiral, diagonals, and more. These techniques will help you place characters and background elements in ways that create balance, focus, and storytelling.

Unlock this book's exclusive benefits now

Scan this QR code or go to `packtpub.com/unlock`, then search this book by name.

9

Perfecting Composition for Visually Striking Art

Composition in art refers to the arrangement of visual elements within an illustration to create a harmonious and eye-catching masterpiece. It involves the use of some of the main elements in art, such as balance, contrast, and flow, to guide the viewer's perspective in our illustration. We can improve our composition in background illustration by using several techniques such as C-shape composition, golden section composition, circular composition, and so on. These techniques can be used in various art creations, such as drawing portraits, character designs, and background scenery.

In this chapter, we'll learn how to use these techniques to make our illustrations look balanced and realistic, especially when drawing background scenery. By the end of the chapter, we'll know how to create good compositions in our art and improve our skills in drawing backgrounds. This will help us understand how to tell stories using background illustrations.

We will cover the following topics with the help of walkthrough examples:

- Getting started with background composition
- Learning how to use C-shape composition in art
- Learning how to use V-shape composition in art
- Learning how to use unbalanced composition in art
- Learning how to use balanced composition in art
- Learning how to use diagonal composition
- Learning how to use cross-composition in art
- Learning how to use circular composition in art
- Learning how to use the Golden Section composition in art

Before beginning this chapter, please read the following important note to ensure that all steps can be followed smoothly. This will help maintain clarity and consistency throughout the process.

> **Important note**
>
> In this chapter, illustrations will be drawn in separate layers to maintain flexibility for adjustments. The layers should be named as follows: *Sketch Layer*, *Composition Layer*, *Contrast Layer*, and *Final Illustration Layer*. This structured approach ensures that each stage of the artwork remains editable, allowing for refinement without affecting previous steps. Keeping layers organized like this makes the creative process smoother and more efficient. I will leave a screenshot of the layers' placement after this note.

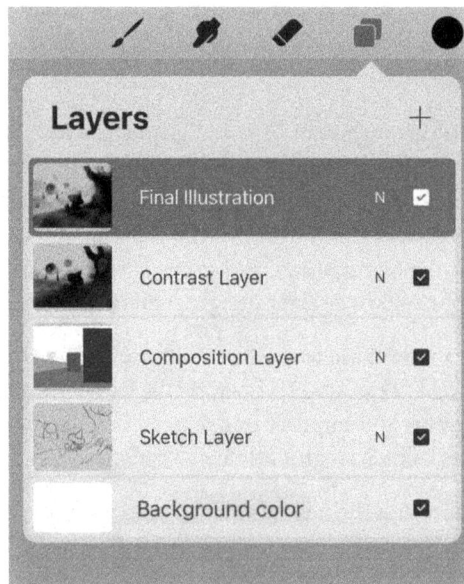

Figure 9.1 – Example layers setting

Getting started with background composition

Composition in art means arranging subjects in an illustration to make it look balanced and lively. This can be achieved by understanding how to place objects, colors, and textures in a way that guides the viewer's eyes, creates feelings, and shares a message. By focusing on these elements, we can make artwork that connects with people. However, as artists, we often struggle to create good compositions for background illustration. In this walkthrough, we'll learn about depth composition techniques to help us in creating a well-balanced and eye-catching background illustration.

Following the steps

Adding depth composition to the background drawing can be done by following these steps:

1. Firstly, come up with a background concept you want to draw. Brainstorm ideas and write them down. You can refer to the steps we covered in *Chapter 7, Brainstorming and Writing Down Ideas*, to guide you through this process. This will help you create a clear and structured plan for your background illustration.

2. Block out the main design elements in different color values, as shown in *Figure 9.2*. This is a fundamental and effective way to establish the structure and flow of your background scene before diving into detailed rendering. By roughly shaping major forms (foreground, middle ground, and background), you're essentially creating a visual roadmap that helps maintain balance, perspective, and storytelling focus throughout the composition process.

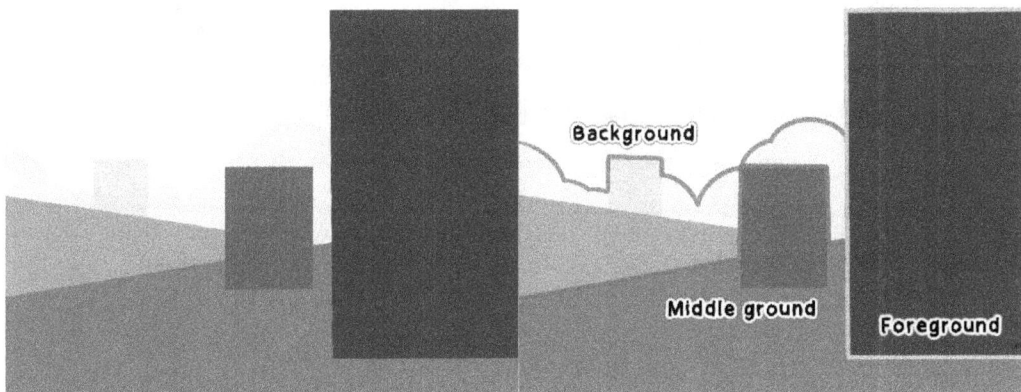

Figure 9.2 – An example of blocking out elements using different color values to improve composition

3. Next, create a background sketch using the ideas we developed in *Step 1*. To add depth to the composition, make the objects that are closer to the viewer appear larger, and draw the objects that are farther away smaller. This technique will help create a sense of dimension and perspective in your background illustration. The main focal point for this background scenery is the character in the middle ground, the little witch, as shown in *Figure 9.3*.

4. Refine the rough sketch by redrawing it into a cleaner version with clear line art. This will help define the details and structure of your composition, making it ready for the next steps in your artwork. I used Procreate's **Vine Charcoal** brush for this and the preceding step.

5. Lastly, apply shadows to the foreground and middle ground areas to enhance the sense of depth and perspective in your artwork. Lower the background's color intensity to push it further into the distance and help the little witch stand out as the focal point. You can achieve this by either lowering the background layer's opacity or gently erasing parts of it using the same brush or the Soft Airbrush in Procreate.

STEP 1

A young witch embarks
on a journey in a
magical place.

STEP 2

STEP 3

STEP 4

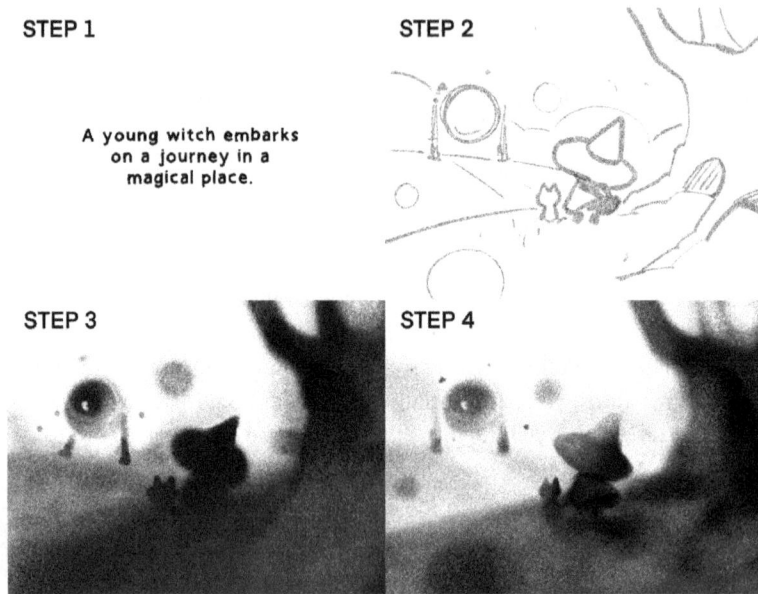

Figure 9.3 – Step-by-step tutorial to improve composition

6. *Figure 9.4* illustrates the outcome of applying the depth composition technique to a background drawing. As demonstrated, the illustration appears well balanced and visually pleasing, making it easy for viewers to understand the story that you share through art.

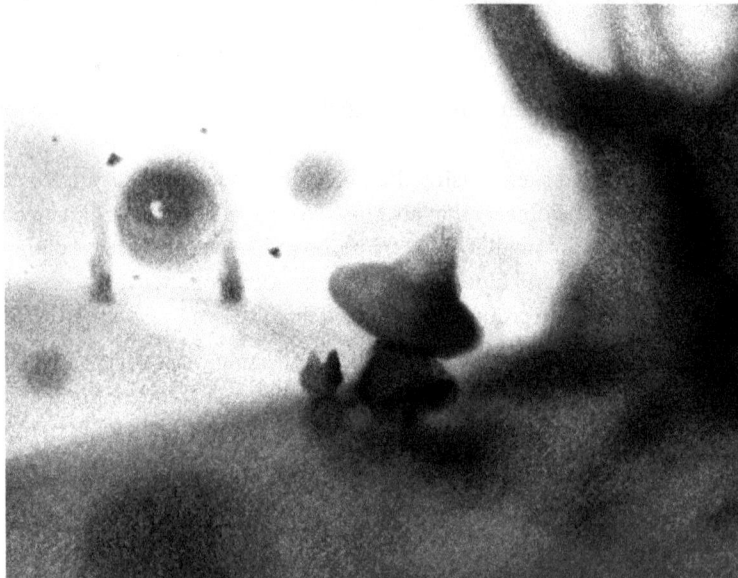

Figure 9.4 – Final result of the illustration

Understanding the technique

To create a good composition, it is important to add a focal point to your illustration. In *Figure 9.4*, I made the little witch my focal point. Once you have decided on and added your focal point, you can proceed with adding depth to create a good composition. To add depth, we can add shadows to the design elements near the focal point in the foreground and the middle ground. This is to ensure that the viewers' eye goes to the focal point first and then to the rest of the illustration.

Please make sure the focal point relates to the object around it to create a harmonious atmosphere and flow. For example, in *Figure 9.4*, the first thing we notice is the little witch and cat, then the tree, and then our eyes slowly move in the direction of the giant mystical orbs. You can add other details along the direction heading into the giant orbs to add more charm to your background scenery.

Common mistakes and how to fix them

As artists, we often struggle to create strong compositions for background illustrations. Let's explore a couple of common mistakes and how to refine them for a more engaging and visually appealing result:

- **Overcrowding the scene**:

  - **Mistake**: Too many details clutter the background, making it overwhelming and difficult to read.

  - **How to fix**: Simplify the composition by reducing unnecessary elements. Use negative space to ensure a clear visual for the scene.

- **Poor eye flow and direction**:

  - **Mistake**: The viewer's eye doesn't move naturally through the scene, making the composition feel scattered.

  - **How to fix**: Use leading lines, curved shapes, or contrast to direct the viewer's eyes toward the focal point. Paths or rivers can help create a natural flow for background scenery.

> **Important note**
>
> To create a good composition, it must consist of at least one main focal point followed by a secondary focal point to guide the direction of the viewer's eyes. A strong composition typically starts with a main focal point. This is what you want the viewer to look at first. After that, having one or more secondary focal points helps lead the viewer through the rest of the artwork, creating flow and visual interest.

Now that we have a basic understanding of how composition works, let's move on and explore other composition techniques that can enhance your illustrations and make them more captivating. We'll start by learning about the C-shape composition.

Learning how to use C-shape composition in art

C-shape composition in art refers to a specific arrangement of elements that forms a C-shaped flow or pathway within the artwork. This composition technique guides the viewer's eye around the piece, creating a sense of movement and leading them to the focal point. The C shape can be formed through strategic shapes and colors that often mimic natural forms, such as the shape of a tree trunk or a crescent moon.

This composition technique helps create a sense of depth and movement, guiding viewers to explore the artwork. Using a C-shape composition can be difficult since it is not easy to find objects that resemble the C-shaped flow. In this walkthrough, we will learn how to apply C-shape composition to our background scenery and how to arrange elements in a curved C layout to create a natural flow that draws the viewer's attention.

Following the steps

Drawing a C-shape composition for background scenery can be done as follows:

1. Start by drawing a C shape on a blank canvas, as illustrated in *STEP 1* in *Figure 9.5*.

2. Identify key elements to include in the composition and determine their placement along the C shape. Mark the areas as follows:

   - *Area 1*: Star (main focal point)

   - *Area 2* and *Area 3*: Tree branch and cat

   - *Area 4*: Little witch

3. Sketch the background scenery, incorporating the important details into their respective areas.

4. Lastly, apply shadows to the foreground and middle ground areas to enhance the sense of depth and perspective in your artwork. Lower the background's color intensity to push it further into the distance and help the little witch stand out as the main focal point. You can achieve this by either lowering the background layer's opacity or gently erasing parts of it using the same brush or a Soft Airbrush.

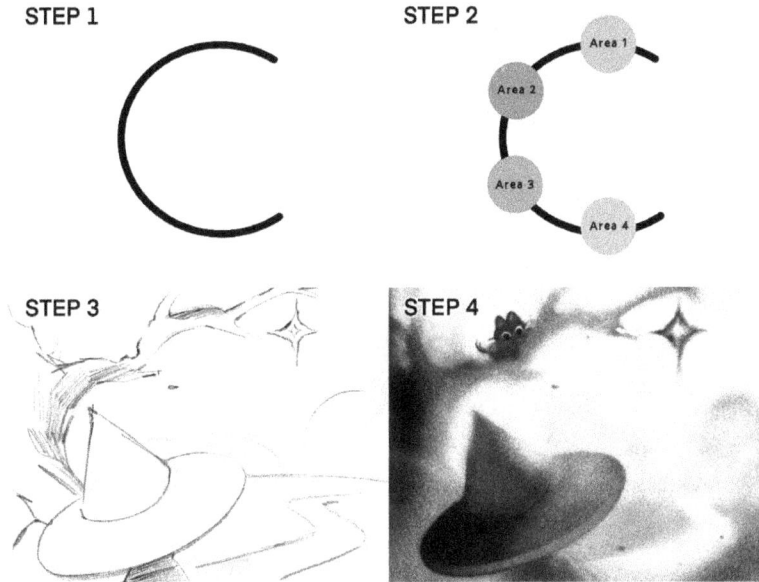

Figure 9.5 – Step-by-step tutorial using C-shape composition

Figure 9.6 shows the results you can achieve by simply following this step-by-step walkthrough:

Figure 9.6 – Final result of the illustration

That's how we apply C-shape composition to background drawings. Let's have a look at how this technique works.

Understanding the technique

Drawing a C-shape composition is the simplest and easiest technique we can apply to our background scenery, as you just draw details along the *C* shape, and you successfully create a good composition. For *Figure 9.6*, I drew a star and the cat as the main and secondary focal points. Then, it was followed by the little witch, the tree, and a long road. From the viewer's point of view, they will focus on the star first, then on the cat, then the tree trunk, followed by the little witch, and lastly, the long road to the horizon. We drew the tree to resemble the *C* shape.

You don't need to actually draw a tree or a perfect *C* to use C-shape composition. You can draw anything as long as the shapes are placed in a curve that leads the viewer's eyes in the shape of a *C*. In *Figure 9.5*, I didn't draw an exact *C*. I just used the idea of the shape to help guide the eye. So, remember, the *C* is just a guide to help you place things in a way that flows nicely; it doesn't have to be perfect.

Common mistakes and how to fix them

While C-shape composition is a powerful way to guide the viewer's eye, we sometimes struggle with making the curve strong enough to create a natural flow. Let's explore a common mistake and how to refine it for a more dynamic and visually engaging result:

- **Mistake**: The focal point is placed outside the curve, disrupting the natural flow
- **How to fix**: Ensure the focal point sits within or near the curve center, so the viewer's eye naturally follows the shape

Now that we've seen how a curve can guide the viewer's eye using C-shape composition, let's try something bolder. Next, we'll explore a V-shape composition, which is perfect for creating drama and directing focus to a powerful point in the scene.

Learning how to use V-shape composition in art

V-shape composition in art refers to a structural arrangement where elements are positioned to form a *V* shape. This creates a sense of movement, direction, and flow within the artwork. This type of composition leads the viewer's eye toward a focal point, typically found at the apex of the *V*, which can be used to emphasize important elements. It can also evoke feelings of stability and balance, as the two sides of the *V* create a sense of harmony while guiding the viewer's gaze.

It is also often used to evoke a sense of drama and action in our works. Using V-shape composition can be difficult to use, as trying to force a *V* shape can lead to cluttered or unnatural scenes. We sometimes struggle to balance the shape with believable depth and atmosphere. In this walkthrough, I will share a step-by-step tutorial to create a perfect V-shape composition for our background drawing.

Following the steps

Drawing a V-shape composition for background scenery can be done as follows:

1. Start by drawing a *V* shape on a blank canvas, as illustrated in *STEP 1* in *Figure 9.7*.

    Identify key elements to include in the composition and determine their placement along the *V* shape. Mark the areas as follows:

    *   *Area 1* and *Area 2*: Trees

    *   *Area 3*: Little witch and cat (main focal point)

2. Sketch the background scenery, incorporating the important details into their respective areas.

3. Lastly, apply shadows to the foreground and middle ground areas to enhance the sense of depth and perspective in your artwork.

For this composition, I've intentionally left the background empty to create a sense of mystery and the unknown. If any background elements are added, they should be rendered with lower color values than those in the foreground and middle ground to maintain proper depth and focus. Let's take a closer look at how the scene was built, step by step using the V-shape composition to lead the viewer's eyes toward a focal point.

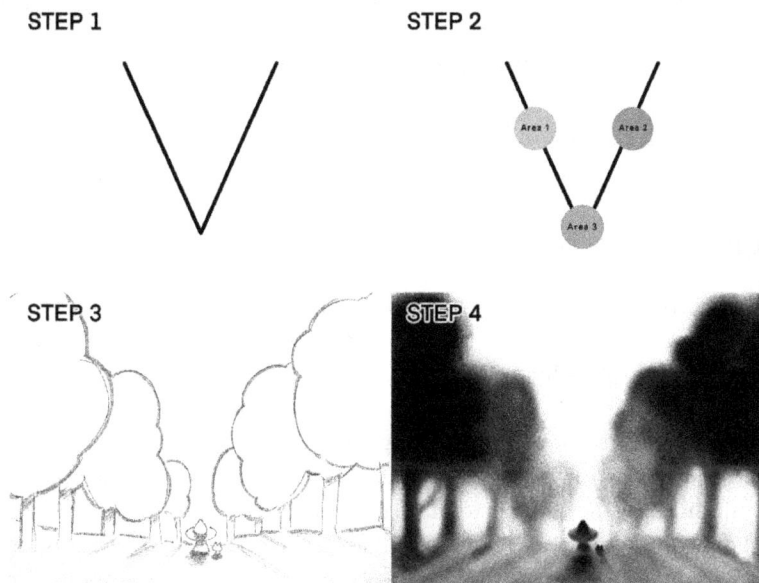

Figure 9.7 – Step-by-step tutorial using V-shape composition

Figure 9.8 shows the results you can achieve by simply following this step-by-step walkthrough:

Figure 9.8 – Final result of the illustration

That's how we apply V-shape composition to background drawings. Let's have a look at how this technique works.

Understanding the technique

V-shape composition can be a bit challenging to apply because it's not always immediately apparent in natural settings. Unlike more obvious compositional structures, the *V* shape often needs to be intentionally constructed or subtly implied. To make it easier, you can draw the details around the *V* shape, and the main object will be drawn where the two lines meet as the main focal point. In *Figure 9.8*, we can see that the trees are drawn pointing toward the little witch and cat. This is to ensure the viewer's eye direction moves toward the little witch and cat that is placed at the apex of the *V*. You can add some details in *Area 1* and *Area 2* to make the illustration more detailed and charming to the audience, such as birds, more detailed foliage, and flowers on the ground. By carefully arranging elements to form a *V* shape, we can guide the viewer's eye toward the main subject and create a strong sense of direction in the scene. Even though this composition may not naturally appear, with thoughtful placement, such as trees pointing inward or added details along the sides, we can create a visually interesting scene for this composition.

Common mistakes and how to fix them

V-shape composition naturally directs attention toward the focal point, but if the structure is too weak, the scene may feel scattered. Let's look at a common pitfall and how to fix it:

- **Mistake**: The focal point is too weak or lacks contrast, making it blend into the background

- **How to fix**: Increase contrast at the apex of the *V* using lighting, saturation, or texture to make the focal point stand out

---

Tips

Aside from trees, you can use mountains and clouds to craft an effective V-shape composition. For example, two mountain slopes converging into a V-shape naturally direct attention to a key element in the scene, such as a winding river or a distant peak. Similarly, clouds form a *V* shape that points toward a character. This arrangement helps highlight the central focus while giving the artwork a sense of movement and balance.

While a *V* shape gives us symmetry and a strong focus, sometimes breaking the balance creates even more visual interest. Let's look at how unbalanced composition uses contrast and tension to keep the viewer engaged.

Learning how to use unbalanced composition in art

Unbalanced composition can be a powerful technique in art, as it creates tension and movement. To use unbalanced composition effectively, consider placing elements asymmetrically within the frame where elements are not mirrored or evenly balanced on both sides but still feel visually harmonious. This might involve positioning a focal point off-center or varying the visual element, such as differences in sizes, colors, or textures. The main goal is to guide the viewer's eye through the piece, creating a sense of dynamism and movement. This technique is often overlooked because we fear it might result in a repetitive or dull composition due to its simplicity. In this walkthrough, I will share a fun and easy way to create an eye-catching background drawing using this composition technique.

Following the steps

Here is how you can create an unbalanced composition for your background scenery:

1. Start by drawing two rectangular shapes in different sizes on a blank canvas, as illustrated in *Figure 9.9*.

2. Identify key elements to include in the composition and determine their placement in the two rectangular shapes. Mark the areas as follows:

    - *Area 1*: Little witch, cat, and tree (main focal point)

    - *Area 2*: Little house

3. Sketch the background scenery, incorporating the important details into their respective areas.

4. Lastly, apply shadows to the foreground and middle ground areas to enhance the sense of depth and perspective in your artwork. Lower the background's color intensity to push it further into the distance and help the little witch stand out as the focal point. You can achieve this by either lowering the background layer's opacity or gently erasing parts of it using the same brush or a Soft Airbrush.

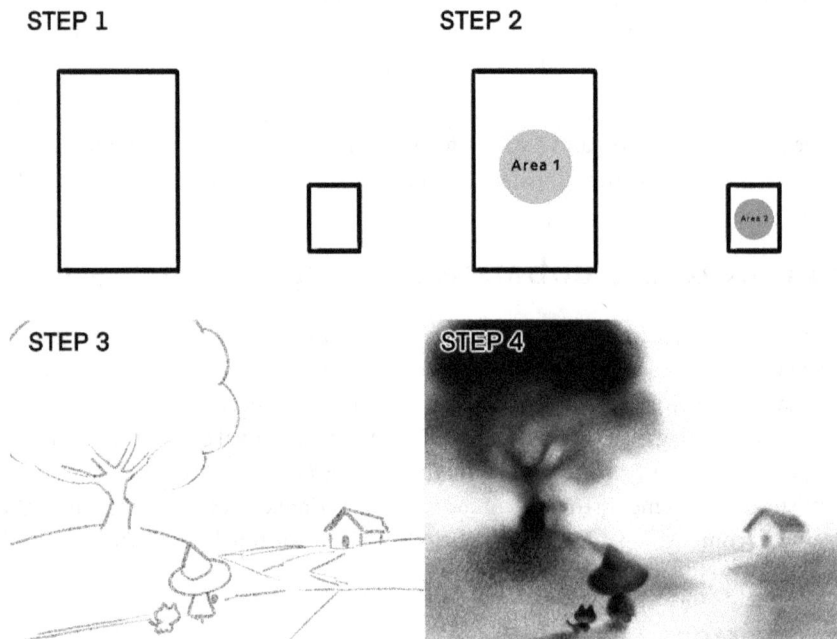

Figure 9.9 – Step-by-step tutorial using unbalanced composition

Figure 9.10 shows the results you can achieve by simply following this step-by-step walkthrough:

Figure 9.10 – Final result of the illustration

That's how we apply unbalanced composition to background drawings. Let's have a look at how this technique works.

Understanding the technique

In *Figure 9.10*, we illustrated a tree, a little witch, a cat, and a little house, with the larger and more detailed elements positioned in the foreground and the smaller elements in the background. By adjusting their sizes, we were able to create a sense of depth and movement in the background scenery. This technique helps establish a strong perspective, naturally guiding the viewer's attention toward the end of the road and drawing focus to the little house at its end.

The main focal points are the little witch, the cat, and the tree, with the viewer's attention naturally guided down the road toward the distant little house. To enhance the composition, you could add more details along the road, such as fences or flowers, to give the scene more charm and a welcoming feel. Alternatively, increasing the contrast on the little witch can make the overall illustration more visually striking and captivating. This background scenery shows how using size, contrast, and direction carefully can make the picture feel deep and engaging. The viewer's eyes naturally follow the road from the front to the small house in the distance, creating a feeling of wonder and warmth, like being invited to walk beside the little witch into the quiet, magical world.

Common mistakes and how to fix them

Unbalanced composition creates movement and tension, but if not handled carefully, it can feel chaotic rather than intentional. Here's how to refine it for a more engaging result:

- **Mistake**: The secondary focal point is too strong, competing with the main subject
- **How to fix**: Reduce detail and contrast in the secondary focal point, so it supports rather than distracts from the main subject

While unbalanced composition creates movement through size contrast and asymmetry, some scenes call for a sense of calm and stillness instead. That's where balanced composition comes in. In the next walkthrough, we'll explore how using symmetry and evenly placed visual elements can help create a peaceful and stable atmosphere in your background illustrations.

Learning how to use balanced composition in art

Balance in composition refers to the even distribution of subjects of the same feature or size in an artwork, creating a peaceful atmosphere. Symmetrical balance involves mirroring elements on either side of a central axis, creating a formal and stable appearance. To effectively use balance, we should consider the placement of elements, the subject's visual appearance, and the overall atmosphere of the background scenery, to ensure that the composition feels stable and peaceful.

This composition is one of the easiest composition techniques, but we tend to avoid it because we are unsure what to draw to create a balanced composition. In this walkthrough, we will learn how to recreate this balance in our background scenery.

Following the steps

Drawing a balanced composition for background scenery can be done as follows:

1. Start by drawing two mirrored rectangle shapes on a blank canvas, as illustrated in *Figure 9.11*.

2. Identify key elements to include in the composition and determine their placement in the two rectangular shapes. Mark the areas as follows:

   - *Area 1*: Fox statue (main focal point)
   - *Area 2*: Fox statue (main focal point)

3. Sketch the background scenery, incorporating the important details into their respective areas.

4. Lastly, apply shadows to the foreground and middle ground areas to enhance the sense of depth and perspective in your artwork. Lower the background's color intensity to push it further into the distance and help the little witch stand out as the focal point. You can achieve this by either lowering the background layer's opacity or gently erasing parts of it using the same brush or a Soft Airbrush.

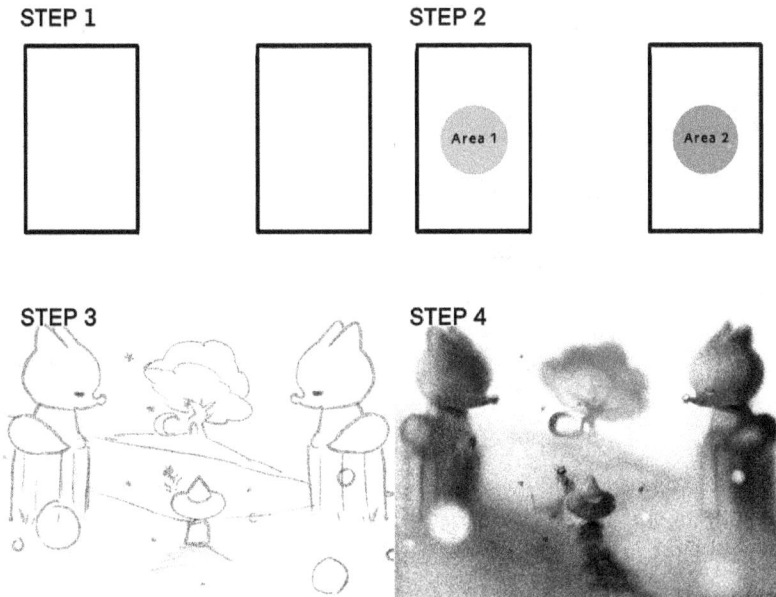

Figure 9.11 – Step-by-step tutorial using a balanced composition

Figure 9.12 shows the results you can achieve by simply following this step-by-step walkthrough:

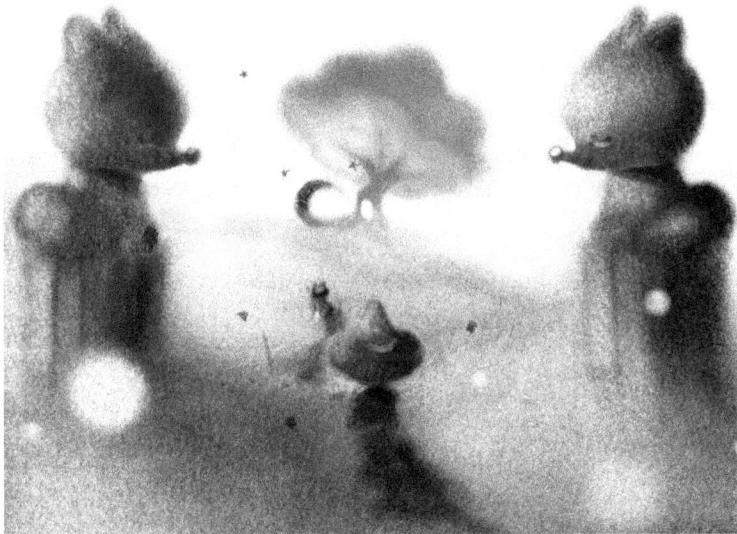

Figure 9.12 – Final result of the illustration

That's how we apply balanced composition to background drawings. Let's have a look at how this technique works.

Understanding the technique

Balanced composition can be created by adding two symmetrical rectangles to a blank canvas, with the main focal points in the center of each (*Area 1* and *Area 2*). In these areas, we drew two fox statues facing each other. To make them stand out, we can add more details on these areas so the viewer's eyes will focus on them first before looking at the whole illustration. In a balanced layout, you can place any design elements in *Area 1* and *Area 2*, such as trees, buildings, or flowers as long as they're similar in height and size. When both sides of your scene feel even, it creates a calm and harmonious composition that's easy for the viewer to enjoy.

Outside of *Area 1* and *Area 2*, we added a scenic background and placed the little witch and cat between the fox statues as a secondary focal point. In the distance, we drew a large tree to suggest that the character is gazing toward it. To make the tree feel more magical, we added a crescent shape under it.

Common mistakes and how to fix them

While balanced composition is one of the easiest techniques to apply, artists sometimes struggle with making it feel natural and engaging. Let's explore a common mistake and how to refine it for a more dynamic and visually appealing result:

- **Mistake**: The main and secondary focal points are too evenly distributed, making it hard for the viewer to know where to focus first
- **How to fix**: Strengthen the primary focal point by adding more detail or contrast to guide the viewer's attention

With an understanding of balanced composition, let's shake things up again! Diagonal composition brings energy and movement into the frame, perfect for scenes that need a sense of motion or direction. Let's look at that next.

Learning how to use diagonal composition

Diagonal composition involves placing two diagonal lines that intersect or lead toward focal points within the artwork, creating a sense of movement and depth. To use this composition, start by determining the main subject and the desired points of emphasis within your piece. Then, create a diagonal line that guides the viewer's eye toward this focal point. This technique helps to establish a strong tension and can enhance the overall storyline of the artwork, making it more engaging and dynamic.

We can practice this composition in our sketches or studies to refine our understanding using this composition. Using this composition can be difficult, especially if we are new to using this technique. In this walkthrough, we will learn how to use this composition technique effectively in our background scenery.

Following the steps

Drawing a diagonal composition for background scenery can be done as follows:

1. Start by drawing a diagonal line on a blank canvas, as illustrated in *Figure 9.13*.

2. Identify the key elements to include in the composition and determine their placement on the diagonal line. Mark the area as follows:

    *   *Area 1*: Hill, little witch, and cat (main focal point)

3. Sketch the background scenery, incorporating the important details into their respective areas.

4. Lastly, apply shadows to the foreground and middle ground areas to enhance the sense of depth and perspective in your artwork. For this composition, I've intentionally left the background empty to create a sense of stillness and the unknown. If any background elements are added, they should be rendered with lower color values than those in the foreground and middle ground to maintain proper depth and focus.

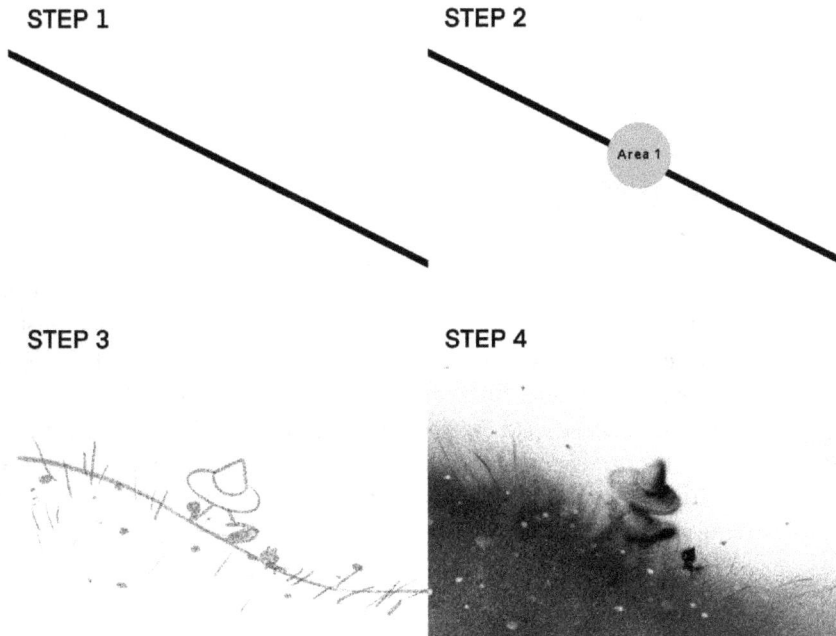

Figure 9.13 – Step-by-step tutorial using diagonal composition

Figure 9.14 shows the results you can achieve by simply following this step-by-step walkthrough:

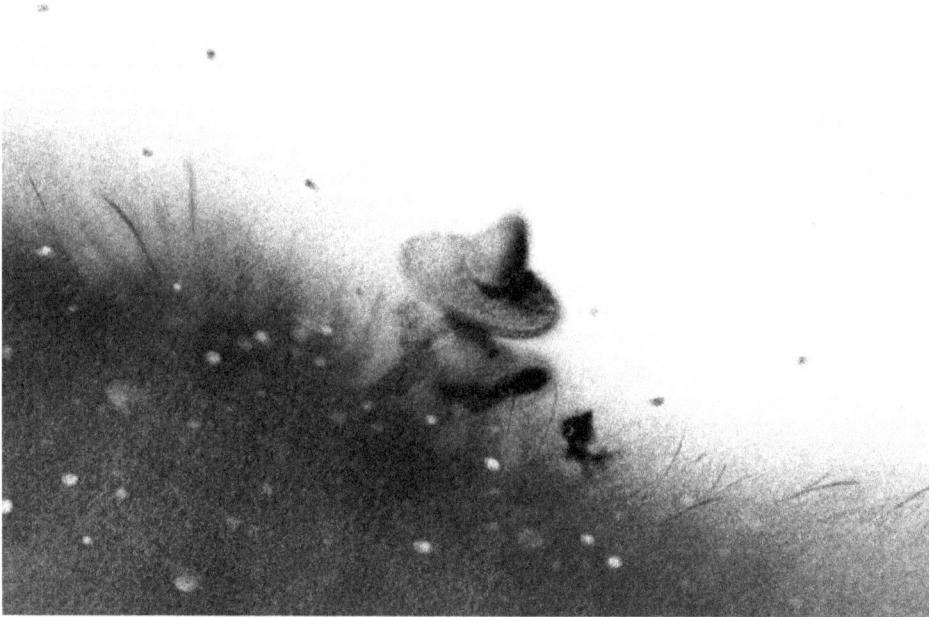

Figure 9.14 – Final result of the illustration

That's how we apply diagonal composition to background drawings. Let's have a look at how this technique works.

Understanding the technique

In this artwork, the diagonal line helps guide the whole scene. I drew it from the top left to the bottom right to gently lead the viewer's eyes across the page. To add a bit of story, I placed a little witch and cat as the main focal point, walking toward something mysterious. This makes people curious and adds a bit of wonder. I added soft touches such as little flowers and grass along the hill to make the journey feel more magical, but I kept it simple so the focus stays on the characters. I left the background mostly empty on purpose. This way, the viewer feels drawn to the hill and the path the characters are taking. If you'd like to add a background, that's totally okay! Just make sure it doesn't take too much attention away from the little witch and cat. This composition style adds a quiet sense of movement and is perfect for peaceful storytelling moments.

Common mistakes and how to fix them

Diagonal composition is great for creating movement, but if the diagonal line doesn't lead to a clear focal point, the composition can feel chaotic. Let's explore a common mistake and how to refine it for a stronger visual impact:

- **Mistake**: The diagonal elements are too weak, making the composition lose its dynamic energy.
- **How to fix**: Strengthen the diagonal line using strong lighting contrasts, dynamic shape, or motion elements such as flowing fabric or wind-swept grass. For example, add strong highlights and more details on the main focal point of the illustration.

Diagonals help lead the eye across the canvas, but cross composition helps us build an even more structured atmosphere. Let's see how intersecting lines can frame a focal point and bring balance with dynamism.

Learning how to use cross composition in art

Cross composition in art refers to the technique of creating a well-balanced background drawing that emphasizes a central focal point. It can create dynamic visual art by using intersecting lines that guide the viewer's eye across the artwork. To create cross composition, we should focus on creating a clear focal point and balancing elements to maintain a harmonious atmosphere. Cross composition can be created by dividing the canvas into four sections using vertical and horizontal lines. We use this composition usually for trees, natural scenery, and so on, such as a boat on a lake. The boat will be drawn on the vertical line, whereas the lake will be on the horizontal line. As an artist, working with composition can be challenging due to its intricate nature. However, in this step-by-step walkthrough, we'll simplify the process and explore how to effortlessly integrate composition into our artwork.

> Tip
>
> While cross compositions are often constructed using intersecting diagonal lines that guide dynamic movement, in this walkthrough, we'll demonstrate a variation using vertical and horizontal lines. Both approaches emphasize the central focal point and balanced layout, so feel free to adapt the cross structure based on the scene's needs or preferences.

Following the steps

Here's how you can create a cross composition for your background scenery—it's simpler than you think:

1. Start by sketching two intersecting lines on a blank canvas, one vertical and one horizontal, to form a cross, dividing the canvas into four sections, as illustrated in *Figure 9.15*.

2. Identify key elements to include in the composition and determine their placement in the two intersecting diagonal lines. Mark the areas as follows:

    • *Area 1*: Clouds

    • *Area 2*: Little witch and cat (main focal point)

    • *Area 3*: Grass field

3. Sketch the background scenery, incorporating the important details into their respective areas.

4. Lastly, apply shadows to the foreground and middle ground areas to enhance the sense of depth and perspective in your artwork. Lower the background's color intensity to push it further into the distance and help the little witch stand out as the focal point. You can achieve this by either lowering the background layer's opacity or gently erasing parts of it using the same brush or a Soft Airbrush.

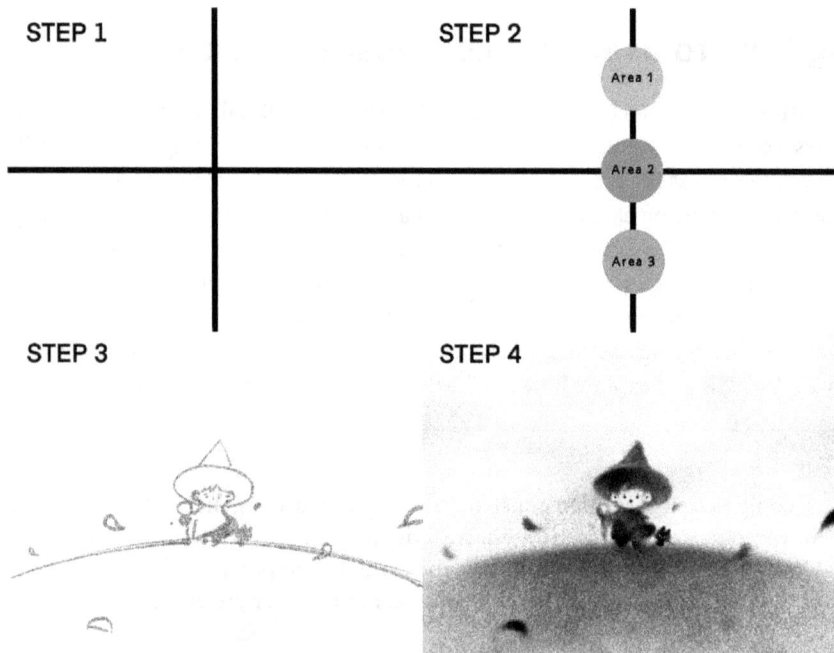

Figure 9.15 – Step-by-step tutorial using cross composition

Figure 9.16 shows the results you can achieve by simply following this step-by-step walkthrough:

Figure 9.16 – Final result of the illustration

That's how we apply a cross composition to background drawings. Let's take a look at how this technique works.

Understanding the technique

To create a cross composition on your blank canvas, start by sketching two intersecting horizontal and vertical lines that form a cross, dividing the canvas into four sections. The main focal point will be drawn at the middle of the canvas where the lines intersect. In *Figure 9.16*, I placed the little witch and cat at the center as the main focal point to help them stand out. I wanted it to feel like they've just discovered something magical, drawing the viewer's attention right to that moment. Placing your main subject here naturally guides the eye to the main focus of your scene. Around them, I added subtle background elements such as distant clouds and a vast grass field to support the main focal point without overshadowing it. To create depth, I drew scattered grass drifting toward the viewer in different sizes. This little touch helps the background feel less flat and makes the whole illustration more full of life.

Common mistakes and how to fix them

Cross composition helps create a strong focal point, but if the intersecting lines don't frame the subject effectively, the composition can feel disconnected. Let's explore a common mistake and how to refine it for a more cohesive result:

- **Mistake**: The background elements overpower the focal point, making it hard to distinguish

- **How to fix**: Reduce contrast or saturation in the background while keeping the focal point sharp and detailed

After working with strong intersecting lines, circular composition offers a softer approach; it leads the viewer's eye around the scene in a smooth, continuous motion. This technique is especially useful when you want a central subject to stand out in an environment. Let's look at that next.

Learning how to use circular composition in art

Circular composition is a technique that involves arranging the main subject in a way that draws the viewer's eye around the artwork in a circular motion. To use circular composition, start by identifying a central focal point that attracts the viewer's attention. From this point, arrange other elements in curves or lines that radiate outward or circle back toward the center, creating a sense of movement.

This composition is usually drawn if you would like viewers to pay attention to what you want to share through art. For example, if you would like to introduce your new character, you can draw it in the center of a crowd to draw the viewer's attention toward your new character. It can be a little difficult to draw using circular composition, as we are not sure what we can draw to resemble circular motion. In this walkthrough, we will learn how to use circular composition easily in our art.

Following the steps

Drawing a circular composition for background scenery can be done as follows:

1. Start by drawing a circle shape on a blank canvas, as illustrated in *Figure 9.17*.

2. Identify the key elements you want to include in your composition and decide where to place them within the circle and around its outer edge. You can label the areas like this:

   - *Area 1*: Moon and little witch (main focal point)

   - *Area 2*: Glowing stars and fireflies

3. Sketch the background scenery, incorporating the important details into their respective areas.

4. Lastly, apply shadows to the foreground and middle ground areas to enhance the sense of depth and perspective in your artwork. Lower the background's color intensity to push it further into the distance and help the little witch stand out as the focal point. You can achieve this by either

lowering the background layer's opacity or gently erasing parts of it using the same brush or a Soft Airbrush.

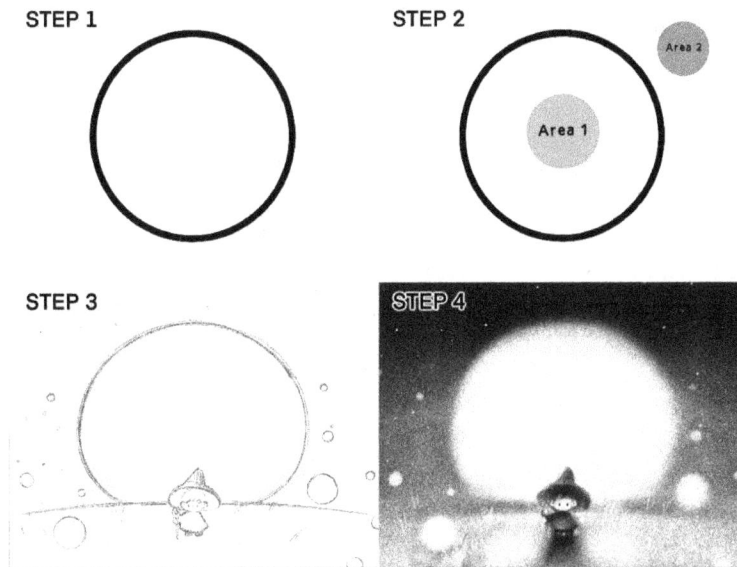

Figure 9.17 – Step-by-step tutorial using circular composition

Figure 9.18 shows the results you can achieve by simply following this step-by-step walkthrough:

Figure 9.18 – Final result of the illustration

That's how we apply circular composition to background drawings. Let's have a look at how this technique works.

Understanding the technique

For circular composition, draw a circle on your canvas as guidance for the main details. In *Area 1*, we will draw our main focal point. In *Figure 9.18*, I chose the full moon and the little witch as the main focal points of the background scene. The moon worked well because its round shape fits nicely with the circular composition. But don't worry, you don't need to draw everything in a perfect circle. As long as your main elements follow a circular motion, the composition will feel balanced. For example, a lake with a roundish shape can work just as beautifully. To add contrast, I placed glowing stars around the moon, making the sky feel lively while helping the moon stand out. I gave the little witch a darker color value, so they'd stand out against the brightness of the night sky and glowing moon behind them. To bring everything together, I added grassy textures to the field and drew a few fireflies. Some fireflies are drawn larger and closer, while others are smaller and farther away. This helps add a sense of depth to the illustration. Just be sure the details around the moon stay soft and subtle so they don't pull attention away from your main focal point.

Common mistakes and how to fix them

Circular composition helps create a smooth, continuous flow, but if the circular motion isn't strong enough, the viewer's eye may wander. Let's explore a common mistake and how to fix it:

- **Mistake**: The focal point is placed outside the circular flow, disrupting the composition
- **How to fix**: Ensure the focal point is within or near the center of the circular arrangement so the viewer's eye moves smoothly around it

Know more...

Aside from ponds, we can use flower beds arranged in circular patterns to give garden scenes a tidy and harmonious look. Curved paths looping around features such as a statue or fountain also naturally create a circular flow, guiding the viewer's attention and adding balance to the composition. These elements work beautifully to recreate the circular effect in landscape drawings!

We've come full circle, literally! Now, let's move on to a more advanced layout: the Golden Section. This timeless composition technique uses nature's perfect ratio to build scenes that feel effortless and striking.

Learning how to use Golden Section composition in art

The **Golden Section**, also known as the **Golden Ratio (1.618)**, is a mathematical proportion that has been used in art and design for centuries to create balanced and visually appealing compositions, as shown in *Figure 9.19*.

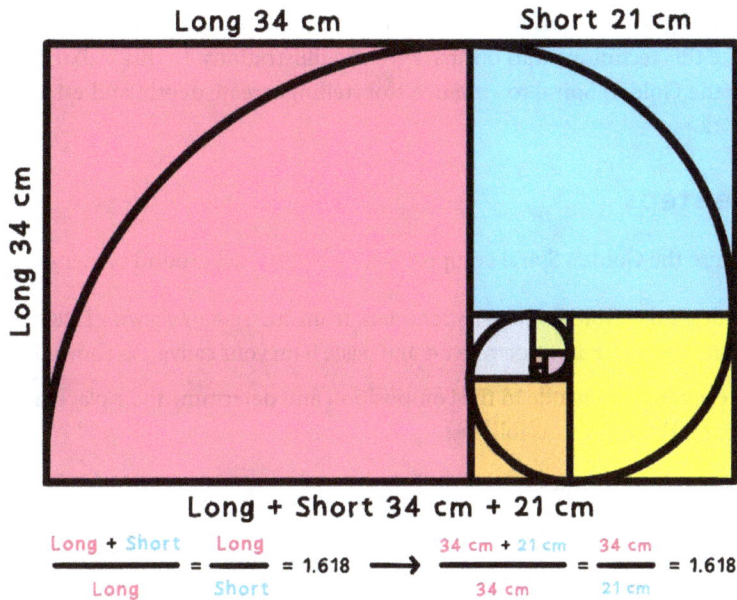

Figure 9.19 – Example of the Golden Ratio (1.618)

One of the most effective ways to apply the Golden Section in art is through the **Golden Spiral**, a structure derived from the Fibonacci sequence. The Fibonacci sequence is a ¥# pattern of numbers where each number is the sum of the two before it. It starts with 0 and 1, then continues like this: 0, 1, 2, 3, 5, 8, 13, 21, 34, and so on. It can be illustrated as shown in *Figure 9.19*. This spiral expands outward, creating a dynamic flow that leads the viewer's attention toward key focal points. By placing important elements along the spiral curve, we can craft compositions that feel effortless yet stand out.

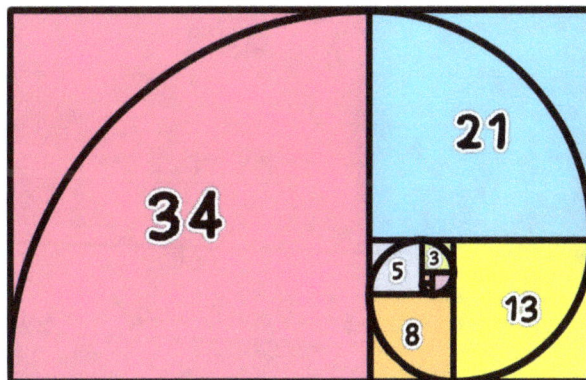

Figure 9.20 – Example of Golden Spiral using Fibonacci sequence

While mastering the Golden Section may seem complex, it can be simplified into practical steps that help us integrate this technique into our background illustrations. In this walkthrough, we will explore how to use the Golden Spiral to enhance storytelling, create depth, and establish a strong visual in your artwork.

Following the steps

Here's how you can use the Golden Spiral composition to design background scenery:

1. Firstly, download the Golden Section template from `https://www.freepik.com/vectors/golden-ratio-template` and paste it on your canvas, as shown in *Figure 9.21*.

2. Identify key elements to include in the composition and determine their placement along the spiral's curve. Mark the areas as follows:

    *   *Area 1*: Fox seen from behind

    *   *Area 2*: Scattered stars

    *   *Area 3*: Tree

    *   *Area 4*: Shining star and little ghost

    *   *Area 5*: Little witch and cat (main focal point)

3. Sketch the background scenery, incorporating the important details into their respective areas.

4. Lastly, apply shadows to the foreground and middle ground areas to enhance the sense of depth and perspective in your artwork. Lower the background's color intensity to push it further into the distance and help the little witch stand out as the focal point. You can achieve this by either lowering the background layer's opacity or gently erasing parts of it using the same brush or a Soft Airbrush.

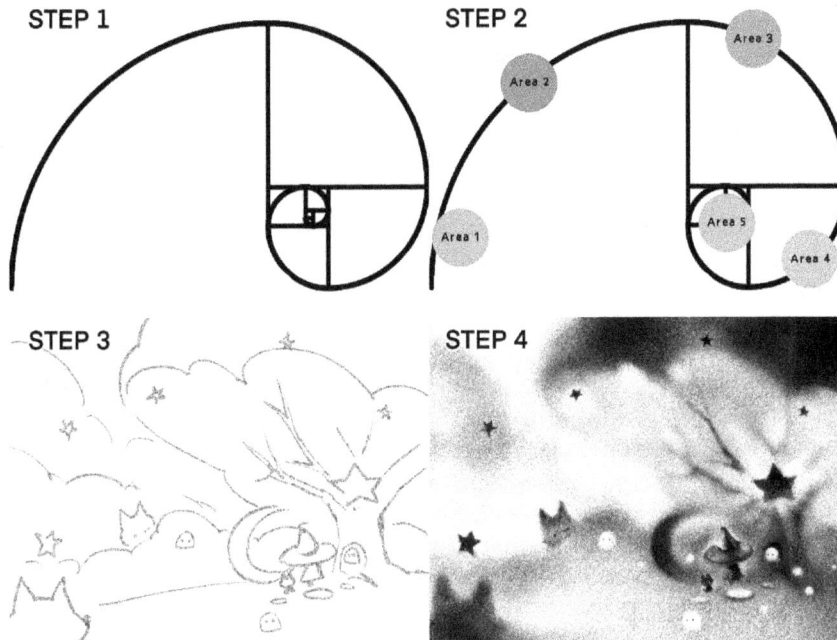

Figure 9.21 – Step-by-step tutorial using Golden Spiral composition

Figure 9.22 shows the results you can achieve by simply following this step-by-step walkthrough:

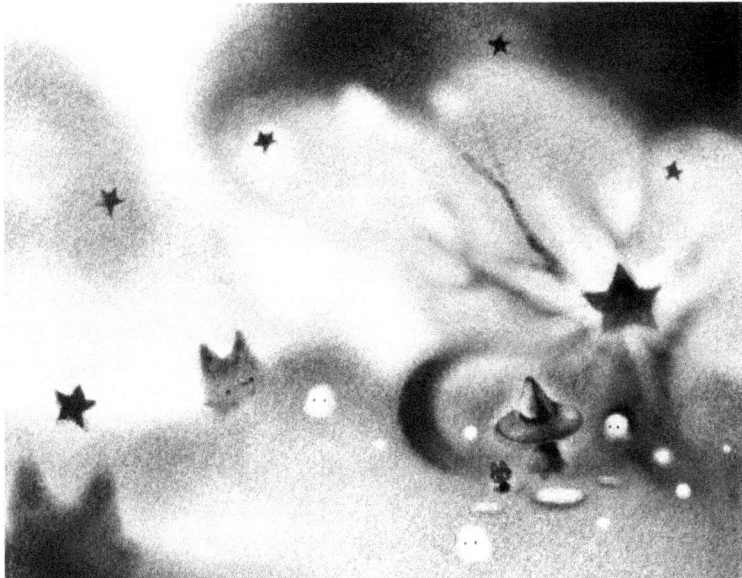

Figure 9.22 – Final result of the illustration

That's how we apply Golden Section composition on background drawings. Let's have a look at how this technique works.

Understanding the technique

Using Golden Spiral composition for background scenery or any kind of drawing in general is the most effective way to create a dynamic and charming masterpiece. This is because the Golden Spiral composition has a good flow, thus helping the viewer move their eyes smoothly to the last focal point. For example, in *Figure 9.22*, I wanted to tell the story of a little witch and cat finally reaching their destination after a long journey.

To convey this narrative using the Golden Spiral, I placed a fox in the foreground, followed by scattered stars leading toward a large tree with a shining star at its top. To guide the viewer's eye further, I included a small ghost at the base of the tree, as if it had been expecting them. Finally, at the end of the spiral (the main focal point), I drew the little witch and cat, marking the conclusion of their journey.

The key to using the Golden Spiral effectively is to place details along the spiral's curve, naturally directing the viewer's attention toward the main focal point. In this case, the little witch and cat are positioned at the end of the spiral, ensuring the composition feels complete and harmonious.

Common mistakes and how to fix them

Golden Section composition is one of the most effective ways to create a dynamic and charming masterpiece, but if the elements don't align properly, the composition can feel unbalanced. Let's explore a common mistake and how to refine it:

- **Mistake**: The spiral is too weak, making the viewer's eye direction unclear
- **How to fix**: Strengthen the spiral by placing smaller details along its curve, reinforcing movement toward the focal point

> Tips
>
> To improve this composition, use a Golden Spiral template as a guide when sketching. You can easily find and download one online by searching for the `Golden Spiral template` on Google Images. Overlay the template on your canvas on a different layer under your Sketch Layer to plan the placement of your focal point and supporting details. This helps your composition flow naturally and align with the spiral. With practice, you'll eventually be able to apply the Golden Spiral intuitively without needing the template. Don't stress too much if you're trying this for the first time. Remember, art is about enjoying the process, not just aiming for perfect results. Have fun experimenting and let your creativity flow!

Know more...

Reflecting on all the compositions we've created in this chapter, combining them allows us to build a storyboard that tells a strong and engaging storyline, as shown in *Figure 9.23*. This storyboard can serve multiple purposes, such as being used for animations or book illustrations. Additionally, it can be a valuable addition to your portfolio, showcasing your storytelling and background design skills to potential clients. This not only highlights your artistic abilities but also helps others understand your creative process. By using the compositions we've explored, you're not just improving your background design skills; you're also learning how to tell compelling stories through art.

Background concept: A young witch embarks on a journey in a magical place.

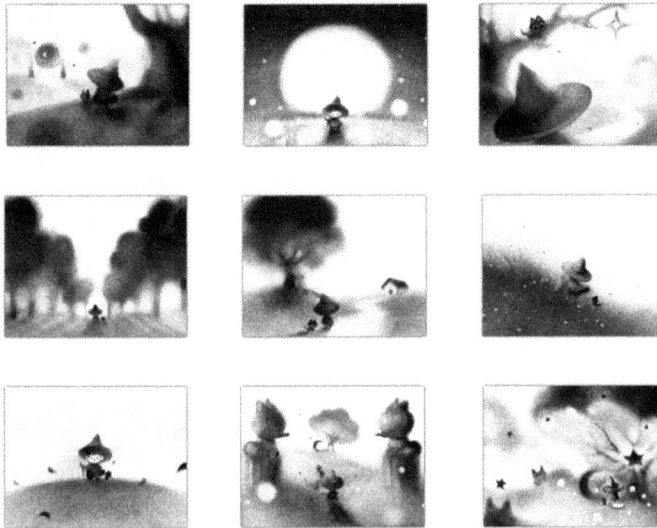

Figure 9.23 – Example of a storyboard

Summary

You've done such a wonderful job learning how to make your drawings more thoughtful and visually pleasing. In this chapter, we explored how placing objects in just the right way can help tell your story clearly and beautifully.

We practiced using shapes such as a *C*, *V*, circle, and spiral to gently guide the viewer's eyes through your scene. We also discovered how balance, depth, and contrast can change how your artwork feels, whether calm and peaceful or full of energy and excitement.

The best part is that you don't need to follow every rule. These techniques are here to guide you, but your imagination always comes first. With every sketch, you're learning to trust your eyes and your ideas more and more.

Keep creating, keep experimenting, and remember, your unique touch is what makes each piece truly special.

In the next chapter, we'll dive into the art of creating captivating landscapes that complement your characters and enhance your storytelling. You'll learn how to set the scene for different times of day—morning, afternoon, evening, and night—by adjusting light, color, and atmosphere. We'll explore how to set the mood, show distance, and use layers to make your scene feel natural and lively.

Unlock this book's exclusive benefits now

Scan this QR code or go to `packtpub.com/unlock`, then search this book by name.

10

Step-by-Step Guide to Drawing Compelling Backgrounds

A background drawing can serve multiple roles, such as establishing the overall mood and atmosphere of a piece, defining the setting and environment, and enhancing storytelling through art. A well-crafted background helps convey your story more effectively, as it can shape the entire tone and influence the perception of the characters within the artwork. Background drawing is important in the art industry because it sets the stage for the main subject of the artwork. A well-drawn background can help create a sense of place and atmosphere, making the scene more believable and engaging for the viewer. It provides context for the main elements, enhancing the overall storytelling and emotional impact of the piece.

Additionally, a good composition can guide the viewer's eye toward the focal points, making the artwork more interesting and balanced. One of the main challenges in background drawing is achieving proper perspective and depth, which can make a scene feel flat or unrealistic if not executed correctly. To make our artwork feel like it has real distance and depth, we can use a few simple tricks. Try drawing objects smaller as they move further away; that's a quick way to show space.

You can also overlap elements, so closer objects slightly cover the ones behind them. This layering helps things feel more natural and three-dimensional. Another helpful tip is using depth perspective: the further away something is, the lighter, blurrier, and less detailed it should appear. These techniques make your drawing feel more realistic and add a sense of space.

In this chapter, we will learn how to draw landscapes at different times of the day, which will help us get better at drawing background scenery.

This chapter will cover the following topics:

- Learning how to draw a serene morning landscape

- Learning how to draw a joyful afternoon landscape

- Learning how to draw a nostalgic evening landscape

- Learning how to draw a peaceful night landscape

- Drawing challenge: Create a background drawing

With the help of walkthroughs, we'll explore how to draw backgrounds representing different times of day: morning, afternoon, evening, and nighttime. Each walkthrough will give you room to experiment, but with plenty of guidance to keep things easy. By the end of this chapter, you'll feel more confident in designing backgrounds that are not only beautiful but also useful for your future projects.

Before beginning this chapter, please read the following important note to ensure that all steps can be followed smoothly. This will help maintain clarity and consistency throughout the process.

Important note

In this chapter, illustrations will be drawn in separate layers to maintain flexibility for adjustments. The layers should be named as follows: *Composition* layer, *Sketch* layer, *Contrast* layer, *Base Color* layer, *Rendering* layer, *Highlight* layer, and *Final Details* layer. This structured approach ensures that each stage of the artwork remains editable, allowing for refinement without affecting previous steps. Keeping layers organized like this makes the creative process smoother and more efficient. Once I begin the rendering process, I will turn off *Composition* layer, *Sketch* layer, and *Contrast* layer. All rendering will be done on a *single layer* to fully take advantage of brush texture and blending effects. However, feel free to use either one layer or multiple layers throughout these walkthroughs, whichever suits your workflow best. The following is a screenshot of the layers' placement:

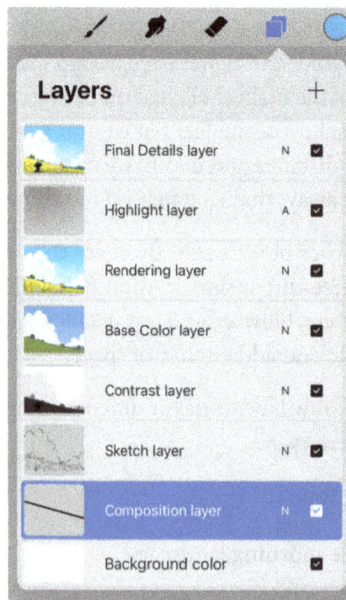

Figure 10.1 – Layers placement for this chapter

Here are the brushes I'll be using in the walkthroughs. Feel free to use these too, or swap in your favorite tools—whatever feels comfortable for your process. The goal is to enjoy the experience and find what works for you:

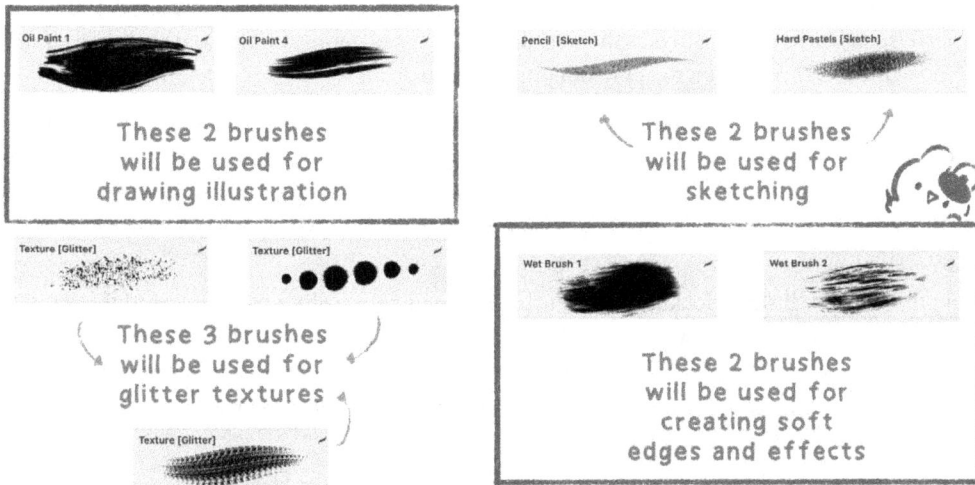

Figure 10.2 – Brushes that will be used in this chapter

Learning how to draw a serene morning landscape

In art, a morning background plays an important role in creating a peaceful atmosphere. The soft and gentle light of dawn can create a sense of calm, relaxation, and inspiration for the audience. We can use soft colors and add shadows of morning light to enhance the depth and texture. Other than that, the quiet atmosphere of morning scenery can evoke a feeling of tranquility, making it suitable for soothing and healing art. Creating a morning background in art can be tricky because you need to blend warm and cool colors to depict the fresh, soft glow of dawn. The light is gentle, so shadows should be subtle and stretched out. For example, warm hues such as orange, pink, and yellow near the horizon gradually shift into cooler blues higher up, making the scene feel peaceful and natural. It might seem tricky at first to balance warm and cool tones to capture that early glow, but don't worry! In this walkthrough, I'll guide you step by step through blending colors to build soft lighting and a serene atmosphere. You'll see how warm sunrise and cool shadows can come together to create a sense of quiet beauty.

Following the steps

Here's how to create a serene morning landscape (see *Figure 10.3*):

1. To begin, select one of the composition techniques introduced in *Chapter 9, Perfecting Composition for Visually Striking Art*, such as the C-shape or balanced composition. For the design shown in *Figure 10.3*, I've chosen to apply **diagonal composition**.

2. Now, sketch the background using the composition technique you picked. I'll draw a sloppy hill with distant trees, hills, and a house to recreate the diagonal composition. For the main focal point, I'll add a little witch and her cat near the front. To make the scene feel deeper, I'll draw flowers across the field, starting with big ones close by and making them smaller as they go farther away.

3. In this step, we'll start blocking details using different color values. Keep in mind that objects closer to the front (foreground) should be drawn with darker colors, while things farther away should be lighter. This helps create depth and make your scene look more realistic. If you need more help, you can check *Chapter 9, Perfecting Composition for Visually Striking Art*, for examples and tips.

4. After that, we'll add the base colors to the background, just like in *Step 4* (see *Figure 10.3*). Since sunrise light is soft and gentle, the sun will be placed low near the horizon. When picking your colors, go for a soft blend and don't use too much contrast, so the scene keeps its calm and peaceful morning vibe.

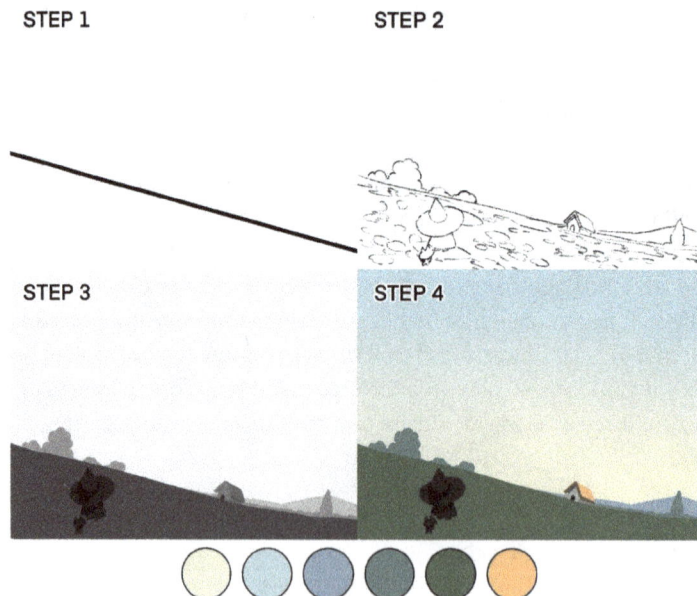

Figure 10.3 – Step-by-step drawing process to create a serene morning landscape

On the *Rendering* layer, begin adding details to the green field, the distant trees, and the far-off hill. In the field, I've included several garden stones leading toward the little house to create flow and guide the viewer's eye. Be sure to stick to the contrast plan we established in *Step 3* so the overall balance and depth stay consistent. For this part, I'll paint everything on a single layer to make full use of the brush textures and blending effects.

Figure 10.4 – Base color for serene morning

On the same layer, let's continue by adding more details to the flowers, the distant trees, and the little house. To add more depth to the background scenery, focus on adding more texture and contrast to the foreground elements, such as flowers and garden stones, so they naturally catch the viewer's attention. Don't forget to consider the light source, as shown in *Figure 10.4*. Since the light source in the morning comes from near the horizon, make sure all your shadows and highlights follow from that lower angle. This helps the entire illustration feel gentle, soft, and natural under the calm glow of the sunrise.

Figure 10.5 – Detailing process for a serene morning scene

Before we finish the illustration, let's gently add highlights where the light source comes from, which is around the horizon. To do this, change the layer's blending mode from **Normal** to **Add**. This helps brighten those areas and creates a soft, glowing effect, which is perfect for sunrise light or a magical mood. Use Procreate's **Soft Brush** with low opacity, so the glow stays soft and doesn't overpower the calm morning atmosphere.

Figure 10.6 – Adding highlight to the serene morning scene

Lastly, let's add the characters to complete the illustration. We do this in the final step so it's easier to color and blend them into the scene. By this point, the background colors are already set, which helps us choose the right tones and lighting for the characters. This way, everything feels balanced and naturally connected.

Figure 10.7 – Final version of the serene morning scene

This is the result of the serene morning illustration. Now, let's dive into the *Understanding the technique* section to give us a better understanding of this walkthrough.

Understanding the technique

Figure 10.8 shows the compilation of the serene morning drawing process:

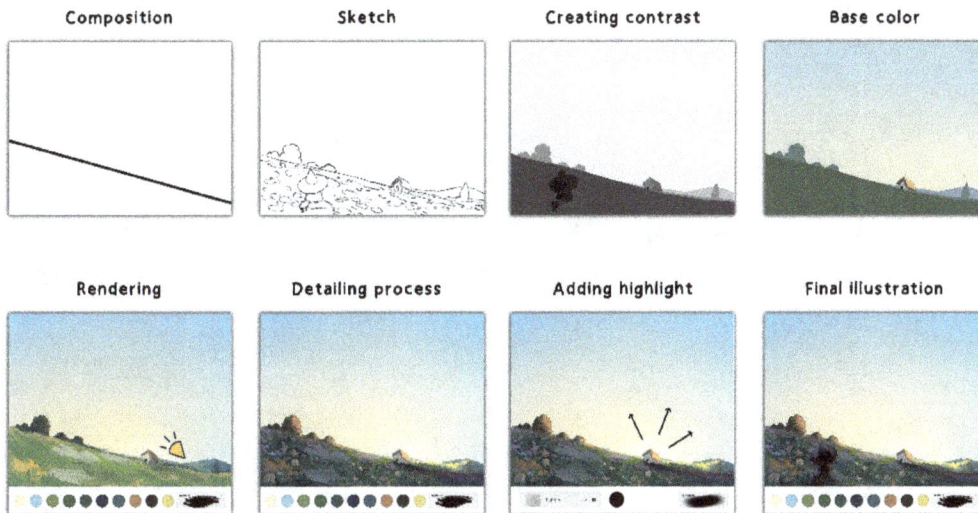

Figure 10.8 – A step-by-step compilation showcasing the serene morning drawing process

A peaceful morning landscape is created by carefully balancing soft colors, subtle textures, and a tranquil mood. The sunrise should serve as the light source, casting soft, stretched-out shadows to reflect the gentle glow of dawn. Applying atmospheric perspective to the trees in the background will help create depth. It can be done by making distant objects' color value appear lighter and hazier while keeping elements that are closer more detailed and contrasted. The color palette should be a blend of warm hues, such as soft oranges or pale yellows near the horizon, transitioning into cooler blues higher up in the sky to maintain the fresh morning feel. All these elements are important because they help to create a calm and peaceful morning scene. To give the morning scene a warm, peaceful feeling, softly brush a glow around the sunrise using the **Add** blending mode and **Soft Brush** set to low opacity

Know more...

Want to make your morning scene feel extra peaceful? Try adding a soft mist above the field or light fog around distant trees using Procreate's **Soft Brush** or **Rainforest Brush**. To gently blend the edges, use the **Smudge** tool for a smooth and natural look. You can also draw gentle clouds drifting across the sky, or a quiet lake softly reflecting the morning colors. These little details add freshness and calm to your artwork, creating a cozy atmosphere full of soft light and peaceful energy.

> **Tip**
>
> To create a more atmospheric perspective in your background, try using **Gaussian Blur** or gently lowering the saturation using the **Hue, Saturation, Brightness** adjustment in Procreate. This helps distant elements look softer and less vivid, making them feel further away and adding a sense of space to your artwork.

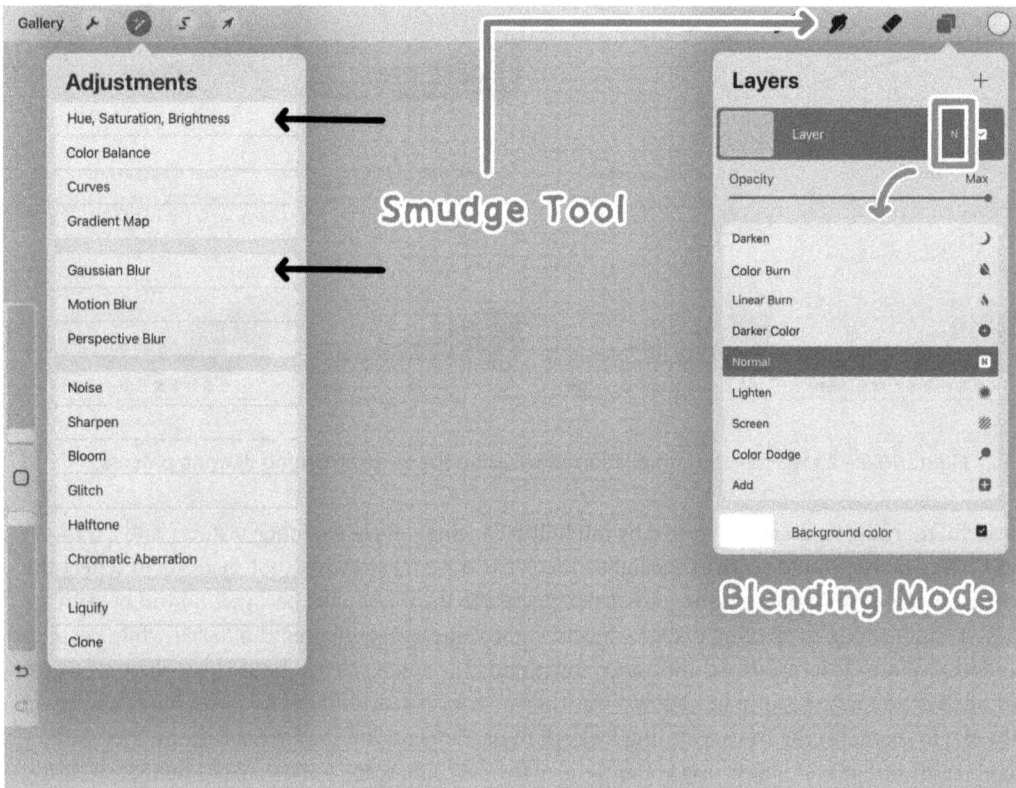

Figure 10.9 – Color palette for a serene morning

Now that we've painted the calm feeling of morning, let's brighten things up. Next, we'll learn how to draw a warm and cheerful afternoon scene.

Learning how to draw a joyful afternoon landscape

In art, an afternoon background often conveys a sense of joy and warmth, symbolizing cheerful moments. It frequently represents the summer season, evoking an energetic and lively atmosphere. The warm, bright light during the afternoon can create an atmosphere that evokes feelings of happiness and excitement, influencing the viewers to feel the same way. Incorporating shadows and light can emphasize forms and details, guide the viewer's eyes, and enhance the overall depth of the illustration, making it more realistic.

An afternoon landscape background can be tricky to draw because of its strong, vivid colors. The sun's position creates unique challenges with shadows and highlights, affecting the overall depth. Additionally, the color palette is somewhat limited, requiring careful balance to achieve the desired effect. To create a good afternoon atmosphere in a drawing, we need to capture the warm, golden sunlight while balancing the cooler shadows. This can be tricky, making afternoon landscapes harder to draw. Instead of avoiding them, practicing color blending and studying how light works can help make it easier. In this walkthrough, we'll paint a joyful afternoon landscape that captures the warmth of the sun and the liveliness of a sunny day.

Following the steps

To create a joyful afternoon landscape, let's follow these steps (see *Figure 10.10*):

1. To begin, select one of the composition techniques introduced in *Chapter 9, Perfecting Composition for Visually Striking Art*, such as the C-shape or balanced composition. For the design shown in *Figure 10.10*, I've chosen to apply **diagonal composition**.

2. Now, sketch the background using the composition technique you picked. I'll draw a sloppy hill with distant trees, hills, big clouds in the background, and a house to recreate the diagonal composition. For the main focal point, I'll add a little witch and her cat near the front. To make the scene feel deeper, I'll draw flowers across the field, starting with big ones close by and making them smaller as they go farther away.

3. In this step, we'll start blocking in the background details using different color values. Keep in mind that objects closer to the front (foreground) should be drawn with darker colors, while things farther away should be lighter. This helps create depth and make your scene look more realistic. If you need more help, you can check *Chapter 9, Perfecting Composition for Visually Striking Art*, for examples and tips.

4. After that, we'll add the base colors to the background, just like in *Step 4*. Since afternoon light is bright and strong, the sun will be higher in the sky. When choosing your colors, focus on tones such as bright blue, yellow, and vivid greens to capture the cheerful energy of the afternoon. Add more contrast between light and shadow to show clear sunlight, but be careful not to make it too harsh; keeping the balance will help the scene feel lively and warm.

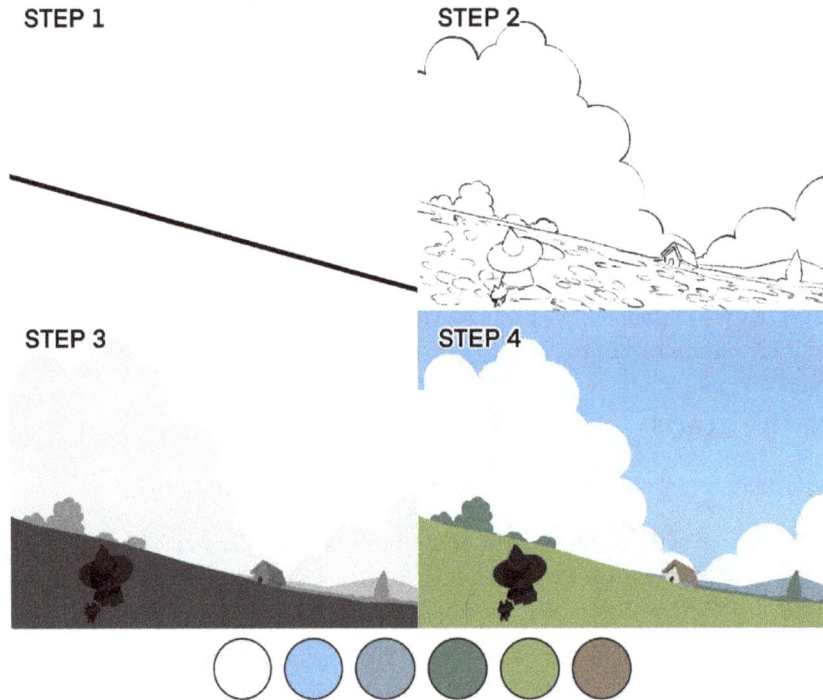

Figure 10.10 – Step-by-step drawing process for a joyful afternoon scene

On the *Rendering* layer, begin adding details to the green field, the distant trees, and the far-off hill. In the field, I've included several garden stones leading toward the little house to create flow and guide the viewer's eye. Be sure to stick to the contrast plan we established in *Step 3* so the overall balance and depth stay consistent. For this part, I'll paint everything on a single layer to make full use of the brush textures and blending effects.

Figure 10.11 – Base color for a joyful afternoon scene

On the same layer, let's continue by adding more details to the flowers, the distant trees, and the little house. To add more depth to the background scenery, focus on adding more texture and contrast to the foreground elements, such as flowers and garden stones, so they naturally catch the viewer's attention. Don't forget to consider the light source as shown in *Figure 10.11*. Since the light source during the afternoon comes from above, make sure all your shadows and highlights follow that direction. This helps the entire illustration feel bright, warm, and naturally highlighted under the afternoon sun.

Figure 10.12 – Detailing process for a joyful afternoon scene

Before we finish the illustration, let's gently add highlights where the sunlight hits the scene, which is from above since it's afternoon. To do this, switch the layer's blending mode from **Normal** to **Add**. This brightens those areas and gives a warm, glowing effect that matches the vibrant afternoon light. Use Procreate's **Soft Brush** with low opacity, so the glow stays natural and doesn't overpower the cheerful, sunny atmosphere.

Figure 10.13 – Adding highlight for a joyful afternoon scene

Lastly, let's add the characters to complete the illustration. We do this in the final step, so it's easier to color and blend them into the scene. By this point, the background colors are already set, which helps us choose the right tones and lighting for the characters. This way, everything feels balanced and naturally connected.

Figure 10.14 – Final version of the joyful afternoon scene

This is the result of the joyful afternoon illustration. Now, let's dive into the *Understanding the technique* section to give us a better understanding of this walkthrough.

Understanding the technique

Figure 10.15 shows a compilation of the joyful afternoon drawing process:

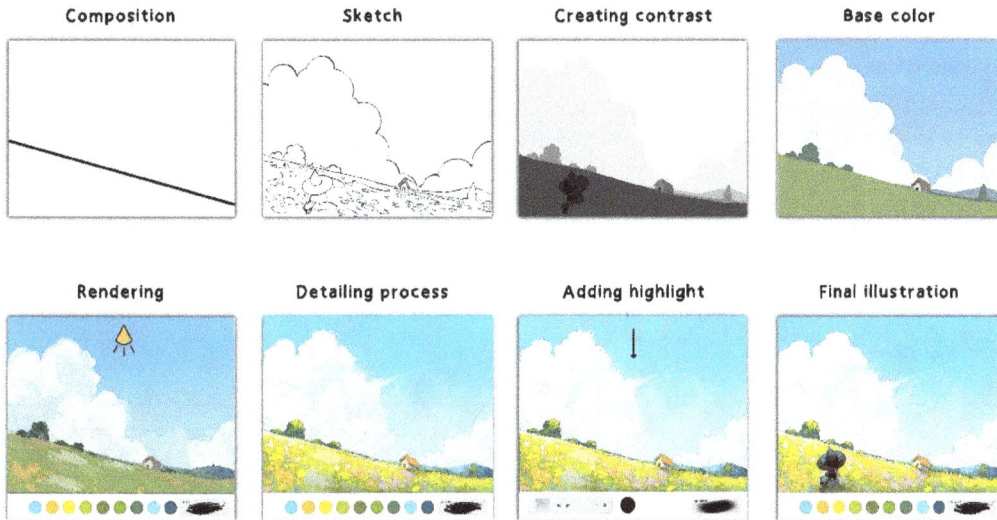

Figure 10.15 – A step-by-step compilation showcasing the joyful afternoon drawing process

When drawing an afternoon scene, focus on capturing the warm, bright light that defines this time of day. Afternoon sunlight creates strong, directional shadows, so observe how objects cast defined shadows and use them to enhance depth in your composition. Balancing warm tones from the sun with cooler shadows will make the scene feel natural and vibrant. The sky often shifts to softer colors, transitioning from bright blue to vibrant blue, as shown in *Figure 10.15*. Pay attention to atmospheric perspective by fading distant elements, such as the trees, with lighter and less saturated colors to create a sense of depth. Including details such as scattered sunlight on leaves, gentle reflections on surfaces, and bright highlights on edges can enhance the realism of the landscape. For example, I added a bright highlight to the green field to make it more glowing and stand out. By using these techniques well, we can create a bright and energetic afternoon scene that feels lively and welcoming to viewers.

Know more...

Afternoon scenes can evoke warm, energetic, or peaceful feelings, depending on how they are drawn. A quiet countryside with golden sunlight feels calm, while a busy city with glowing afternoon colors feels lively. To make the scene look real, adding small details such as soft grass, scattered leaves, and textured clouds helps. To recreate gentle lighting in your afternoon scene, try using blending modes such as Add or Soft Light:

- **Add** is perfect for a bright and glowing effect. It highlights and adds warmth to areas where sunlight hits.

- **Soft Light** gives a natural, gentle brightness that blends softly with surrounding colors. It is ideal for creating smooth transitions and glowing edges.

Using these modes with **Soft Brush** at low opacity will help your lighting look warm, dreamy, and natural effortlessly.

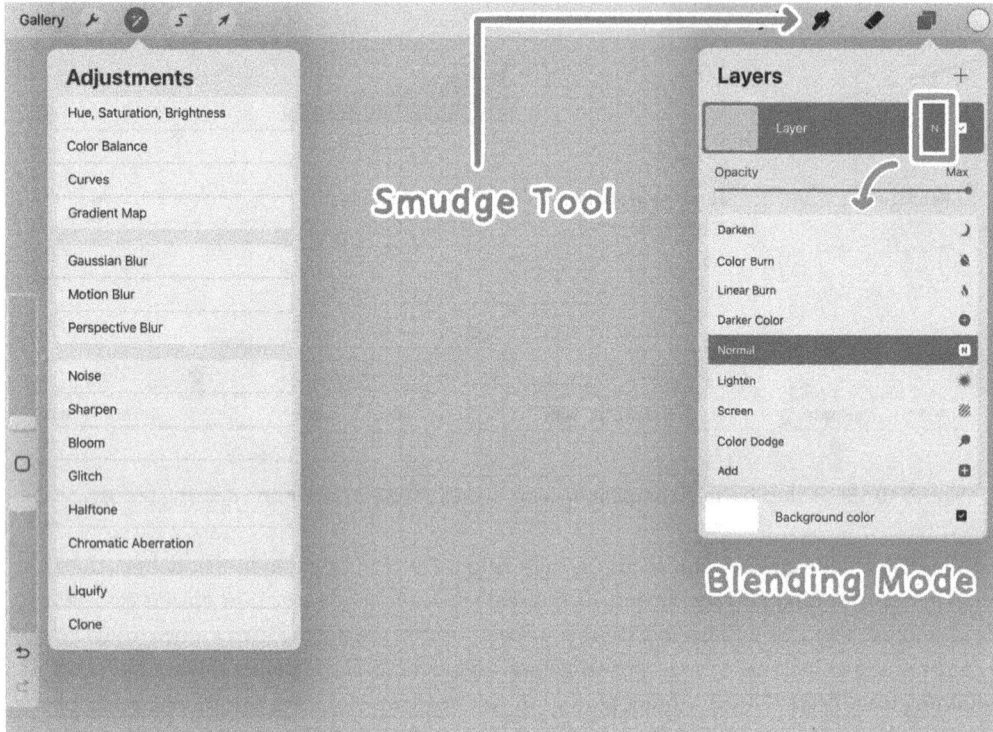

Figure 10.16 – Screenshot of Procreate tools

After a sunny afternoon, the light begins to soften. Let's move on to the cozy glow of evening and explore how to create a peaceful, nostalgic sunset.

Learning how to draw a nostalgic evening landscape

Evening landscapes often invoke a specific emotion and interpretation, with the warm hues of lighting creating a sense of safety and longing. We can use the evening atmosphere to create a nostalgic moment that can evoke a sense of happiness or sadness in the viewer. It is suitable for emotional illustrations such as farewell scenes or happy events. Adding warm glows, such as the light from a setting sun, can make an evening landscape feel inviting and peaceful. The gentle warmth enhances the mood, creating a comforting and nostalgic atmosphere that draws the viewer in. However, one of the biggest challenges is capturing the subtle, shifting light of evening and balancing warm and cool colors effectively. If you're new to background drawing, this can be challenging, but with the right approach, it becomes easier. In this walkthrough, we'll explore how to paint a nostalgic feeling by blending orange and purple hues, adding a gentle sunset glow, and painting shadows from the low sun near the horizon.

Following the steps

To create a nostalgic evening landscape, you can follow these steps (see *Figure 10.17*):

1. To begin, select one of the composition techniques introduced in *Chapter 9, Perfecting Composition for Visually Striking Art*, such as the C-shape or balanced composition. For the design shown in *Figure 10.17*, I've chosen to apply **diagonal composition**.

2. Now, sketch the background using the composition technique you picked. I'll draw a sloppy hill with distant trees, hills, big clouds in the background, and a house to recreate the diagonal composition. For the main focal point, I'll add a little witch and her cat near the front. To make the scene feel deeper, I'll draw flowers across the field, starting with big ones close by and making them smaller as they go farther away.

3. In this step, we'll start blocking in the background details using different color values. Keep in mind that objects closer to the front (foreground) should be drawn with darker colors, while things farther away should be lighter. This helps create depth and make your scene look more realistic. If you need more help, you can check *Chapter 9, Perfecting Composition for Visually Striking Art*, for examples and tips.

4. After that, we'll add the base colors to the background, just like in *Step 4*. Since sunset light is warm and golden, the sun will sit low near the horizon, casting a soft glow across the scene. When choosing your colors, aim for smooth blends of oranges, browns, and a hint of pinks and purples. Avoid strong contrast, so the overall mood stays calm and nostalgic, just like a peaceful evening atmosphere.

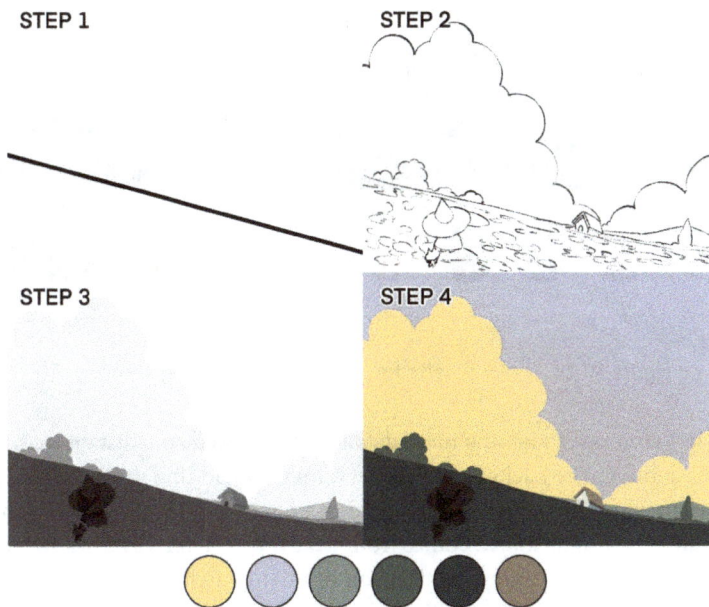

Figure 10.17 – Step-by-step drawing process for the nostalgic evening scene

On the *Rendering* layer, begin adding details to the green field, the distant trees, and the far-off hill. In the field, I've included several garden stones leading toward the little house to create flow and guide the viewer's eye. Be sure to stick to the contrast plan we established in *Step 3* so the overall balance and depth stay consistent. For this part, I'll paint everything on a single layer to make full use of the brush textures and blending effects.

Figure 10.18 – Color palette for the nostalgic evening scene

On the same layer, let's continue by adding more details to the flowers, the distant trees, and the little house. To add more depth to the background scenery, focus on adding more texture and contrast to the foreground elements, such as flowers and garden stones, so they naturally catch the viewer's attention. During sunset, the light source comes from near the horizon, casting a warm glow across the scene. Just like in *Figure 10.19*, make sure all shadows and highlights follow that direction to keep everything looking natural and consistent with the evening atmosphere.

Figure 10.19 – Detailing process for the nostalgic evening scene

Before we finish the illustration, let's gently add highlights where the sunset light hits the scene around the horizon. To do this, switch the layer's blending mode from **Normal** to **Color Dodge**. This brightens those areas and adds a warm, glowing effect that fits beautifully with the golden sunset mood. Use Procreate's **Soft Brush** at low opacity so the light stays smooth and doesn't overpower the peaceful evening atmosphere.

Figure 10.20 – Adding highlights for the nostalgic evening scene

Lastly, let's add the characters to complete the illustration. We do this in the final step so it's easier to color and blend them into the scene. By this point, the background colors are already set, which helps us choose the right tones and lighting for the characters. This way, everything feels balanced and naturally connected.

Figure 10.21 – Final version of the nostalgic evening scene

This is the result of the nostalgic evening illustration. Now, let's dive into the *Understanding the technique* section to give us a better understanding of this walkthrough.

Understanding the technique

Figure 10.22 shows the compilation of the serene morning drawing process:

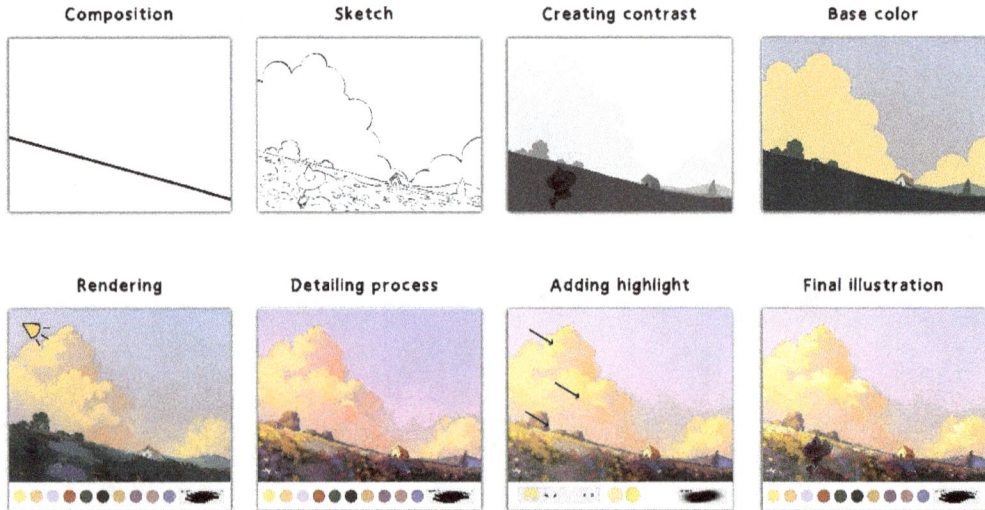

Composition	Sketch	Creating contrast	Base color

Rendering	Detailing process	Adding highlight	Final illustration

Figure 10.22 – A step-by-step compilation showcasing the nostalgic evening drawing process

When drawing an evening scene, focus on creating a warm and peaceful feeling with soft, warm colors, such as yellow and orange hues. Evening light has a golden glow that slowly fades into purples with a hint of pink, so mixing these colors will help set the right mood. It can be done using **Gaussian Blur** easily. For sunset scenes, shadows appear longer and softer as the sun lowers, making the atmosphere nostalgic. Adding small details such as flecks of light, glowing surfaces, or tiny stars can make the scene feel more real. Distant objects should look lighter and less detailed to create depth. Whether you're drawing a quiet countryside or a busy city at sunset, using the right lighting and colors will bring out the beauty of the nostalgic evening.

Know more...

To create a nostalgic atmosphere, dark shapes such as trees, fences, or buildings can frame the sunset and make it feel more personal and nostalgic. Their simple outlines stand out against the colorful sky, guiding the viewer's eye to the warm glow of the setting sun. This creates a peaceful and emotional mood, making the scene feel more meaningful. Now, we'll step into the night and learn how to paint a calm and dreamy nighttime scene.

Learning how to draw a peaceful night landscape

A peaceful night landscape is perfect background scenery for those who would like to convey a feeling of calmness and solitude. The scene can feature calm nighttime scenery with a moon reflecting on the lake. Night background is often used to describe a feeling of tranquility, thus, we can draw night landscapes if we would like to convey a feeling of calmness. By adding darkness to create contrast, we can evoke emotions ranging from solitude to a mysterious or uneasy atmosphere, making it a suitable choice for storytelling and artistic expression. Drawing a night background presents several challenges, due to the limited use of colors and light sources. To create a realistic night atmosphere, we must have a deep understanding of contrast and be able to balance out cool and warm color tones.

Working with dark colors can feel daunting at first as they might seem overpowering or hard to control, especially if you're more comfortable with lighter tones. But don't worry; in this walkthrough, I'll show you how to build a night atmosphere step by step. We'll learn how to use contrast to add depth, and how to mix warm and cool colors to keep things balanced and beautiful.

Following the steps

To create a peaceful night landscape, you can follow these steps (see *Figure 10.23*):

1. To begin, select one of the composition techniques introduced in *Chapter 9, Perfecting Composition for Visually Striking Art*, such as the C-shape or balanced composition. For the design shown in *Figure 10.23*, I've chosen to apply **diagonal composition**.

2. Now, sketch the background using the composition technique you picked. I'll draw a sloppy hill with distant trees, hills, and a house to recreate the diagonal composition. For the main focal point, I'll add a little witch and her cat near the front. To make the scene feel deeper, I'll draw flowers across the field, starting with big ones close by and making them smaller as they go farther away.

3. In this step, we'll start blocking in the background details using different color values. Keep in mind that objects closer to the front (foreground) should be drawn with darker colors, while things farther away should be lighter. This helps create depth and make your scene look more realistic. If you need more help, you can check *Chapter 9, Perfecting Composition for Visually Striking Art*, for examples and tips.

4. After that, we'll add the base colors to the background, just like in *Step 4*. Since nighttime has very little natural light, focus on using darker tones such as deep blues, pale yellows, and muted grays. The moon and stars are usually the main light source for nighttime, so they will determine the placement of highlights and shadows in your scene. Since the moon and stars give off a soft, cool light, be sure to use gentle, low contrast shading. Avoid strong contrast to preserve the calm, quiet mood of a peaceful night scene.

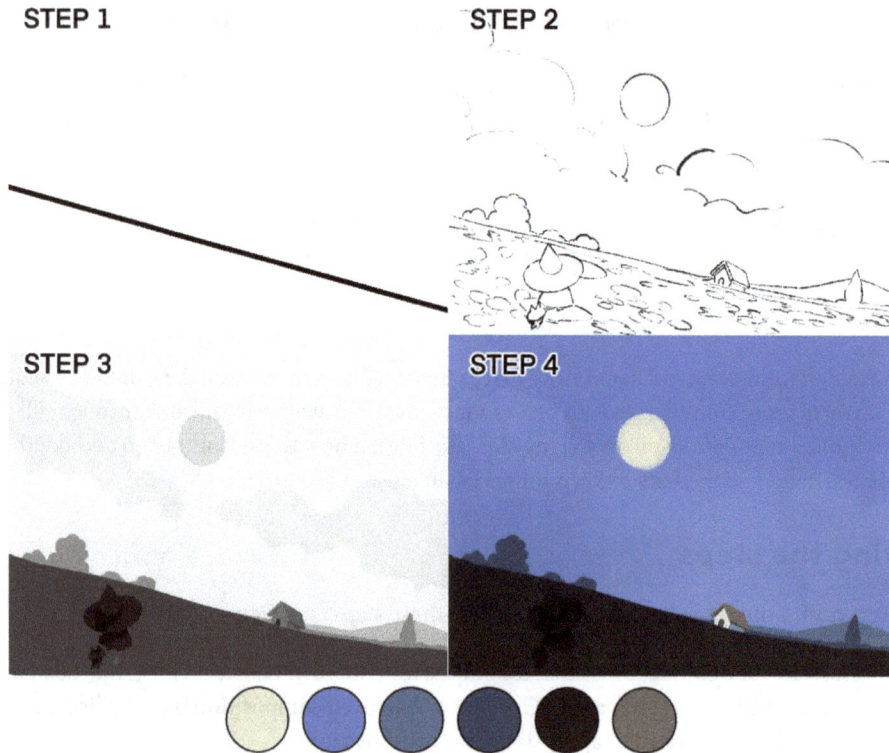

Figure 10.23– Step-by-step drawing process for a peaceful night

On the *Rendering* layer, begin adding details to the green field, the distant trees, soft clouds in the background, and the far-off hill. In the field, I've included several garden stones leading toward the little house to create flow and guide the viewer's eye. Be sure to stick to the contrast plan we established in *Step 3* so the overall balance and depth stay consistent. For this part, I'll paint everything on a single layer to make full use of the brush textures and blending effects.

Figure 10.24 – Color palette for a peaceful night scene

On the same layer, let's continue by adding more details to the flowers, the distant trees, the moon, the stars, and the little house. To add more depth to the background scenery, focus on adding more texture and contrast to the foreground elements, such as flowers and garden stones, so they naturally catch the viewer's attention. Remember to consider the light source, just like in *Figure 10.24*. At night, the light usually comes from the moon and stars, which are positioned higher up in the sky. This means your shadows and highlights should follow that same gentle direction, helping the whole scene feel calm and consistently lit by the night sky.

Figure 10.25 – Detailing process for a peaceful night

Before we finish the illustration, let's softly add highlights where light sources such as the moon or stars shine from above. To do this, change the layer's blending mode from **Normal** to **Color Dodge**. This will gently brighten parts of the scene and give a subtle, warm glowing effect that fits the quiet and magical feeling of a night setting. Use Procreate's **Soft Brush** with low opacity, so the glow stays soft and doesn't overpower the calm nighttime atmosphere.

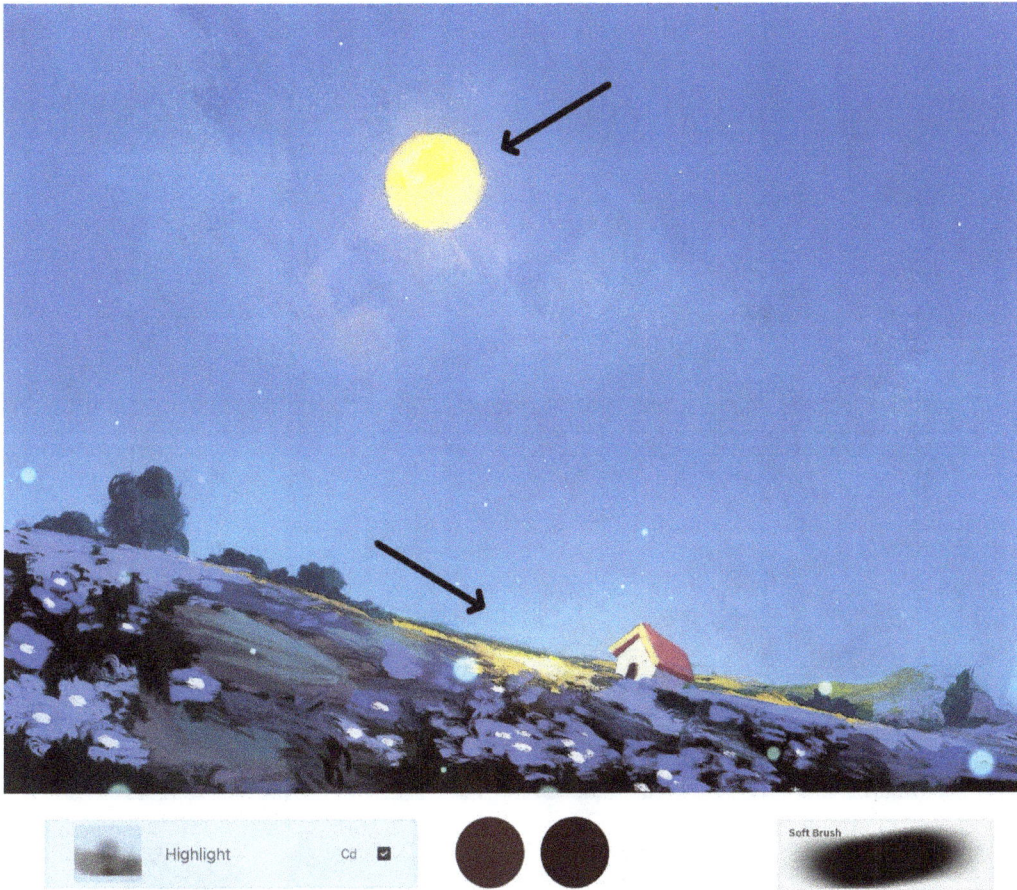

Figure 10.26 – Adding highlights for the peaceful night scene

Lastly, let's add the characters to complete the illustration. We do this in the final step so it's easier to color and blend them into the scene. By this point, the background colors are already set, which helps us choose the right tones and lighting for the characters. This way, everything feels balanced and naturally connected.

Figure 10.27 – Final version of the peaceful night scene

This is the result of the peaceful night illustration. Now, let's dive into the *Understanding the technique* section to give us a better understanding of this walkthrough.

Understanding the technique

Figure 10.28 shows a compilation of the serene morning drawing process:

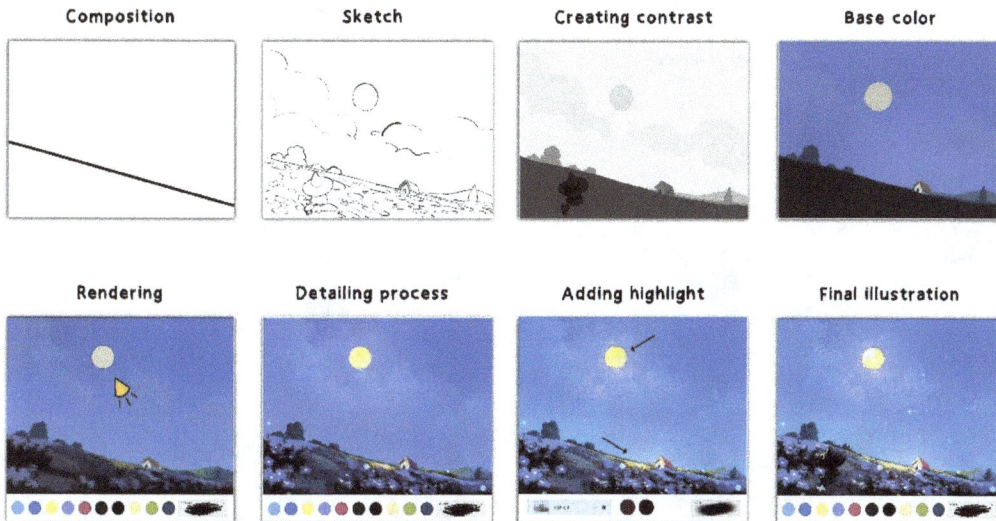

Figure 10.28 – A step-by-step compilation showcasing the peaceful night drawing process

When drawing a nighttime scene, focus on creating a calm effect using deep blues and blacks to represent the night sky. Adding a subtle gradient on the night sky and scattered stars can enhance the mood and bring realism to the setting. Light sources, such as the moon or glowing stars, play an essential role in nighttime scenery as they cast soft lighting and gentle shadows. Since night scenes are usually dim and soft, try not to use very strong or bright contrasts. Keeping the lighting gentle will make the artwork feel more natural and calmer.

We can create smooth transitions between light and shadow using smudge tools to create a natural look. Adding bright highlights, such as on the flower field and the little house, can make the nighttime scene more realistic. Depth perspective is also important in nighttime scenery. Distant objects should appear muted and less detailed to emphasize the vastness of the night. Whether you're illustrating a peaceful countryside under a starry sky or a busy cityscape, lighting adjustments will help convey the mood and emotion of the nighttime setting. You can use the **Curves** tool in Procreate to gently adjust the contrast and colors in your artwork. It helps you fine-tune the overall mood and balance without making things too strong or harsh.

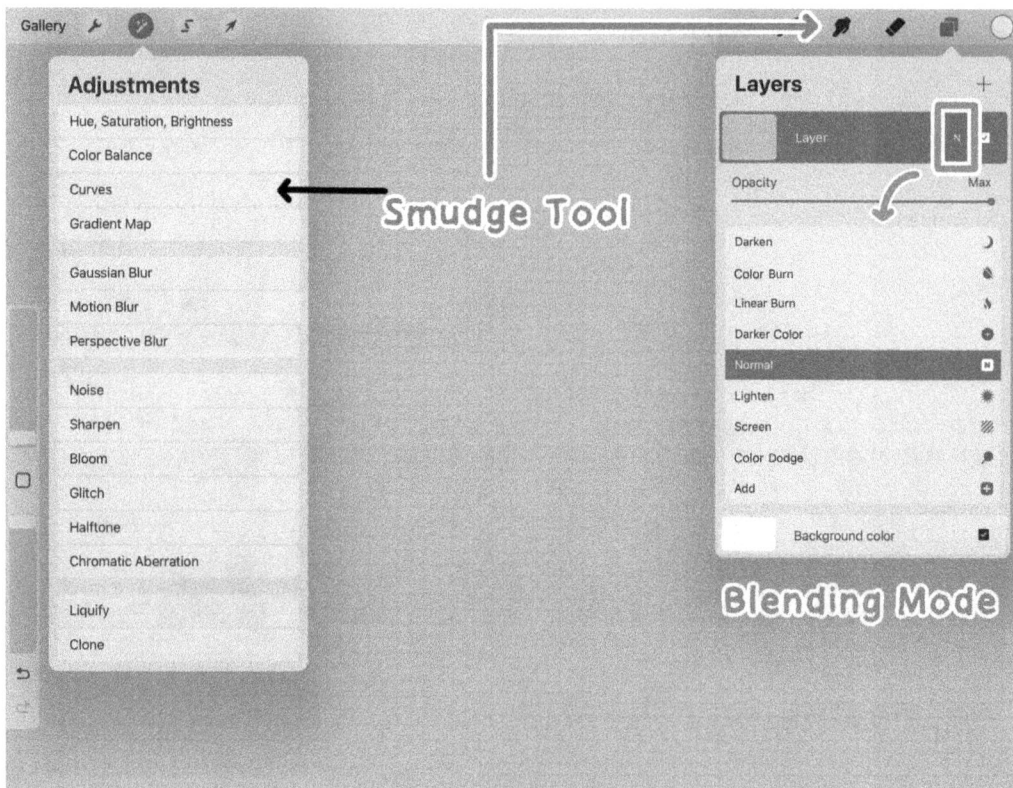

Figure 10.29 – Screenshot of Procreate tools

Know more...

To create a warm nighttime scenery, we can draw a glowing moon, lanterns, or city lights to make the nighttime scene feel warm and inviting. Adding a soft glow effect using **Soft Brush** makes the light look more natural. You can use blending modes, such as **Color Dodge**, to recreate bright and warm glows on the object surfaces.

Color Dodge in Procreate is perfect for creating glowing light effects and vibrant highlights. It's especially useful when you want to make areas of your artwork look bright and magical.

Here's how **Color Dodge** works in Procreate: it brightens mid-tones and highlights, making colors stand out with vivid energy. This blend mode is perfect for adding glow to light sources such as lanterns, fireflies, or magical auras. It also helps create a dreamy or radiant atmosphere, enhancing the mood of your artwork beautifully.

To use it, do the following:

1. Create a new layer above your artwork.

2. Tap the layer "N" to open **Blending Mode**.

3. Choose **Color Dodge**. Use a soft brush with darker colors (such as brown) and low opacity for best results.

Up next, you will create your very own background drawing. Let's take everything we've learned and create something wonderful together.

Drawing challenge: Create a background scenery

Background drawing in digital art is important as it creates the setting and mood of the piece, providing context for the viewer. To create a good background drawing, we need to have good depth to create a sense of space that will attract the viewer's attention to explore our art at a deeper level. It also allows us to showcase our skills in perspective, color, and detail, helping us to get better at telling a story through art. Ultimately, backgrounds help the storytelling become more engaging and give more context to the viewer. One major challenge in background drawing is balancing detail and the story we want to share. We must learn how to balance out the details without overwhelming the scene. Creating realistic backgrounds can be challenging and time-consuming. In industries such as animation and game design, strict deadlines and high-quality expectations make it even more difficult, often adding pressure on artists to work efficiently while maintaining detail and accuracy.

This final walkthrough is all about bringing together everything you've learned about composition, color, lighting, and storytelling and letting your imagination shine. In this challenge, we'll create an original background scene from start to finish.

Following the steps

In this final walkthrough of the book, we will explore how to design our own background scenery and create a stunning masterpiece. Here's how to bring your vision to life (see *Figure 10.30*):

1. Firstly, choose one of the composition techniques we learned about in *Chapter 9*, such as C-shape composition or balance composition. For the design shown in *Figure 10.30*, I will use **double diagonal composition**.

2. Next, sketch the background using the composition style you chose. I'll draw a shooting star and big, fluffy clouds. To highlight the double diagonal composition, I've placed the shooting star falling toward the left side of the illustration, while the green field gently leans to the right. These opposite directions create a strong visual flow and help make the scene stand out more.

3. In this step, we will clean up the sketch to make the design clearer and ready for coloring.

4.   Then, we will decide on the light source placement and use shades of gray to create a contrast base for the background scenery, as shown in **STEP 4** in the following figure. I will create an afternoon setting for this background scenery, where the lighting is bright and the colors are vibrant. Since the afternoon atmosphere naturally has strong contrasts, the illustration will feature bold highlights and deep shadows, as demonstrated in **STEP 4** in *Figure 10.30*.

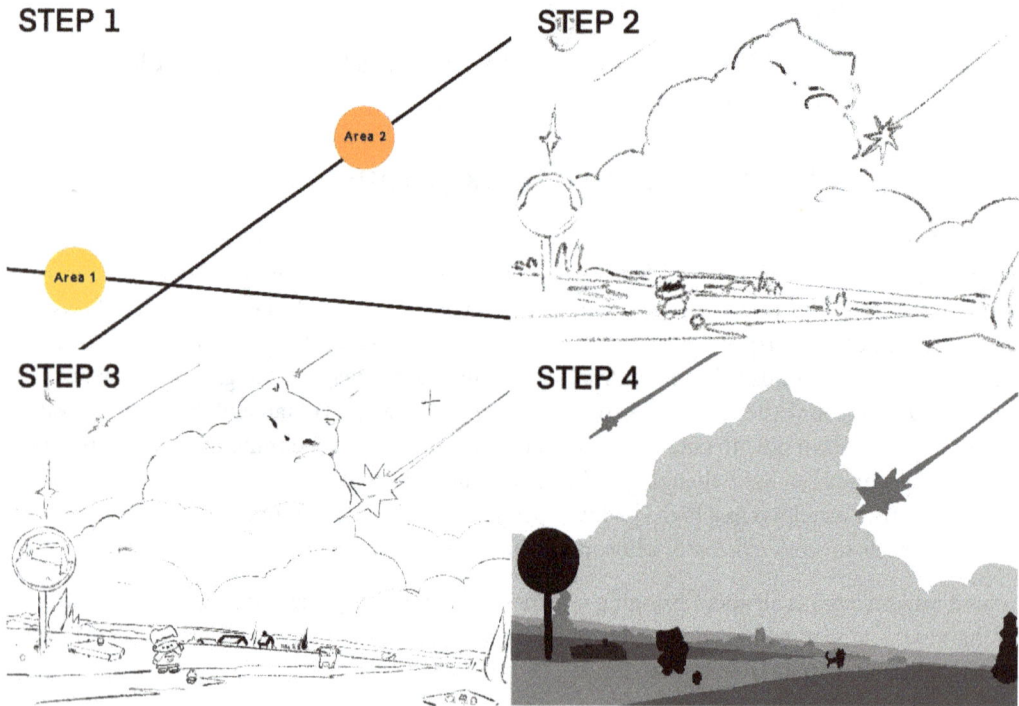

Figure 10.30 – Step-by-step drawing process for the background scenery

Prepare a color palette for the background scenery. I will use the color palette shown in *Figure 10.31*.

Figure 10.31 – Color palette for the background scenery

Paint the background scenery using the color palette by following the color contrast we created in *Step 4*.

Figure 10.32 – Base color for background drawing

Lastly, for the final touches, refine the rendering and enhance the background by adding details such as flowers, shadows, and lighting. These elements will bring depth and vibrancy to the scene, completing the illustration beautifully. I'm using the **Oil Paint** brush from *Chapter 1* to create a background scenery with the look and feel of a traditional oil painting.

Figure 10.33 – Final version of the background drawing

Lastly, share your work on social media using the #HappyyuBook hashtag on Instagram or X (Twitter). I will reshare them.

This is the result of drawing background scenery. Now, let's dive into the *Understanding the technique* section to give us a better understanding of this walkthrough.

Understanding the technique

Creating a dreamy and magical background is all about mixing soft colors, storytelling, and playful details. We start by picking a composition style, such as double diagonal, to lead the viewer's eye and build a strong visual flow. Then, we sketch the scenery with big clouds, shooting stars, and gentle hills in the background to bring that composition to life.

Using a base color palette, as shown in *Figure 10.31*, we paint the sky and background in smooth blends that suit the time of day. For brighter settings, such as afternoon, bold highlights and shadows, as in *Figure 10.33*, help the scenery feel warm and full of energy. In the foreground, adding details such as soft flowers, grassy fields, and garden stones adds depth and makes the scene feel alive. Small touches, such as a cozy cottage, a character with a little companion, or magical skies, help tell your story better.

Once everything is rendered as shown in *Figure 10.34*, the scene blends beautifully like a finished painting. To add a gentle glow and brighten the background, I use **Soft Brush** on a layer set to **Add** blending mode. This helps bring light and magic into the final illustration.

Drawing mission: Let's create together!

It's time to bring your vision to life! You've learned how to build backgrounds with color, light, and storytelling, and now it's your turn to create your own. Choose your favorite composition, decide on the mood or time of day, and build a scene that speaks to you.

Picture a quiet hill just before nighttime. The sky is glowing with warm orange light as a peaceful little village gets ready for a night full of stars. Small lanterns light up the paths, and a distant cozy cottage sits on the hillside with a soft, warm glow.

Your main character is a cheerful traveler carrying a bag of stars. They walk calmly toward the house with their little animal friend beside them.

As you draw, think about the feelings you want to evoke. Is it calm, magical, or maybe a little mysterious? Use everything you've learned about composition and lighting to tell your story. Every flower, rock, cloud, and shadow can help bring the mood to life. When you're done, feel free to share your artwork on Instagram or X (Twitter) using the #HappyyuBook hashtag, or tag @gummyy.y and @happyyu_ so we can see and celebrate your beautiful work. If you'd like some help or feedback, you can reach out at happyyudrawing@gmail.com. I'd be so happy to guide you!

Summary

You've reached the end of this book… but your journey is just beginning!

You've made it to the final page, but your art journey is just getting started! There are still so many scenes to sketch, colors to play with, and stories to tell. Thank you for drawing with me. It's been a joy to create together, share ideas, and explore the beauty of art. I hope this art journey leaves you feeling inspired, encouraged, and excited to keep drawing from your heart.

Creating a background landscape involves a deep understanding of color harmony and composition and a clear storyline. By understanding how these elements work, we can create a good background drawing that will help us to bring our art career to the next level.

As we reach the end of this book, remember that art is a continuous journey of learning, experimenting, and growing. Every brushstroke, every composition, and every technique you've practiced contributes to your unique creative works. Whether you're painting serene landscapes, dynamic scenery, or simple illustrations, the skills you've developed will help you bring your ideas to life with confidence.

Art is not about perfection; it's about expression, storytelling, and discovering your own style. Keep challenging yourself, stay curious, and never be afraid to draw new things. The more you draw and try new ideas, the better you'll get and the clearer your artistic style will become. Every time you practice, you improve and learn more about what works best for you.

Don't compare your progress with other people; instead, continue your art journey at your own pace. It's important to remind ourselves about why we started this art journey whenever we feel discouraged. Lastly, keep going and draw things that you like instead of following trends. In that way, you will attract genuine supporters and a community that truly appreciates your work.

Thank you again for learning with me through this book. I hope the tips and techniques we have explored together help you to build trust in your skills and joy in your art. Now, go ahead, grab your brush, open your canvas, and let your creativity shine. The world is waiting to see your beautiful art and unique imagination. Let's keep learning, keep creating, and take our next steps with joy and all the new skills we've unlocked. I can't wait to see what you draw next!

Index

A

analogous schemes
 creating 120-122
Apple Pencil 177
atmospheric perspective 48, 168

B

background color
 exploring 24-26
 using, technique 23
 using, to set mood 21
 warm color tones, using 22
background composition
 drawing 215, 216
 errors, fixing 217
 techniques 217
background landscape
 creating 279
background scenery
 drawing 275-279
 drawing, with one-point perspective 75, 76
 drawing, with three-point perspective 78-80
 drawing, with two point-perspective 76-78
 technique 278, 279

B (continued)

balanced composition 226
 drawing 226-228
 errors, fixing 228
 technique 228
blending modes 33
bright afternoon scene, with light and shadow
 illustrating 98-100
 illustrating, technique 100
bright light source
 identifying 91-93
brushes
 information 6, 7
 materials 2-5
 styles, exploring 7, 8
 textured brush 5

C

calm night scene, with light and shadow
 illustrating 104-106
 illustrating, technique 106
character designs
 brainstorming and sketching 192
 brainstorming and sketching, steps 192, 193
 brainstorming and sketching, technique 194, 195

finalizing 195
finalizing, steps 196, 197
finalizing, technique 197, 198
character designs, from different perspectives
drawing 198
drawing, steps 198, 199
drawing, technique 199, 200
character, into background drawing
blending 209
blending, steps 209-211
blending, technique 211, 212
character sheet, for portfolio
preparing 202
preparing, steps 203-206
preparing, technique 206
character, to background drawing
adding 206
adding, steps 207, 208
adding, technique 208
circular composition 234
drawing 234-236
errors, fixing 236
technique 236
color and composition
connection 165-167
techniques 167, 168
color contrast 136
ColorDrop 156
color emotion 152
applying 152
examples 153
happy atmosphere, techniques 155
heartwarming atmosphere, techniques 164
integrating, into sketch 182, 183
intense atmosphere, techniques 162
learning, to create happy
    atmosphere 153-155

learning, to create heartwarming
    atmosphere 162, 163
learning, to create intense
    atmosphere 160, 161
learning, to create mysterious
    atmosphere 158, 159
learning, to create sad atmosphere 156, 157
mysterious atmosphere, techniques 160
relevance 153
sad atmosphere, techniques 158
color harmony
using, in art 145-149
color harmony, with Procreate
analogous schemes, creating 120-122
complementary schemes, creating 122-124
creating 118
creating, techniques 126, 127
monochromatic schemes, creating 118-120
triadic schemes, creating 124-126
color palette
random colors, selecting
    techniques to create 141
random colors, selecting to create 139-141
color palette, with Gradient Map tool
creating 142-144
creating, techniques 144
color value
significance 127-130
using, in art 127-130, 145-149
using, techniques in art 130
complementary schemes
creating 122-124
composition 213, 214
background composition 214
contrast, in art
improving 136-138
improving, techniques 138
using 145-149

cool color tones
  using and applying 132-134
  using and applying, techniques 134, 135
cross composition 231
  creating 231, 233
  errors, fixing 234
  technique 233
C-shape composition 218
  drawing 218, 219
  errors, fixing 220
  technique 220
Curves tool 273

D

delicate trees
  drawing 29-31
depth of field 55
detail perspective 55-59
  technique 59
diagonal composition 228, 246
  drawing 229, 230
  errors, fixing 231
  technique 230
double diagonal composition 275

E

eye level 65

F

facial expressions
  drawing 200
  drawing, steps 200-202
  drawing, technique 202

fence
  drawing 37, 38
Fibonacci sequence 237
flower field scene
  drawing 33-35
fluffy clouds
  drawing 28, 29

G

Golden Section composition 236
  errors, fixing 240
  example 237
Golden Spiral composition 237
  example 237, 238
  technique 240
  using 238-240
gravel
  drawing 35, 36
green field
  drawing 40, 41

I

ideas
  brainstorming 172, 173
  writing down 172, 173
illustration
  finalizing 184-188

J

joyful afternoon landscape
  creating 253-258
  techniques 258, 259

L

lake
drawing 41, 42
layer opacity 180
lighting and shading
mastering, technique 111-114
mastering, ways 107-111
lighting and shadows
observing, on rough surfaces 86, 87
observing, on shiny surfaces 84-86
observing, technique 88
observing, with real-life images
and reference images 84
lighting and shadow, techniques 89
bright light source, identifying 91-93
identifying 93
soft light source, identifying 89-91
linear perspective
identifying, in real-life images 65
little houses
drawing 38, 39

M

monochromatic schemes
creating 118-120
mood board
creating, for references 173-176

N

natural perspective, in background drawing
applying 48-51
applying, technique 51
detail perspective 55-59
size perspective 52-55

nostalgic evening landscape
creating 260-266
technique 266

O

one-point perspective 60, 61
identifying, in real-life images 65
used, for drawing background scenery 75, 76

P

**peaceful morning scene, with
light and shadow**
illustrating 94-97
illustrating, technique 97
peaceful night landscape
creating 267-275
technique 273
Procreate 1

R

random colors
selecting, techniques to creating
color palette 141
selecting, to creating color palette 139-141
reference images
color palette based, preparing on 11-13
selecting 9-11
technique 13
using, for inspiration 8

S

serene morning landscape
creating 245-250
customizing 251, 252

technique 251
simple composition, for background drawing
requirement 14
using 13
using, steps 14-16
using, technique 16, 17
size contrast 136
size perspective 52-55
technique 55
sketch
color emotion, integrating into 182, 183
improvising 179-181
snow
drawing 43, 44
soft light source
identifying 89-91
soothing grass
drawing 32, 33
story
finalizing 184-188
improvising 179-181
storyline
sketching out 177-179

T

texture contrast 136
texture material, for illustration
adding 17-21
applying 17-19
preparing 17
three-point perspective 63
identifying, in real-life image 71-74
technique 64, 65
used, for drawing background scenery 78-80

transform tools 180
triadic schemes
creating 124-126
two-point perspective 61, 62
identifying, in real-life image 68
used, for drawing background scenery 76-78

U

unbalanced composition 223
creating 223-225
errors, fixing 226
technique 225

V

vanishing point 65
V-shape composition 220
drawing 221, 222
errors, fixing 223
technique 222

W

warm color tones
using and applying 130-132
using and applying, techniques 134, 135
warm evening scene, with light and shadow
illustrating 101-103
illustrating, technique 103

‹packt›

packtpub.com

Subscribe to our online digital library for full access to over 7,000 books and videos, as well as industry leading tools to help you plan your personal development and advance your career. For more information, please visit our website.

Why subscribe?

- Spend less time learning and more time coding with practical eBooks and Videos from over 4,000 industry professionals
- Improve your learning with Skill Plans built especially for you
- Get a free eBook or video every month
- Fully searchable for easy access to vital information
- Copy and paste, print, and bookmark content

At www.packtpub.com, you can also read a collection of free technical articles, sign up for a range of free newsletters, and receive exclusive discounts and offers on Packt books and eBooks.

Other Books You May Enjoy

If you enjoyed this book, you may be interested in these other books by Packt:

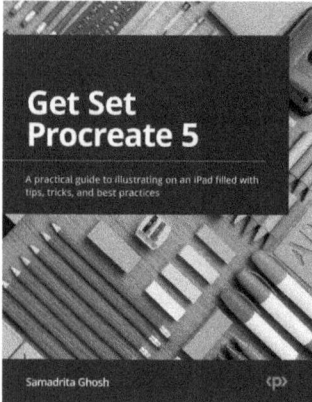

Get Set Procreate 5

Samadrita Ghosh

ISBN: 978-1-80056-300-1

- Become well-versed with the fundamentals of Procreate
- Personalize the Procreate application to suit your workflow
- Gain preliminary knowledge of the tool to further explore it for your artwork
- Speed up your workflow with gestures and shortcuts
- Explore, edit, and create a wide range of brushes with the help of Brush Library and Brush Studio
- Use assisted drawing tools to enhance your accuracy
- Learn animation using Procreate s Animation Assist tools
- Get up-to-date with the new features of Procreate 5.2 like Page Assist and 3D painting.

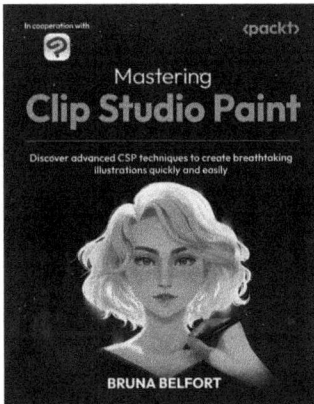

Mastering Clip Studio Paint

Bruna Belfort

ISBN: 978-1-80512-403-0

- Design a personalized CSP workspace to boost your productivity
- Refine your artistic process for a seamless creative workflow
- Use drawing tools such as vector layers and rulers for precise line art
- Get the most out of layers and blending modes for more dynamic and imaginative results
- Customize brushes with advanced brush settings
- Master tool selection, coloring techniques, and adjustment layers for polished results
- Find out how to manipulate 3D objects in your illustrations
- Leverage CSP's 3D capabilities to sculpt intricate lighting systems and backgrounds

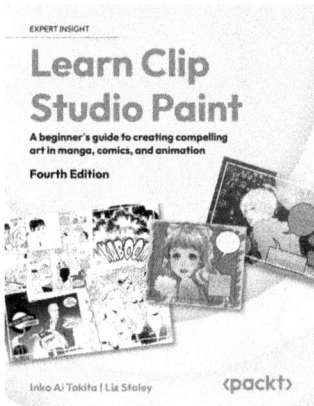

Learn Clip Studio Paint - Fourth Edition

Inko Ai Takita, Liz Staley

ISBN: 978-1-83588-658-8

- Organize layers to make your artwork easy to edit
- Customize tools and brushes to draw compelling characters
- Implement inking and coloring techniques in your art
- Craft engaging comic panel layouts
- Employ layer masks and screentones for professional results
- Use 3D models to learn poses for your characters
- Explore animation basics to bring your artwork to life
- Leverage Clip Studio Paint's vast library of assets
- Export your creations for various platforms, including print and web

Packt is searching for authors like you

If you're interested in becoming an author for Packt, please visit `authors.packtpub.com` and apply today. We have worked with thousands of developers and tech professionals, just like you, to help them share their insight with the global tech community. You can make a general application, apply for a specific hot topic that we are recruiting an author for, or submit your own idea.

Share Your Thoughts

Now you've finished *Procreate for Digital Artists*, we'd love to hear your thoughts! Scan the QR code below to go straight to the Amazon review page for this book and share your feedback or leave a review on the site that you purchased it from.

`https://packt.link/r/183508298X`

Your review is important to us and the tech community and will help us make sure we're delivering excellent quality content.

www.ingramcontent.com/pod-product-compliance
Lightning Source LLC
Chambersburg PA
CBHW080549270326
41929CB00019B/3245